understanding
CHRISTIAN DOCTRINE

understanding
CHRISTIAN
DOCTRINE

IAN S. MARKHAM

Blackwell
Publishing

BLACKWELL PUBLISHING
350 Main Street, Malden, MA 02148-5020, USA
9600 Garsington Road, Oxford OX4 2DQ, UK
550 Swanston Street, Carlton, Victoria 3053, Australia

First published 2008 by Blackwell Publishing

1   2008

Library of Congress Cataloging-in-Publication Data

Markham, Ian S.
    Understanding Christian doctrine / by Ian S. Markham.
        p. cm.
    Includes bibliographical references and index.
    ISBN 978-1-4051-3152-0 (hardcover : alk. paper)—ISBN 978-1-4051-3153-7 (pbk. : alk. paper)
1. Theology, Doctrinal.   I. Title.

BT75.3.M3 2007
230—dc22

                                                                                    2007013128

A catalogue record for this title is available from the British Library.

Set in 10.5/13 pt Minion by Graphicraft Limited, Hong Kong
Printed and bound in Singapore by C.O.S. Printers Pte Ltd

The publisher's policy is to use permanent paper from mills that operate a sustainable forestry policy, and which has been manufactured from pulp processed using acid-free and elementary chlorine-free practices. Furthermore, the publisher ensures that the text paper and cover board used have met acceptable environmental accreditation standards.

For further information on
Blackwell Publishing, visit our website at
www.blackwellpublishing.com

For my funny and charming nieces

Nicola Sowden
Abbie Sowden
Lizzie Markham
Ellen Sowden

CONTENTS

ACKNOWLEDGMENTS

2007 is the year that I was ordained into holy orders; it is also the year when I was called, invited, and elected to become the 14th Dean and President of Virginia Theological Seminary. The growing sense of call to the priesthood has run parallel with a deepening commitment to formation within a tradition – in my case the Episcopal tradition. This book was written as part of my priestly formation: I wanted to be clear about the faith I was called to serve.

There are many who have helped me on this journey. The home of my childhood celebrated and affirmed faith. My father, now eighty, imparted the most precious gift of all – the capacity to see the divine all around me. For that gift, I am enormously grateful. For the many childhood friendships, especially, Sue Burns, Philip Hadley, Jane Shepherd, Peter Wotton Jr, Shaun Coates, and Don and Harvey McQuillan-Wright. For the conversation partners at University and beyond, especially, Charles Williams, Giles Legood, Melanie Phillips, Richard Burridge, George Newlands, Mark Wallace, Jane Compson, Shannon Ledbetter, Lewis Ayres, Gareth Jones, Martyn Percy, Kenneth Newport, Andrew Hodge, Gillian Cloke, R. John Elford, Simon Lee, Keith Ward, Leslie Houlden, and in particular Sophia Weber (who is now living in Germany).

Most of this book was written while serving as Dean at Hartford Seminary. I am grateful to the President, Heidi Hadsell, who gave me the space to write. For Kelton Cobb, who read the entire manuscript and improved it in countless ways. Yvonne Bowen was my Executive Assistant, who provided crucial help at various stages. Karen Rollins was the Director of Enrollment Management and Registrar, who kept the educational part of the Seminary going. While distracted on the writing of this book, Christy Lohr, Worth Loomis, and Uriah Kim took responsibility for editing *Reviews in Religion and Theology*. Hartford Seminary welcomes Muslims and Jews. The challenge of explaining the concepts of the Trinity and the Incarnation to these traditions has helped the book considerably. Particular conversations with Abdullah Antepli, Ingrid

Mattson, Yehezkel Landau, Tubanur Yesilhark, and Ibrahim Abu-Rabi were especially helpful.

The stable center of my life is my wife and son. Thank you Lesley and Luke for the countless gifts you bring to my life every day.

Once again I am delighted to work with Blackwell publishers. I am enormously grateful to Rebecca Harkin, the Commissioning Editor, who provided advice, support, and guidance, which significantly improved the book. Faith Bell helped me at various stages. And anonymous readers did what they could to make sure that this book realizes the ambitious goals it has set. To all, I am grateful.

As this book was being finished, my five siblings and I decided to have a non-spouse vacation. We went skiing in the French Alps. A delightful week with them made me realize my enormous debt to them: they have shaped me in more ways than I can start to describe. So thank you Rosemary, Anthony, Jacqui, Debbie, and Michael.

Leaving all the spouses behind caused some consternation. The growing family is a complete delight. So allow me to take this opportunity to thank Paul, Nicola, Paddy, Eric, and Bev. It is the joy of the growing family, which provokes me to dedicate this book to my nieces. Nicola Sowden (age 33) is the heart and soul of any party: Abbie Sowden (age 24) is elegance personified; Lizzie (age 9) is cheerful and bubbly; and Ellen (age 5) is the great-niece, who makes everyone smile. Thank you for everything you give.

Many of the persons listed above would want to take issue with some (or perhaps all) of the arguments in this book. So I take this opportunity to express my gratitude, while recognizing that I take complete responsibility for the contents of this book.

INTRODUCTION

We are going to embark on a journey – a journey that starts with the problems with belief and culminates with a discussion of the Christian beliefs about the end of the world. The "we" here is simply the author and the reader. The reader can be in a variety of different places. Many of you will be Christians – an umbrella term that embraces considerable diversity. Some of you will be clinging on to faith – finding the orthodox story of a creator God who redeems humanity through Christ difficult to affirm. Others are firmly located in a particular tradition, for example, the Roman Catholic or Baptist traditions. Other readers are non-Christians. Perhaps you are an atheist or agnostic who suspects that Christianity belongs to a pre-scientific era. You might be an adherent of another faith tradition – a Muslim, Jew, Buddhist or Hindu. I have tried to write this book so we can all walk this journey together. For the agnostic or atheist, I hope this book will be a challenge. Along with reasons for the fundamental beliefs, I have attempted to provide an attractive, plausible account of the Christian faith that takes the problems seriously. For those who are in another faith tradition, I have attempted to make connections with other faith traditions – sometimes alluding to similarities or confronting key differences. At the end of the book, I trust you will understand some of the debates within Christianity and reasons why Christians talk in certain distinctive ways (e.g. about God being triune). For the Christians, I am offering a particular account of the faith, which will contrast markedly with others.

One primary goal in writing this book was to be accessible. It is aimed at the student or the intelligent lay person. At every point, there are aids to help understanding – a glossary and brief vignettes of key theologians. In each chapter, I attempt to provide an overview of Christian attitudes to the topic. So there is a map of the main arguments and issues within the Christian tradition. However, unlike most textbooks, which are exclusively descriptive, this book has an argument. It takes positions.

The reason for this is that the hardest skill for any student to learn is how to decide what she thinks is true. The risk in teaching Christian theology is that one presents the options – in a detached, fair, way – and then leaves the impression that all options are equally valid and legitimate. Students find themselves becoming relativists (there are many options and no rational way of deciding between them). To counter this tendency, this book attempts both to describe positions and to decide between positions. Using the reflection questions at the end of each chapter, students are invited to disagree with my judgments. While I am countering the relativist tendency of many modern textbooks, I am not seeking to imply that I have all the right answers. God is complicated, which means doctrine is also. We need students of theology to continue to challenge the "received" answers. But we do so on the assumption that there are better and worse ways of making sense of God. We are on the quest for the truth; and our arguments are often a valuable way of discovering that truth.

Clarifying the Vantage Point

Having admitted that this book seeks to model theological judgments, it might help if I set out precisely what vantage point is taken. All of us are rooted. We are shaped by a culture, a language, and various traditions. I am an Englishman, living in the United States. As an Episcopalian, I am heavily shaped by the Anglican tradition. With its affinity for natural theology, the emphasis on the Incarnation, the high view of sacraments, readers may recognize an Anglican approach in the text.

In summary I argue in *Understanding Christian Doctrine*, for the following positions. First, *natural theology is a legitimate enterprise.* Of the three approaches delineated in chapter three (the Schleiermacherian, Barthian, and Thomist), I argue that the classical Catholic approach of Thomas Aquinas is the one to follow. We need to start with our shared human experience of life – an experience shared by all people. Granted this does not get us to the triune God revealed in Christ, but it does get to a sense of the transcendent who created this world. Treating the arguments inductively, I suggest that they are sufficiently persuasive for rational belief in God.

Second, *Christian doctrine is the Christian response to the problem of evil.* Unifying many of the chapters is the idea that it is in the narrative of Christianity that we find the response to the mystery of evil and suffering. Traditional theodicies, I argue in chapter five, are insufficient. Instead the Christian response is the story of the Fall, the claim that God was in Christ dying on the cross, the action of the Spirit in the world, the gift of the sacraments, and the promise of God in the life to come. None of these explain why God allows evil and suffering. But they do locate the problem in a narrative where God takes the complete responsibility for the hurt and pain within God's creation.

Third, *this is a liberal theology*. The word "liberal" needs to be reclaimed. It is not liberal in the sense of increasing skepticism about the truth claims in Christianity. The liberalism of the Anglican theologian Don Cupitt, who finally decided that even an objective God must go, is tantamount to atheism. The theologian should struggle with doctrines. In this book, I defend the Trinity and the Incarnation as indispensable aspects of the Christian understanding of God and God's relations to the world. But this book is liberal in the sense of affirming the generous heart and disposition of Christian orthodoxy. As I argued in *A Theology of Engagement*, the orthodox Christian tradition is deeply committed to taking reasons seriously, learning from non-Christian sources, and interpreting experience appropriately. This book is "liberal" in that sense. It is also liberal in the sense of wanting to learn from those more progressive theologies that are emerging (feminist and liberationist). Trying to find the balance between representing the traditional debate and including some of these neglected contemporary voices has been difficult. And there are sections where I am still not sure I have it quite right.

It is not necessary to go into further details of my argument in this book. Suffice it to say, this book is written out of the conviction that the drama of God in Christ continues to be good news for humanity. Tragically, there are many people who have encountered versions of the gospel who have been enslaved rather than liberated. The challenge is to the struggle with the message and to allow the God of love, who is calling us to love each other more deeply, to emerge.

Chapter 1
FINDING A WAY IN

LEARNING OUTCOMES

By the end of this chapter you should be able to:

- understand why some people find religion so implausible
- have a sense of some of the responses that a person of faith might make

STRUCTURE

- The social dimension
- Why bother with the Christian worldview?
- Problems: (1) It looks like religion is on the way out; (2) Science has displaced religion; (3) Metaphysics is impossible; (4) Agnosticism makes more sense; (5) Religion is horrid and cruel; (6) Faith is just a psychological projection
- The next stage

Much of the world is very religious. Despite all the predictions to the contrary, our world seems to be getting more religious rather than less. However, as an Englishman living on the east coast of America, I am aware that many students find it difficult to understand a religious worldview. So, in this opening chapter, we shall start by looking at some of the problems that a typical, thoughtful, European or American student might have with religion. Before we get to the doctrines of the Trinity or atonement, we need to understand why the religious discourse matters.

So let us start with the following questions: What makes some people atheists and agnostics and others persons of faith? This is the starting point of this book. Why do some people find it easy to believe, while others find it all so incomprehensible?

The Social Dimension

Perhaps because the founders of sociology were skeptical of religion, it is often assumed that the social explanation for religion is evidence for atheism. **Émile Durkheim**'s famous critique was one of the first. In his *The Elementary Forms of Religious Life* (1912), Durkheim argued that religion provides a socializing force. It brings people together. He establishes his argument by examining "primitive" forms of religion. However, Durkheim has no interest in simply describing the past; instead he visits the past with a view to establishing the truth about the nature of religion for the present. The central claim of the book, Durkheim explains,

> is that religion is something eminently social. Religious representations are collective representations which express collective realities; the rites are a manner of acting which take rise in the midst of the assembled groups and which are destined to excite, maintain or recreate certain mental states in these groups.[1]

As a result, religion and morality become closely connected. Religion is society's way of imposing certain shared moral values; this, Durkheim thought, explains why moral values seem to have a transcendent feel.

Whether or not Durkheim is right (and he is probably right about much), he offered an explanation for religion which recognized the power of our "socialization" to account for our worldview. Atheists and agnostics are sometimes tempted to dismiss a person's religious beliefs as "simply a result of their upbringing." This approach to religion has its roots in Durkheim's sociology.

The truth, however, is that perhaps we are all "indoctrinated." Many agnostics and atheists grew up in an agnostic and atheist environment: as children they never learned the discourse of faith. For the truth is that faith is learned. Much like language, it

ÉMILE DURKHEIM (1858–1917)

On April 15, 1858 Émile Durkheim was born of Jewish parents in Épinal, Lorraine in France. Early on he was recognized as exceptionally gifted and it was not surprising that he was admitted and flourished at the École Normale Supérieure (the premier University in Paris). In 1882, he became a philosophy teacher. In 1887, he moved to Bordeaux, where he started to articulate a distinctive approach to the social sciences and in 1913, he moved to Paris. During the First World War, he assisted with the war effort; and he also had to cope with the tragic loss of his son André who died in 1916. Plagued by illness throughout his life and devastated by the death of his son, he died on November 15, 1917.

LUDWIG WITTGENSTEIN (1889–1951)

Wittgenstein was born on April 26, 1889 in Vienna, Austria. He was baptized and buried a Roman Catholic, although he was very sensitive to his Jewish heritage (his father's parents converted from Judaism to Protestantism). Wittgenstein's academic interests started in mechanical engineering and then moved into aeronautics. It was his love of mathematics that provoked his interest in philosophy. He started work with Bertrand Russell (1872–1970) at Cambridge University. His family was extremely rich; in 1913 he inherited a fortune that he then gave away. In 1922 he published his only book *Tractatus Logico-Philosophicus*, which he believed solved all the problems of philosophy. Becoming, for a short time, an elementary school teacher in Austria, he returned to Trinity College Cambridge in 1929, renouncing his earlier work and determined to revisit the primary issues. The mature Wittgenstein was published after his death in *Philosophical Investigations*. He died in April 1951.

becomes part of the furniture of your mind. In the same way that a particular language is learned in a home, so is a particular faith discourse. In the same way that love of country is "instilled" so is love of God.

This was a key insight of **Ludwig Wittgenstein**. Wittgenstein is a complex thinker and disagreements about the interpretation of his work abound. However, Wittgenstein recognized that there are many different ways in which language operates. Language is used in a variety of different ways, with different "rules" governing the particular discourse (or language-game). Subsequent commentators on Wittgenstein, for example, D. Z. Phillips, have suggested that different communities use language in different ways.[2] Atheists operate within one community and use language in one way, while believers operate within a different community and use language in a different way.

So religion might well be a result of "social conditioning," but the point is that everything is. The agnostic and atheist lack of awe is equally a result of social conditioning. The fact that we have all been indoctrinated does not mean that we cannot be rationally reflective. There are still good reasons for believing. There are better and worse forms of indoctrination.

At this point, the reader might object: but if this is true, if we are all socially determined, then how do we explain "conversions"? How does one explain a conversion from faith to atheism (perhaps due to a tragic death of a relative) or from Christianity to Islam or from atheism to faith?

At this point, it is also necessary to introduce "reason." As children, we learn from our parents; we learn a language, a set of values, and a religion. As we encounter different languages, values, and religions, we start to interrogate the worldview given to us by our parents. We ask questions about difference and the reasons for the differences. Language differences we cope with fairly easily; but differences of value and religion are much harder to handle. It is important to use our capacity to think and reason in these difficult areas. And when it comes to religious disagreements, we should use our minds to evaluate which religion makes more sense of the complexity of our experience. Naturally, due to the fact that each person has been shaped by a multitude of different factors, the weighing by reason of the multitude of different factors (some of which are very particular to an individual's journey) will produce different results. So when it comes to "conversion," reason often meets social conditioning in interesting ways. Social conditioning remains significant. In the same way a person can grow up thinking in one language, so it is possible for a person to learn a second language and start thinking in that one instead. Learning a second language is difficult. Ideally you must live and submerge yourself in a different culture. But many people manage to do this and as a result start to think differently. What is true in language is also true in religion. Atheists become Christians and Christians become atheists because of the company they choose. The choice of company creates a challenge to the received worldview of their youth. As a person rationally reflects on two different worldviews, he or she makes a choice.

So a key question then is what sort of group we decide to mix with? We all come to the conversation with a certain givenness: my parents introduced me to faith. But as we grow older, so we decide to select our own conversation partners. The choice of conversation partner is crucial. So on a religious level: If I opt to find a group of

Pentecostals then, it is likely, I shall slowly become a Pentecostal; if I opt for a group of Roman Catholics, then I might become a Catholic and so on. On a political level: If I gravitate towards a group of white supremacists, then there is a danger I shall slowly become racist. However, if I opt to read, watch, and gravitate towards people sympathetic to Michael Moore, then it is likely I shall become a liberal. It is at the point of deciding who we are going to let influence us that we have certain options. And it is at this point we should read. Books open up many different worldviews. It is at this point we can give our reason a more prominent role to evaluate the evidence, explore the implications, and decide which worldview we want to let shape us. This is important: Reason and arguments are important players. We need to think about who we are going to read. I should think about a disagreement provoked by reading a book written by someone with whom I am in disagreement. Just because I am conditioned (i.e. there is a certain givenness) does not mean that there are not reasons for my worldview. And as you read this book you will see that I have been shaped by a range of influences – atheists, agnostics, Muslims, Jews, and Buddhists are all important conversation partners. This book is about Christian doctrine; it wants to open up, in a sympathetic, way the Christian worldview.

Why Bother with the Christian Worldview?

A book about Christian doctrine needs to assume that the story of the Christian drama is worth examining and makes sense of the complexity of the world. However, the assumption does need some defending. In the next chapter, we shall examine the whole project of natural theology and the arguments for the existence of God. In the rest of this chapter however, we shall describe and respond to some of the main reasons why people find faith rather implausible.

Problem 1: it looks like religion is on the way out

If you are sitting in Germany or Holland, then it looks like religion is in trouble. Pop into a church and you will find it a gathering place for the elderly. Anyone 40 years old and younger has better things to do with their Sundays. The secularization thesis – whose most able contemporary defender is Steve Bruce – seems to be vindicated.

There are various versions of the secularization thesis. One popular version states that with the rise of modernity, science, and technology, the pre-modern nature of religion would become increasingly apparent. Where gods and spirits explained the weather, we now have the science of meteorology. Where witch doctors used to heal, antibiotics now cure. As modernity spreads across the world, so religion will decline. A more sophisticated version stresses the problem of socialization. Steve Bruce writes:

> We may want to explain the secularity of some elite groups (such as professional scientists) by the impact of science and rationalism, but to understand the mass of the population it is not self-conscious irreligion that is important. It is indifference. The primary cause of indifference is the lack of religious socialization and the lack of constant background affirmation of beliefs.[3]

So, for Bruce, the problem is that people have just stopped caring; they have stopped being interested in religion.

However, the secularization thesis is not supported by the data. Statistically, Asia, the Middle East, South America, and Africa are all robustly religious, even though they have McDonalds, satellite television, and increasingly modern medicine. The United States remains deeply religious. A virtually unchanged 40 percent of Americans sit in Church every week (or at least think they do) and almost all of them insist that their faith is vitally important.[4] Even in Europe we find many people believing even if they don't belong. Grace Davie has documented the ways in which religious life in Europe seems to be "mutating" but not disappearing. Grace Davie writes:

> For particular historical reasons (notably the historic connections between Church and State), significant numbers of Europeans are content to let both churches and churchgoers enact a memory on their behalf (the essential meaning of vicarious), more than half aware that they might need to draw on the capital at crucial times in their individual or their collective lives. The almost universal take up of religious ceremonies at the time of death is the most obvious expression of this tendency; so, too, the prominence of the historic churches in particular at times of national crisis or, more positively, of national celebration. Think, for example, of the significance of European churches and church buildings after the sinking of the Baltic ferry *Estonia*, after the death of Princess Diana or after the terrifying events of 11 September 2001.[5]

Countries with a church tax system continue to collect revenue, even if the donors don't actually attend. And when a crisis erupts, argues Davie, churches are suddenly "used" as a mechanism of coping with the trauma. Although this might not be a particularly demanding form of religious life, it is still very much there. It is undoubtedly true that modernity has not created thousands of atheists and agnostics. Scratch a European and you will find underneath the apparent indifferent exterior, a person interested in "New Age" movements and "spirituality." The few atheists and agnostics assume that most of their friends are just like them. This is not true. The world is full of people of faith.

Problem 2: science has displaced religion

Nevertheless my agnostic conversation partner might retort: Since science has explained the world far more effectively than religion ever could, is it not the case that religion ought to be disappearing?

It is true that the story of the religion and science debate often looks like that. Along came the Copernican revolution and the Church – on the basis of Aristotle (384 BCE–322 BCE) – opposed it. Galileo – who had decisive evidence that the earth is spinning around the sun – was placed under house arrest by the Roman Catholic Church.[6] Along came Charles Darwin, with his elegant hypothesis of natural selection that contradicts the historicity of Genesis 1, and the Church offered implausible alternative accounts, such as the young earth hypothesis or that the earth was created with the appearance of age.

It is undoubtedly true that overall the Church did not react wisely to the story of science. In my view, it created a needless battle. We shall see in chapter two how the New Physics has proved to be a friend of religion. The Church should have never worried about the cosmology of the universe: it was mainly the authority of Aristotle which was at stake; and although Aristotle is important, he is not that important. As we shall see in chapter six, we should have never argued with science on Genesis 1. The Victorian Church seemed to have lost sight of the genre of the creation stories. When God said "Let there be light," we shouldn't imagine a big mouth uttering words. Instead we see that the creation is brought about by the words of God, which means that through creation we can see God disclosing Godself. The genre of the creation story is closer to poetry: it was never intended as a historical account.

Science, I shall argue in chapter two, needs theism (a belief in a personal God). But for now, we shall note that the charge is definitely not proven.

Problem 3: metaphysics is impossible

Metaphysics is literally "after the physics." The term was originally used by Aristotle. However, in this context, we are using the term to describe all attempts to describe ultimate reality. It was **Thomas Huxley** who first coined the expression "agnostic" in the nineteenth century. He explained:

> When I reached intellectual maturity, and began to ask myself whether I was an atheist, a theist, or a pantheist; a materialist or an idealist; a Christian or a freethinker, I found that the more I learned and reflected, the less ready was the answer; until at last I came to the conclusion that I had neither art nor part with any of these denominations, except the last. The one thing in which most of these good people were agreed was the one thing in which I differed from them. They were quite sure that they had attained a certain

---

THOMAS HUXLEY (1825–95)

Huxley was born in Ealing, London, on May 4, 1825. His father could only afford to send Thomas to school for two years. However, thanks to Huxley's passionate interest in reading, he managed to get a scholarship to study at Charing Cross Hospital. Trained as a surgeon, he traveled around the world in the Navy collecting marine invertebrates. When Charles Darwin published *The Origin of Species*, Huxley became his most outspoken supporter. In June 1860, he was the respondent to Archbishop Samuel Wilberforce. He is best known for his contributions in science, but he also wrote widely on politics, religion, and ethics. He died on June 29, 1895.

"gnosis" – had more or less successfully solved the problem of existence; while I was quite sure I had not, and had a pretty strong conviction that the problem was insoluble. And, with Hume and Kant on my side, I could not think myself presumptuous in holding fast by that opinion. [. . .] So I took thought, and invented what I conceived to be the appropriate title of "agnostic." It came into my head as suggestively antithetic to the "gnostic" of Church history, who professed to know so much about the very things of which I was ignorant; and I took the earliest opportunity of parading it at our Society, to show that I, too, had a tail, like the other foxes. [Quoted in *Encyclopedia of Religion and Ethics*, 1908, edited by James Hastings MA DD][7]

In popular usage the word "agnostic" often means unsure. Huxley, however, believes it is impossible for puny little people to know about ultimate reality. Here we are in the middle of space–time, stuck on a small planet in an insignificant solar system, which is part of many solar systems. How on earth (pun intended) could we ever work out with any meaningful confidence what the source of all this is like? Huxley insisted that the only proper answer is to surrender to our ignorance. We cannot and never will know.

Again a full response to this will be developed in chapter two. For now let us think a little about Huxley's expectations for knowledge. Let us try a thought exercise: imagine, if you can, your brain on a laboratory bench attached to a powerful computer. Imagine further that there are five leads (one for each sense) attached from your brain to the computer. Let us suppose that this computer generates the impression of your body (your physical appearance) and then all the subsequent experiences that your body enjoys. Let us further imagine that the computer program is interactive: So when your mind makes a decision, the experiences generated by the computer change. Now consider the following question: is it possible that this could be the case? Can you disprove the possibility that your mind is not attached to a computer and everything you experience is just a computer generated experience?

Now of course it is possible that this is true. But no one believes it is. There are some possible explanations, which we need to exclude because they are so extremely improbable. It is true the external world might not exist, but we all know it does. And we certainly all behave as if it does.

There are many complex events, of which we are right in the middle, that we attempt to explain. We attempt to formulate a hypothesis to make some sense of the event, for example, the nature of the brain, the mystery of love, and the powerful bonds between a parent and a child. Just because it is complicated and we are part of what we are trying to explain, we do not simply surrender to agnosticism. It is true that there are many possible explanations for these things. It is also true that complete certainty is impossible, but we can still distinguish between accounts that are more likely and less likely.

One sickness that pervaded modernity was this absurd expectation for knowledge – if we cannot be completely and utterly sure then we cannot claim to know.[8] Alasdair MacIntyre in *Whose Justice? Which Rationality?*[9] has described the damage that this sickness has caused. Many Europeans reasoned thus:

1 Knowledge depends on complete certainty.
2 We cannot be certain of anything – including whether there is an external world and what is true in metaphysics.
3 Therefore we have no knowledge.

With this reasoning, European culture invented relativism. Each culture has different beliefs; there is no way of knowing which culture has the true beliefs; therefore we must just resign ourselves to our ignorance and culturally-conditioned beliefs.

The big mistake underpinning relativism is an unreasonable expectation for knowledge – the quest for complete certainty. Where did this absurd expectation for knowledge come from? Most historians of ideas blame **René Descartes**. Living in the seventeenth century, he was responsible for raising, in an acute way, the whole modern problem of epistemology. In his *Meditations on First Philosophy* (1641),[10] Descartes set out on his quest for a sure foundation for all knowledge claims. He starts the first meditation by asking the question whether the external world exists and decides that he cannot exclude the possibility that he is dreaming. In the second meditation he reflects on the nature of mathematics and logic. Can he be sure that $2 + 2 = 4$? He decides that he cannot be sure because it is possible that a malignant demon is tampering with his mind. (Incidentally, at this point Descartes is in deep trouble because a malignant

RENÉ DESCARTES (1596–1650)

Descartes was a Frenchman, born in 1596 near Tours. With an initial Jesuit education, he discovered a passion for mathematics. He trained in law and then joined the Dutch military. He started writing in 1619 and ranged widely: he wrote on optics, meteorology, and geometry. But it was when he moved to Amsterdam that he started work on his best known work *Discourse on the Method* (1637), which was followed by *Meditations on First Philosophy* (1641). In 1649, Queen Christina of Sweden asked him to become a philosophy tutor in Stockholm. However, his health could not cope with the demands being placed upon him and he died in 1650.

demon that is tampering with his rational processes means that he cannot any longer have any confidence in the power of reason and deduction and therefore he cannot rationally justify any further steps in his argument.) Nevertheless, on he goes. So is there anything about which Descartes can be certain? After much thought he decides that he is sure of one proposition (a proposition is a fact-asserting sentence). He is sure that he – Descartes – doubts everything. Hence he arrives at his famous: *cogito ergo sum* – I think therefore I am.

Descartes's achievement was to set up an impossible standard for knowledge: a standard that his own argument does not reach. One does not know until one is completely sure. If one works with this standard for knowledge, then it is not surprising that one does not know very much. Everything is in trouble: science, knowledge that another loves me, mental activity, and of course metaphysics.

Knowledge claims must make certain assumptions. Science assumes both the existence of the external world and that this world is intelligible. So every scientific hypothesis could be doubted. However, we find ourselves persuaded of a scientific hypothesis (for example the rather elegant hypothesis of natural selection to explain the fossil record and the development of life on earth) because of its explanatory power. A good hypothesis explains the data in a simple (without recourse to complicating entities or improbable factors) and comprehensive way.

On one level the claim that "God is" can be treated much like a scientific hypothesis. As we shall see in the second chapter, we live in a complex world. We need to explain the reality of love, the order in nature, our religious experience, and our sense of moral obligation. The best explanation for this complex data will, I suggest, be the claim that God exists.

BLAISE PASCAL (1623–62)

In his short life of 39 years, Pascal shaped the disciplines of mathematics, science, and philosophy. Educated by his eccentric father, Pascal exhibited a natural capacity for mathematics. After his father died, Pascal was required to administer his father's estate, which he combined with an interest in scientific experimentation and continuing to make developments in geometry and philosophy. His best known philosophical works are *Pensées* (published 1842) and *Provincial Letters* (published 1657).

Problem 4: agnosticism makes more sense

Where problem 3 stresses the impossibility of metaphysics, this problem wants to stress the positive attractions of agnosticism. Even allowing for the promise in the next chapter that theism will be presented as the best explanation for the complex data of the world, it still leaves many questions unanswered. There are many religions in the world, which one has the truth? Is the experience of God an Allah, a Trinity, a Brahman, or just a Buddha-Nature?

The problem here can be illustrated by looking at the following thought-exercise. Imagine you are sitting in the middle of a large room. Around the edge of this room is one representative of all the major religious traditions in the world. Along with the major traditions – Hindus, Buddhists, Sikhs, Jews, Christians, and Muslims – some of the smaller and more recent traditions – Ba'hais, Mormons, and New Age advocates – are represented. Each person is given half a day to present his or her tradition. Your task is to decide which tradition is true. Each person is a superb and effective communicator; so each tradition has an equal chance. How would you decide which one is true?[11]

The problem here is that even if (and this remains a big if) one can argue for some divine reality, we are still left with the problem that we "don't know" which religion best represents the interests of the divine.

Now, thinking about this problem introduces another dimension to being "religious." Reasons are clearly central: However, it is equally important to recognize the centrality of practices. A decision for faith is not simply a matter of belief. Religion has as much to do with practice as belief. It was **Blaise Pascal** who saw this most closely with his famous wager. The argument breaks down into five steps.

1 Let us assume that the agnostic is right and that we cannot be sure if there is a God.

Pascal starts from the place of the agnostic. He is assuming, as John Hick puts it, "epistemological agnosticism" (i.e. there is no rational way of knowing for sure whether God is or is not).[12]

2 Nevertheless the agnostic must make a choice.

Now this is Pascal's insight. A decision must still be made. The reason why a decision is forced is because faith is to be practiced. And with practices you cannot be agnostic. So, for example, I am either going to pray or not pray. If I try to decide not to decide, then I end up not praying. Or I am going to go to Church or not go to Church. If I decide not to decide, then I don't go to Church. All agnostics behave like atheists. They, in effect, make a decision. So Pascal explains:

> Yes; but you must wager. It is not optional. You are embarked. Which will you choose then? Let us see. Since you must choose, let us see which interests you least. You have two things to lose, the true and the good; and two things to stake, your reason and your will, your knowledge and your happiness; and your nature has two things to shun, error and misery. Your reason is no more shocked in choosing one rather than the other, since you must of necessity choose. This is one point settled. But your happiness? Let us weigh the gain and the loss in wagering that God is. Let us estimate these two chances. If you gain, you gain all; if you lose, you lose nothing. Wager, then, without hesitation that He is.[13]

Embedded in the above quotation is the rest of the argument, which then runs as follows:

3 If you opt for unbelief and get it right, then you will have extinction; if you opt for unbelief and get it wrong, then you risk damnation.
4 If you opt for belief and get it wrong, then you will get extinction; if you opt for unbelief and get it right, then you will get eternal life.
5 So gamble on happiness: you have nothing to lose and everything to gain.

Much has been made of the problems with the argument. Pascal assumes that there is really only one religious option, but this ignores the sheer range and diversity of religions in the world. Many faithful believers are unhappy with faith being turned into a prudent gamble. However, his major challenge to the agnostic remains: faith is to do with behavior. With behavior you cannot be agnostic.

Agnostics like to imagine they are in between atheism and belief. However, Pascal points out to them that this is largely an illusion. Agnostics behave like atheists: they like to imagine all the options are still open, but in terms of behavior they don't go to church or pray. They live like atheists. Agnosticism only makes sense if atheism is true.

Naturally this still leaves the problem embedded in the thought-exercise. Religious diversity is a major challenge. In chapter nine, we shall look at the challenge of religious diversity in some detail. Suffice it to say for now, it is important to remember that there is a fundamental agreement across religious traditions: they all agree that atheism is mistaken. And when it comes to the disagreement, it is very easy for us to imagine that each religion is completely separate from every other religion. The truth is that there is endless interplay and development between traditions. Judaism gave birth to Christianity and Islam. Hinduism is the root of Buddhism. Islam and Hinduism shaped Sikhism. Furthermore, given the complexity within each religion, there is hardly a religious idea which isn't found within each tradition. So for example, Hinduism is often depicted as pantheistic (God is in all), while Christianity is seen as theistic (there is a personal God separate from creation). Yet Hinduism has theistic strands and there are Christians who are pantheistic in their understanding of God.

As a lifestyle option, agnosticism doesn't exist. And I want to suggest that the problem of religious diversity is not a decisive argument for agnosticism. Indeed the universal witness of these religions, that there is a transcendent entity, is a major challenge to the agnostic.

Problem 5: religion is horrid and cruel

For some critics of religion, the problem with religion is less intellectual and more moral. The problem with religion, these critics complain, is that often it is linked with violence. A. N. Wilson states the problem thus:

> Religion is the tragedy of mankind. It appeals to all that is noblest, purest, loftiest in the human spirit, and yet there scarcely exists a religion which has not been responsible for wars, tyrannies, and the suppression of the truth. Marx described it as the opium of the people; but it is much deadlier than opium. It does not send people to sleep. It excites them to persecute one another, to exalt their own feelings and opinions above those of others, to claim for themselves a possession of the truth. If we read St Paul's famous hymn to Charity in his Epistle to the Corinthians, we see an incomparably exalted view of human virtue. "Charity suffereth long, and is kind. Charity vaunteth not itself . . . rejoiceth not in iniquity, but rejoiceth in the truth." When we consider the behavior of the huge preponderance of religious people and religious organizations in the history of mankind, we come to realize that Religion is the precise opposite of what St Paul calls Charity. Religion, far from suffering long, makes a point of establishing itself as the sole highway to salvation, and brooks no dissent from those who have the temerity to disagree with it. Religion is not kind; it is cruel. Religion does not rejoice in the truth. In fact,

all the major religions go out of their way to suppress the truth and to label those who attempt to tell the truth as heretics. Religion vaunteth itself, is puffed up; but worse: by trying to bring good things to pass, it brings very evil things to pass. Like a human psychopath it is a war with all its own best instincts, because it knows, if these impulses were followed, it would destroy itself.[14]

Wilson goes on to document countless illustrations of the cruelty of religion: the damaging role that religion has played in Northern Ireland and Israel/Palestine; the history of religious wars, the intolerance towards those that disagree with a religion (especially the Salman Rushdie controversy), and the reluctance of the Church to take progressive ethical positions (for example on the rights of women). The temptation is to conclude that religion is a deeply destructive entity: even if the world isn't going to outgrow religion, it does not deserve any encouragement.

Such is the power of religion, it is important to recognize that religion is often a force for evil in the world. For a person of faith, the study of religious history is deeply painful. One cannot evade the history of Christian anti-Semitism or the brutality of the Crusades or the propensity of the Church to support patriarchy rather than justice. One must resist the temptation to distinguish between "true religion," which does not do these wicked things, and "bad religion," which is religion being used by political and economic entities for unjust ends. It is clear that many of the most devout were involved in heinous acts. Popes that no doubt prayed and loved Jesus did authorize the Crusades; Muslims who prayed five times daily have become suicide bombers and blown up many innocent people; and it was Bible-believing Christians in the Dutch Reformed Church who constructed a Biblical justification of apartheid. Sincere people of faith have behaved in extremely wicked ways.

Yet in the same way it would be wrong to condemn secularism and secularists because of the abuses of Stalin's regime, so one should not condemn religion because of its evil and violent past. The truth about the evils exercised in the name of religion should not obscure us from other truths. Religion has, for example, provided us with Mahatma Gandhi, Martin Luther King, Desmond Tutu, and Mother Teresa. Religion has inspired amazing music and poetry. Religion has helped millions of people cope with seemingly unbearable tragedy. Religion has underpinned the campaign for civil rights and justice. Although it is true that if religion did not exist, we would not have had the Crusades; it is also true that we would not have had the concept of human rights.[15]

The fact that religious people have often behaved in deeply wicked ways does not mean that the claims underpinning the religious worldview are false. It might all be true. At this stage, to proceed with the rest of the book, we simply need a sense that Christianity is worth investigating. The violent history of religions is not, I suggest, a sufficient reason to refuse to investigate the truth claims of Christianity.

Problem 6: faith is just a psychological projection

It was **Sigmund Freud** who argued that religion is our own projection of our earthly father (who provides comfort and security) into the skies. In *The Future of an Illusion*, he explains:

> As we already know, the terrifying impression of helplessness in childhood aroused the need for protection – for protection through love – which was provided by the father; and the recognition that this helplessness lasts throughout life made it necessary to cling to the existence of a father, but this time a more powerful one. Thus the benevolent rule of a divine Providence allays our fears of the dangers of life; the establishment of a moral world-order ensures the fulfillment of the demands of justice, which have so often remained unfulfilled in human civilization; and the prolongation of earthly existence in a future life provides the local and temporal framework in which these wish fulfillments take place.[16]

Freud goes on to argue that given this is so manifestly what religion is, it is unlikely to be true. Therefore understanding the pyschological cause of religion will help us free ourselves from its influence.

Freud is right on one level. All beliefs about the world have a psychological cause. I believe that $2 + 2 = 4$. The psychological cause of this belief was an intimidating elementary school teacher, who taught me the basics of mathematics. However, the psychological cause has nothing to do with the truth or falsity of the belief. One is guilty of the Genetic Fallacy when one confuses a psychological cause with the truthfulness of a belief. As we saw when we looked at Durkheim: we are all socially-conditioned. In the same way there is a psychological explanation for all beliefs: there is a psychological explanation for the atheist and agnostic. Furthermore a religious person could argue that all Freud has done has been to identify the God-given mechanism that creates the need for the transcendent. In other words, God wanted humans to draw a parallel between the "ideal" earthly parent and the heavenly one. The psychological doorway to belief that Freud has identified is the one that God always intended.

The Next Stage

In this opening chapter we have looked at six reasons why faith is viewed as problematic. There are many other reasons, for example the problem of evil and suffering. However, given that the problem of evil and suffering is a major theme in this book, we shall take this difficulty with us into the rest of the book. In this chapter, I have confined the discussion to defending the following: first the persistence of religion;

SIGMUND FREUD (1856–1939)

Brought up a Jew in Vienna, Austria, Freud developed the broad outlines of modern psychology. He spent much of his life working with Joseph Breuer. One of their key ideas is that many neuroses are a result of traumas developed in childhood. Freud and Breuer parted company when Freud increasingly stressed the centrality of sexual attitudes in childhood. Freud's finest work is probably *The Interpretation of Dreams* (published in 1900).

second, science is not an enemy of religion; third, the legitimacy of metaphysical claims; fourth, the impossibility of living as an agnostic; fifth, the violent history of religions does not justify the refusal to examine the truth claims of Christianity; and finally, a psychological explanation is compatible with religion being true.

With these preliminaries out of the way, we now need to start the important work of exploring Christianity in some detail.

QUESTIONS FOR REFLECTION AND DISCUSSION

- Can you think of any other major obstacles to faith, which are not considered in this chapter?
- Take one of the responses to a problem in this chapter and reflect on how an agnostic might disagree with the response.
- Do you think that modernity is slowly and gradually undermining religious belief?
- Why has the relationship between science and religion been so difficult? What can be done to improve the relationship?

GLOSSARY

Agnostics: at a popular level, the term describes people who are not sure whether God exists. More technically, an agnostic is a person who thinks that we can never know the truth about metaphysics

Atheists: people who do not believe in the existence of God. Some atheists are also "secular humanists" (i.e. people who believe that society should be free from religious influences and affirm the importance and value of humanity)

Genetic fallacy: the view that to identify a social or psychological genesis for a view or position precludes the possibility that the view or position is true

Metaphysics: literally, beyond physics. Any attempt to describe ultimate reality

Relativism: the view that certain disagreements (especially religious and moral) are unresolvable and one's perspective will be determined by one's culture

Secularization: the process that has seen in Western Europe a decline in the significance of religious institutions in society.

Notes

1 Émile Durkheim, *The Elementary Forms of Religious Life* (1912, translated 1915, New York: The Free Press, 1965), p. 22.
2 For D. Z. Phillips see *Wittgenstein and Religion* (Basingstoke: Palgrave Macmillan, 1994).
3 Steve Bruce, *God is Dead: Secularization in the West* (Oxford: Blackwell, 2002), p. 240.
4 Gallup is responsible for the fairly consistent statistic that 40 percent of Americans are in Church every week; the challenge to this statistic is from the work of Kirk Hathaway who has argued that we do not find in the actual congregations the expected number for this statistic to be true. Even if the statistic speaks to the "intention" of most Americans, it remains true that this reflects on a deep religious commitment. It is not evidence for the secularization thesis. See K. Hadaway, P. Marler, and M. Chaves, "A symposium on church attendance," *American Sociological Review* 63 (1) (1988): 111–45.
5 Grace Davie, *Europe: The Exceptional Case. Parameters of Faith in the Modern World* (London: Darton, Longman, and Todd, 2002), p. 19.
6 I should stress that with the advantage of hindsight it is easy to be very critical about the players in the Copernican revolution. There were plenty of thoughtful people who had strong arguments against Galileo.
7 Thomas Huxley, as quoted in http://www.infidels.org/news/atheism/sn-huxley.html.
8 This is a complex area. One distinction, which is popular amongst philosophers, is to concede that knowledge does require certainty, but that rational belief does not. Given that certainty about the existence of the world is not available, I would want to suggest that "knowing" cannot entail certainty. To eliminate every theoretical area of uncertainty would mean that we would not even know that tables and chairs exist. My view is that knowledge claims can

make certain basic assumptions. This is developed further in Ian Markham, *Truth and the Reality of God* (Edinburgh: T. & T. Clark, 1999).

9 Alasdair MacIntyre, *Whose Justice? Which Rationality?* (Notre Dame, IN: University of Notre Dame Press, 1988).

10 Descartes first sketched out the argument in 1637 in his *Discourse on Method*. However, his *Meditations on First Philosophy* is his best known work and is a fuller formulation of the argument (translated from the Latin by Donald A. Cress (Indianapolis, IN: Hackett Publishing Company, 1979)).

11 I have used this thought exercise in several places in my work. It was originally developed in my *A World Religions Reader*, 2nd edition (Oxford: Blackwell, 2000), p. 17.

12 See John Hick, *Faith and Knowledge*, 2nd edition (London: Collins Fount, 1978).

13 Blaise Pascal, *Pensées* as found at http://www.ccel.org/p/pascal/pensees/pensees04.htm.

14 A. N. Wilson, *Against Religion* (London: Chatto and Windus, 1991), pp. 1–2.

15 I am assuming that the language of human rights owes much to the Roman Catholic development of the concept of natural law. I defend this claim in my *Theology of Engagement* (Oxford: Blackwell, 2003).

16 Sigmund Freud, *The Future of an Illusion*, translated by W. D. Robinson-Scott. Revised and newly edited by James Strachey (London: The Hogarth Press and the Institute of Psycho-Analysis, 1973), pp. 30–1.

chapter 2
THE
THEISTIC
CLAIM

LEARNING OUTCOMES

By the end of this chapter you should be able to:

- know about the arguments for and against natural theology
- appreciate the complexity of concepts such as "proof" and "argument"
- understand the traditional arguments for God's existence
- understand why the author finds these arguments sufficient as a basis for faith

STRUCTURE

- Natural theology
- Arguments for the existence of God – the Cosmological argument, and the Ontological argument
- The Design argument
- Contemporary physics
- Additional arguments – from religious experience, from moral experience, from love, and from music and art

For many young people growing up in Europe, secular humanism is the way forward. The term "secular" has its roots in the **Enlightenment** and captures the decreasing power of religious institutions in society. The term "humanism" has its roots in the **Renaissance** and its meaning has evolved into the affirmation of humanity without reference to God.[1] The creed of the modern secular humanist believes that science has displaced God. Paul Kurtz and Edwin Wilson write in their *Humanist Manifesto* that "traditional dogmatic and authoritarian religions that place revelation, God, ritual, or creed above human needs and experience do a disservice to the human species."[2] The problem, they explain, is that religion does not meet the basic rational requirements for belief:

> Any account of nature should pass the tests of scientific evidence; in our judgment, the dogmas and myths of traditional religions do not do so. Even at this late date in human history, certain elementary facts based upon the critical use of scientific reason have to be restated. We find insufficient evidence for belief in the existence of a supernatural; it is either meaningless or irrelevant to the question and survival of the human race. As nontheists, we begin with humans not God, nature not deity.[3]

ENLIGHTENMENT

An intellectual movement that shaped the eighteenth century. It started in Europe and had a significant impact on America. Key thinkers include John Locke (1632–1704), David Hume (1711–76), Voltaire (1694–1778), Rousseau (1712–78) and Immanuel Kant (1724–1804). Of these Kant is the most important. It tended to distrust authority, believing instead in the importance of reason and good argument.

RENAISSANCE

This is a French and Italian movement, which developed in the fourteenth and fifteenth century. Inspired by the classical period of ancient Greece, it advocated "humanism." Given that most of the members of this movement were Roman Catholics, the term "humanist" did not have the anti-religious connotations that it has today. They wanted to celebrate human achievements because they believed that humanity was the crowning point of God's creation.

Given there is no God, the authors go on to argue, we have all the more reason to embrace each other and embrace the world in which we live.

It is important that we respect this growing tradition of secular humanism. At various points it provides an important challenge to faith. It forces faith to engage constructively with science. Secular humanism requires faith to confront its ambivalent role in the history of civil rights both for women and blacks (and, increasingly, other minorities). However, while conceding the importance of the conversation with secular humanists, it is wrong to imagine that they have all the good arguments. Indeed, it is my view that the better arguments are on the side of belief. The entire project of "natural theology" was dedicated to demonstrating the coherence and reasonableness of faith.

Natural Theology

Although many Christian thinkers believed that there were good arguments for belief, it was the thirteenth-century Dominican Friar **Thomas Aquinas** who is most often given the credit for distinguishing revealed from natural theology. Aquinas believed that all people, by virtue of their God-given rationality, should be able to use their

THOMAS AQUINAS (1225–74)

Thomas was born at Roccasecca, which is near Aquino in Italy. He was educated at Monte Cassino Abbey, then later at the University of Naples. Much to the surprise of his family, he decided to become a Dominican friar. He moved to the University of Paris, where he found himself at the center of many of the main controversies of his day. His great achievement was to weave together the Augustinian tradition with the thought of Aristotle. His major work is the *Summa Theologica* (a book intended for beginners!), which he never finished. After celebrating the Eucharist on December 6, 1273, he had a mystical experience that made it impossible for him to complete his massive project. Apparently when asked why he had stopped writing, he explained that "all that I have written seems to me like straw compared with what has now been revealed to me." He died three months later.

minds and establish three truths about God. The first is that God is; the second is the nature of God; and the third is the immortality of the soul. In other words there are good arguments for these three truths, which means that humans everywhere should accept them. This is the realm of natural theology. Matters such as the atonement, the Incarnation, and the Trinity depend on God revealing these truths to us. We cannot use our reason to work these truths out. Instead we depend on God revealing these truths to us in the life, death, and resurrection of Jesus, which is documented in the Bible and affirmed by the Church. This aspect of theology is revealed theology.

There are plenty of contemporary Christian thinkers who believe that natural theology is problematic. The first major worry is a widespread feeling that it no longer works. Some suspect that Immanuel Kant (1724–1804) has irretrievably damaged the traditional arguments. Later in this chapter, we shall look at some of the main arguments and their objections.

It is, however, worth reminding ourselves of the point made in chapter one about "expectations." These arguments are bound to be in trouble if the expectation is that one must arrive at a formulation of the argument that every rational person must accept. This is a very demanding definition of "proof." Strictly, the only arguments that satisfy this expectation are mathematical and logical. Consider, for example, the mathematical truth that two added to two will always equal four. Provided the words and concepts are understood, no rational person can disagree with that assertion.

Once we move beyond this very narrow range, problems immediately arise. It is true that water boils at 100°C at standard pressure. This truth is a result of repeated observations: however, we are assuming that (a) an external world exists in which there is water, and (b) that which is true in the past will be true in the future. Both of these assumptions are contestable.[4] With a strict definition of "proof" these arguments do not succeed.

It might be objected that at least in the world of science, unlike the world of religion, we find sound deductive argument. With a deductive argument, if the reasoning is sound and the premises are true, then the conclusion must follow. So to take the classic example:

1 A bachelor is an unmarried man
2 John is a bachelor
3 Therefore John is an unmarried man.

This is a model deductive argument: the first premise is the definition of the term bachelor; the second is an empirical observation; and the third must follow logically.

Much of the debate in philosophy of religion has assumed a high expectation of proof and treated the arguments as deductive arguments. However, these expectations are not met by science, let alone law. Instead scientific arguments are probability arguments (given all this data, the hypothesis that provides the most probable explana-tion is this one) rather than straightforward deductive arguments. Richard Swinburne in *The Existence of God* revisits many of the traditional arguments (in particular the argument from Design) and illustrates that treated as a probability argument the Design argument, for example, is sound and potentially persuasive.[5]

Perhaps the best way to look at these arguments is to use the analogy of a murder trial in a court of law. The courts are never totally sure as to who did the murder; instead they work with the criterion that a case must be proved "beyond reasonable doubt." It is possible that aliens planted the evidence on the suspect but this would be beyond reasonable doubt. The task then for the court is to examine all of the clues and determine whether the narrative suggested by the prosecution makes the best sense of the evidence. Total certainty is impossible; every result is contestable (even a confession – some are forced, others reflect mental instability). But one concedes that judgments must be made. And we work within the constraints forced upon us.

So if we have similar expectations for our arguments for God's existence as we do for legal arguments (in a court of law, where one is trying to persuade a jury) or scientific arguments (the best explanation for the data), then the traditional arguments can and do persuade people.

The second worry is more theological. For many in the Reformed tradition, natural theology is a denial of the centrality of the revelation of God in Christ. The most eloquent example of this was **Karl Barth**. Barth's opposition to natural theology was shaped by his experience in Nazi Germany. Barth explains why natural theology became the question of the 1930s:

> The question became a burning one at the moment when the Evangelical Church in Germany was unambiguously and consistently confronted by a definite and new form of natural theology, namely, by the demand to recognize in the political events of the year 1933, and especially in the form of the Godsent Adolf Hitler, a source of specific new revelation of God, which, demanding obedience and trust, took its place beside the revelation attested in Holy Scripture, claiming that it should be acknowledged by Christian proclamation and theology as equally binding and obligatory . . . If it was admissible and right and perhaps even orthodox to combine the knowability of God in Jesus Christ with His knowability in nature, reason, and history, the proclamation of the Gospel with all kinds of other proclamations – and this had been the case, not only in Germany, but in the Church in all lands for a long time – it is hard to see why the German Church should not be allowed to make its own particular use of the procedure.[6]

Barth's objection is simple: once one accords the logical possibility of knowledge of God outside the revelation of God in Christ, then one accords the possibility that Adolf Hitler is a new revelation. Given the latter is abhorrent, it is important that the Church witness exclusively to the revelation of God in Christ. In addition, Barth explains

KARL BARTH (1886–1968)

Karl Barth was born in Basle, Switzerland on May 10, 1886. After a good training in nineteenth-century liberal theology he became a Pastor. It was as he saw all his teachers supporting the madness of the First World War that he started to believe that there was a fundamental problem with this approach to theology. After writing a commentary on the Book of Romans, he became a leading advocate of "dialectical theology" sometimes called "crisis theology." His major work was *Church Dogmatics,* which runs to some thirteen volumes. He was a major inspiration to the Confessing Church during the Nazi period and the author of the Barman Declaration.

elsewhere, it is a grave mistake to treat revealed theology as the conclusion of natural theology. He writes:

> In a word, the covenant of grace which is from the beginning, the presupposition of the atonement, is not a discovery and conclusion of "natural theology." Apart from and without Jesus Christ we can say nothing at all about God and man and their relationship one with another.[7]

This touches on a wider Barthian theme. All knowledge of God depends on God's disclosure to us. Natural theology, for Barth, is a human conceit. It presumes that puny humans can use their minds to work out the ultimate truths of the universe. (At this point, Karl Barth sounds rather like our agnostic.) Instead we must trust God to reveal the truth to humanity. The central claim of Christianity is that the nature of God is revealed decisively in the life, death, and resurrection of Jesus of Nazareth.

Karl Barth raises some important questions. He is right to insist that knowledge of God ultimately depends on revelation. It is true that we are creatures in the middle of the creation; any claims about the ultimate character of the creation depend on God revealing the truth to us. However, there are three reasons why natural theology is helpful. First, it is justified and grounded in the Biblical witness. The Design argument is, in embryo, in St Paul's epistle to the Romans. There Paul writes:

> Ever since the creation of the world his invisible nature, namely, his eternal power and deity, has been clearly perceived in the things that have been made. So they are without excuse. (Romans 1:20)

Second, the ultimate claim of natural theology is simply that there is a God who is revealing. The two issues of God's existence and God's revelations need to be distinguished. Natural theology concentrates on the existence of God: once the existence of God has been established then the location of true revelation is the next stage of the conversation. Third, one can and should recognize that the capacity of the human to detect the purposes of God in creation is itself revelation. It was Emil Brunner who helpfully suggested that natural theology could be properly called natural revelation. The God of Jesus is also the God who created the world. We are connecting with the former when we meditate on the latter.

Most theologians see "theology" very much in the process of natural theology. Karl Rahner argues that the capacity of the human to reason from nature to God is evidence for the intrinsic freedom of the human soul.[8] And most theologians would not accept Karl Barth's claim that if one concedes God's revelatory activity in nature, then one must concede the possibility that Adolf Hitler is a revelatory activity of God. To accept one need not involve accepting every such claim. And a simple criterion for distinguishing true claims to revelation from false ones is simply the compatibility of the revelatory claim with *what we already know of God revealed in Scripture*.

Natural theology is a helpful, legitimate tool for discerning the validity of the Christian story. It is to those main arguments that we now turn.

Arguments for the Existence of God

The arguments for the existence of God are bound to be complex and difficult. So what follows is difficult material: However, given our subject matter, this is not surprising. Let us start our discussion with two very traditional arguments for the existence of God. These are the Cosmological argument and the Ontological argument. The Cosmological argument has been formulated in several different ways. I shall concentrate on the two main ways.[9] The first treats it as an argument about the origins of the universe. The second is derived from **Gottfried Leibniz** and makes use of a version of his "Principle of Sufficient Reason."

The first has a redoubtable defender in William Lane Craig. For Craig, the question is simple: how did the universe begin? Craig argues that the enduring Big Bang theory provides decisive empirical evidence that the universe had a beginning. The idea of the universe starting by itself from nothing is too absurd to contemplate. Therefore one needs to postulate a creator.[10] A major difficulty with this argument is in the work of Stephen Hawking. Quentin Smith makes use of Hawking to argue that his quantum cosmology provides an alternative, namely a self-contained universe, having no

GOTTFRIED WILHELM LEIBNIZ (1646–1716)

Leibniz was a prolific and distinguished German philosopher, who contributed to a wide variety of disciplines. He is probably best known for his contributions to mathematics. He was born and educated in Leipzig. Much of his life was spent in the service of the aristocracy: first the Baron of Boineburg and later the Duke of Hanover. He died on November 14, 1716 in Hanover.

boundary or edge, and therefore not needing a beginning. For Hawking, the universe is finite but it did not have an origin.[11]

This approach has significant problems. Although many religious people have thought of God as the agent responsible for the start of the universe, it is especially attractive to "deists" (those who believe in a creator God, who does not interfere in the running of the universe, but simply starts the universe). The God of theism (belief in a personal God who creates, sustains, and maintains the universe) is the sustainer of all that is: then and now. God is not the great first cause, somewhere back in the mists of time. In fact, when Aquinas discusses the creation of the universe, he implies that rationally his preference is to believe, like his Greek "masters," that matter is eternal, but on the basis of Genesis 1 he accepts that the universe had a beginning.[12] But both his Cosmological argument and his faith would be intact if it were shown that the universe was infinite. Craig concedes this point in passing,[13] but fails to see that it undermines the entire enterprise of the book. The English physicist John Polkinghorne (1930–) places the Hawking question into the appropriate context, when he writes:

> Of course, the first thing to say about that discourse is that theology is concerned with Ontological origin and not with temporal beginning. The idea of creation has no special stake in a datable start to the universe. If Hawking is right, and quantum effects mean that the cosmos as we know it is like a kind of fuzzy spacetime egg, without a singular point at which it all began, that is scientifically very interesting, but theologically insignificant ... Creation is not something he (i.e. God) did fifteen billion years ago, but it is something that he is doing now.[14]

Certainly the second form of the Cosmological argument is not particularly interested in the origin of the universe. This type of cosmological argument appeals to some form of Leibniz's "principle of sufficient reason."

Leibniz's Cosmological argument works from two principles: the first is the law of contradiction; and the second is the principle of sufficient reason. The first is no problem. It simply means that two contradictory assertions cannot both be true. The assertion "this is a chair" cannot be compatible at the same time pointing to the same object with "this is not a chair." The second, however, is subject to much discussion. Leibniz states it as follows: "And that of sufficient reason, in virtue of which we held that no fact can be real or existent, no statement true, unless there be a sufficient reason why it is so and not otherwise, although most often these reasons cannot be known to us."[15] This principle has proved enormously important for understanding the structure of the Cosmological argument, because almost all versions appeal to this principle in some form. So let us look at Leibniz's argument with care. Craig helpfully schematizes it in the following way:

1 Something exists.
2 There must be a sufficient reason or rational basis for why something exists rather than nothing.
3 This sufficient reason cannot be found in any single thing or in the whole aggregate of things or in the efficient causes of all things.
  (a) Things in the world are contingent, that is, determined in their being by other things such that if matter and motion were changed, they would not exist.
  (b) The world is simply a conglomeration of such things and is thus itself contingent.
  (c) The efficient causes of all things are simply prior states of the world, and these successive states do not explain why there are any states, any world, at all.
4 Therefore, there must exist outside the world and the states of the world a sufficient reason for the existence of the world.
5 This sufficient reason will be a metaphysically necessary being, that is, a being whose sufficient reason for existence is self-contained.[16]

When faced with this argument, the literature has been preoccupied with two issues. The first is the validity of the 'principle of sufficient reason'. Attacks have come from a variety of directions. The skeptical philosopher David Hume (1711–76) asked, if one has explained each part of the universe, then what further is there to explain?[17] We know that each part of the universe is explicable in terms of prior states and natural laws, and that is sufficient.

One might feel with Richard Swinburne that an explanation is required for the natural laws.[18] However, even if, with Gaskin, this is granted as a legitimate question, then Gaskin cannot see any reason why the answer cannot simply be that there is no explanation. Gaskin writes, "What Leibniz establishes with unrivalled clarity is the insight that in the last resort explanation of the laws of change and of the existence of the physical universe (if the universe is of finite duration) cannot come from within it. What is not established is that it must come from outside. There may indeed be no explanation."[19]

The second objection rests with the conclusion. Is the idea of a metaphysically necessary being coherent? The difficulty is that most of us find it quite easy to imagine any existing entity not existing. If anything that exists could be conceived of as not existing, then no being could be logically necessary.[20]

It is at this point that the Cosmological argument meets Ontological argument. The Ontological argument was originally formulated by **Anselm** in his *Proslogian*. It is now agreed that there are two forms of the arguments.[21] The first is as follows:

1 Consider the idea of God.

The argument is a prayer: it is an exploration of the concept of God.

The concept of God involves, as a minimum, the greatest conceivable being or as Anselm puts it when addressing God: "that you are something greater than which cannot be thought."[22]

Our whole notion of God, derived from worship, is the "maximally perfect being."[23] God cannot be surpassed. This is one of the reasons why God is "all-powerful, all-loving, and all-knowing."

2 There is a difference between an entity in the imagination and an entity in reality. God would not be the greatest conceivable being if the idea was simply in the imagination.

For a greater entity would be one that exists both in the mind and reality.

ANSELM OF CANTERBURY (1033–1109)

Anselm was born in Aosta, Italy. In 1059 he joined a Benedictine monastery at Bec in France. The Prior of the abbey was Lanfranc, who later became Archbishop of Canterbury. When Lanfranc moved to Canterbury, Anselm became the Prior and later in 1093 succeeded Lanfranc as the Archbishop of Canterbury. He was a gifted theologian and developed the Ontological Argument, as well as writing a key work on the atonement. He had endless disagreements with the King of England (King William II), which led to occasional periods of exile. He died in England in 1109.

Anselm offers an analogy with a painting. He writes: "For it is one thing for something to exist in a person's thought and quite another for the person to think that thing exists. For when a painter thinks ahead to what he will paint, he has that picture in his thought, but he does not yet think it exists, because he has not done it yet. Once he has painted it he has it in his thought and thinks it exists because he has done it."[24]

3   Given God is the greatest conceivable being, God must exist both in the mind and reality.

The great critic of this argument was **Kant**. Now Kant was responding to Descartes's version of the argument, which is a little different from Anselm's. The heart of his objection can be summed up in the now famous slogan "existence is not a predicate." The problem, complains Kant, is that you cannot treat existence as a quality that something either has or does not have. When you look at an advert for a car: the advert lists many qualities of that car (a sun roof, air bags, engine etc). It would be surprising to find in the list – existence. If the car doesn't exist, then it cannot have any qualities. The problem for Kant is that Descartes (and to this version of Anselm's argument) is adding existence on as if it were a quality like any other: but it is not a quality like any other.

It was Norman Malcolm (1911–90) in a famous article in 1960 who spotted that Anselm did have a response to Kant.[25] The second form of the Ontological argument works with a concept of "necessary existence." For this argument to work, the distinction between "contingent" and "necessary" existence needs to be understood. Contingent existence is the type that we all know about and appreciate. Contingent

IMMANUEL KANT (1724–1804)

Considering the impact of Kant's life, everyone marvels at its simplicity. He was born in the East Prussian city of Königsberg (modern day Kaliningrad in Russia); he studied at the University of Königsberg, and then was employed at the University as a tutor and professor for over forty years. It is often said that Kant lived such a regular and ordered life that his neighbors could set their clocks by the time of his daily stroll. Although this is probably apocryphal, it is true that he never traveled more than fifty miles from Königsberg. With a deep pious faith, he brought together the insights of Newtonian physics with philosophy, introducing a set of distinctions that continues to dominate contemporary philosophical discussion.

means "it could be otherwise or not at all." It carries connotations of being dependent and caused. So my study chair is black, but it could have been white. It exists but if the factory making this chair had gone bankrupt before the chair was made, then it wouldn't have existed. It continues to exist, but someone strong could destroy the chair. Almost everything we experience (see or touch) in this universe is contingent.

Now necessary existence is the opposite. It is the idea of something "not contingent." It is not dependent and not caused. It is a self-explanatory entity. So an entity with necessary existence cannot be imagined to not exist: its non-existence is inconceivable. The nearest analogy we have to this type of existence is mathematics. If you add two to two, then you always get four. In any conceivable universe then, four is the result. If this idea makes sense, then the question becomes: which sort of existence would an infinitely perfect being have?

So now a different argument is evolving. The initial steps are the same:

1 Consider the idea of God.
2 The concept of God involves, as a minimum, the greatest conceivable being.

But at this point, the argument shifts:

3 The greatest conceivable being would not be the greatest conceivable being unless it had necessary existence.

If the greatest conceivable being had contingent existence, then that is not as great as a being that has necessary existence. Although it is true that God could be infinite, all-powerful, all-loving, all-knowing and contingent (just happen to exist), it is not as great as having all those qualities and being necessary.

1 A necessary being is one whose non-existence is inconceivable.

We are now considering an idea of God whom we cannot imagine not existing. It is not coherent to say that we think the idea of God involves necessary existence, but doesn't exist. If the idea of God involves necessary existence, then we are imagining an entity that cannot not exist.

2 If God's non-existence is inconceivable, then God must exist.

Critics have concentrated on whether the idea of a necessary being is coherent (self-contradictory or not). Incoherence can be established in one of two ways. First the idea might be vacuous. It might not have any content. However, the concept has content: the analogy with mathematics is helpful. We are envisaging a different type of existence that only God has. Granted that the idea is stretching human language to the limits, but this is inevitable in theology. The idea of a self-explanatory being, which if sufficient to explain all logically possible contingent worlds must be logically necessary, clearly has content. The second way is to show that the idea is self-contradictory. The above account is not obviously self-contradictory. If we can envisage the opposite (i.e., entities which are dependent and caused) then surely it is logically possible to envisage an entity non-dependent and uncaused. The onus of proof when it comes to accusations of incoherence must rest with those who make the charge.

The Cosmological arguments start with the reality of the world around us. In the stronger of the two forms it asks the question: "what explanation do we give for this complex world around us?" A sufficient explanation needs a necessary being, which both seems to make sense, and would then entail envisaging an entity that we cannot imagine not existing. For the contemporary philosopher Keith Ward, the Cosmological argument together with the Ontological argument is sound. He writes:

> The structure of the argument in the so-called Cosmological and Ontological proofs is thus essentially the same. Both are arguments which are primarily philosophical, not experimental: that is to say, they are concerned with analysis of certain concepts, especially those of "necessity", "causality", "explanation" and "value". This is not just a matter of defining terms at will, but of trying to achieve a coherent, consistent, elegant, and illuminating conceptual account of reality.[26]

It is possible to disagree with these arguments. We are not in a position to announce that all rational people must believe in God by virtue of these arguments. However, the arguments are strong. Using our court of law analogy, they provide good reasons for belief. When we look at a new born baby or a beautiful flower, we find ourselves asking the question – why does anything exist at all? And the argument here is that the only adequate explanation for the miracle of anything existing is God.

The Design Argument

Whereas the Cosmological argument marveled at the fact that anything existed, the Design argument marvels at the intricate way in which everything fits together. This argument was supremely popular in the eighteenth and early nineteenth centuries. William Paley's (1743–1805) famous book *Natural Theology or Evidences of the Existence and Attributes of the Deity* (1805) was a bestseller when it came out. He draws an analogy between the universe and a watch. In the same way that you cannot help but deduce an intelligent designer from the intricate workmanship of the watch, so,

DAVID HUME (1711–76)

Born in Edinburgh, his father died when he was two. As a result he was raised by his mother who hoped that David Hume would become a lawyer. However, his interest was in philosophy. He studied at the University of Edinburgh. Although a distinguished philosopher with an engaging and clear writing style, he found it difficult to make a living. His best seller, *A History of England,* was written when he was the Librarian to the Edinburgh Faculty. However, he is best remembered for his *A Treatise of Human Nature* (1739–40), *Enquiries Concerning Human Understanding* (1748), *Concerning the Principles of Morals* (1751), and *Dialogues Concerning Natural Religion* (1779), which was published posthumously.

argued Paley, you cannot help but deduce an intelligent designer from the intricate workmanship of the world.

It is widely assumed that the Scottish philosopher **David Hume** fatally undermined the argument in his *Dialogues Concerning Natural Religion*, published before Paley's book. The dialogues purport to be a conversation between Philo (a skeptic), Demea (an advocate of a rigid orthodoxy) and Cleanthes (an advocate of the Design argument). Although the narrator Pamphilus acclaims Cleanthes the winner, Philo tends to get the better of the arguments. And Philo has three main difficulties with the traditional Design argument.[27]

First, the basic argument is a trick. By drawing a parallel between the world and a human artifact, the suggestion is then offered that something analogous to human decision and creativity is responsible for the world. However, the parallel between the world and a human artifact is in fact weak. There is much dissimilarity. Perhaps the world is much more like a giant crustacean or cauliflower. However, these analogies would not suggest a designer.

Second, there are naturalistic explanations for the order which do not require a designer. David Hume was writing a long time before Charles Darwin (1809–82). However, we now know that one reason why the world fits together so remarkably is because that which didn't "fit in" didn't survive. The remarkable harmony of our eco-system is due to a process of evolution that started with prokaryotic cell organisms emerging 3,000 million years ago. It was not that God fitted everything together in the seven days of creation; but those aspects of the process that did not fit in did not survive.

Third, the argument does not get to God. At best one might affirm the existence of a designer. But this need not be the creator God revealed in Scripture. One problem with the argument is that only some aspects of the world are emphasized in the analogy. While it is true that the order of the world is remarkable, it is also true that there is considerable evil and suffering in this world. What sort of designer introduces the balance of nature where animals feed on each other? If these features of the world are emphasized, then one would logically deduce that the creator of the world must be a sadist or cruel. The designer might be part of a committee of fairly inept trainee gods. All in all, suggested Hume, the argument is very limited.

The temptation at this point is to concede that the Design argument is weak. However, before doing so, let us remind ourselves that simply because there are some arguments against a position does not mean that the position itself is untenable. Even in the clearest of cases, where it seems obvious that the accused is guilty, an imaginative attorney can construct arguments that undermine the prosecution's arguments. We should revisit the form in which the argument was originally stated. And we still need to weigh the arguments for and against.

When Paley formulated his version of the argument, the primary arguments were found in biology. Paley, for example, makes much of the intricate nature of the eye. However, contemporary forms of the arguments are more likely to draw on cosmology and physics. It is here that remarkable data is being collected that does suggest strongly that the universe is designed.

Contemporary Physics

Where the original design argument was threatened by discoveries in biology (in particular the theory of evolution), the modern design argument is entirely comfortable with the account of the universe emerging from contemporary physics. The narrative of a universe emerging 15 billion years ago and becoming the home in which complex sentient creatures exist is a remarkable one. We now know how precise the mathematics needed to be for our type of universe to emerge. If the universe had been only slightly different, then life would not have emerged. The physicist Paul Davies explains:

> The large scale structure and motion of the universe is equally remarkable. The accumulated gravity of the universe operates to restrain the expansion, causing it to decelerate with time. In the primeval phase the expansion was much faster than it is today. The universe is thus the product of a competition between the explosive vigor of the big bang, and the force of gravity which tries to pull the pieces back together again. In recent years, astrophysicists have come to realize just how delicately this competition has been balanced. Had the big bang been weaker, the cosmos would have soon fallen back on itself in a big crunch. On the other hand, had it been stronger, the cosmic material would

have dispersed so rapidly that galaxies would not have formed. Either way, the observed structure of the universe seems to depend very sensitively on the precise matching of explosive vigor to gravitating power. Just how sensitively is revealed by calculation. At the so-called Planck time (10^{43} seconds) (which is the earliest moment at which the concept of space and time has meaning) the matching was accurate to a staggering one part in 10^{60}. That is to say, had the explosion differed in strength at the outset by only one part in 10^{60}, the universe we now perceive would not exist. To give some meaning to these numbers, suppose you wanted to fire a bullet at a one-inch target on the other side of the observable universe, twenty billion years away. Your aim would have to be accurate to that same part in 10^{60}.[28]

It does look fixed. It looks intended. It looks as if there was a decision made that it was important to have life in this universe. And there are so many factors that need to be managed: the order of the universe needed vast quantities of negative entropy; the lack of black holes, which one would expect to dominate a chaotic universe; the uniform structure and behavior of the universe beyond the light horizon; and the fundamental constraints of nature (i.e. those basic entities that have the same numerical value throughout the universe and across all time). As Paul Davies sums up: "There seems to be no obvious reason why the universe did not go berserk, expanding in a chaotic and uncoordinated way, producing enormous black holes. Channeling the explosive violence into such a regular and organized pattern of motion seems like a miracle."[29]

The term "Anthropic Principle" has been coined to partly explain this remarkable order that makes life possible. Coined originally by the astrophysicist Brandon Carter in 1973, the Principle suggests that all the remarkable variables in the universe have precisely the right values for life to appear. John Barrow and Frank Tipler have distinguished between the "Weak Anthropic Principle" and the "Strong Anthropic Principle."[30] The weak version says no more than the fact that because we – as observers of this universe – exist, then inevitably our description of the universe will be consistent with that fact. The strong version insists that the universe must be the way it is to enable observers to emerge within it. John Polkinghorne suggests the "Moderate Anthropic Principle," "which notes the contingent fruitfulness of the universe as being a fact of interest calling for an explanation."[31] He explains:

[T]here is the hint of an amazing anti-Copernican revolution. We don't live at the center of the universe, but it does look as though the very fabric of the cosmos has been given a character which is required if the emergence of beings like us is to be a possibility. There seems to be the chance of a revised and revived argument from design – not appealing to Paley's Cosmic Craftsman working within physical process (which process science explains in a way not requiring intervention by such a God of the gaps) – but appealing to a Cosmic Planner who has endowed his world with a potentiality implanted within the delicate balance of the laws of nature themselves (which laws science cannot explain since it assumes them as the basis for its explanation of the process). In short, the claim would be that the universe is indeed not "any old world" but the carefully calculated construct of its Creator. The Strong Anthropic Principle is then seen to be an intuition of teleological truth, but of a theological rather than a scientific character.[32]

Physicists have been debating the significance of this data. And it is worth examining alternative explanations for this order and the way, mathematically, it makes possible the emergence of life. One of the most popular alternative explanations is that there is a portfolio of universes (all of which exist) and we just happen to be in the one which mathematically enables life to emerge. Naturally we are not in a position to exist in any of the other universes. Hugh Everett in 1957 postulated the "parallel universe" theory to explain the quantum measurement paradox. This involves the universe splitting as a result of an electron to enable two options to be realized simultaneously. With physicists postulating multiple universes in one domain, it was attractive to suggest that there are many (perhaps an infinite number) of universes of which only a small number produce life.

Now there is no scientific evidence (almost by definition) for the multiple-universe theory. As Polkinghorne writes, "Rather it is a metaphysical guess. Its interest lies in the fact that they feel that by making such guesses people clearly feel there is really something calling for an explanation. To my mind a metaphysical speculation of equal coherence and greater economy is, there is just one universe, anthropologically finely-tuned because it is the creation of a Creator who wills it to be capable of fruitful purpose."[33]

Again in the court of law, I want to suggest, it is my judgment that the balance of probabilities lies with belief.[34] The picture emerging from cosmologists involves a universe so intricate and remarkable that there must be a being responsible for it.

Additional Arguments

Many discussions of natural theology stop with the big three arguments (Cosmological, Ontological, and Design). However, there are many other pointers to faith that are worth giving a mention. Naturally all of these pointers could be developed (to deal with each of them properly would really require an entire book). The pointers I shall examine are (a) religious experience, (b) moral experience, (c) love, and (d) music and art.

Religious experience divides into two types: the first is the "sense of God" that countless individuals have had at some time in their life. This is often very unspectacular.

It might be triggered by a beautiful sunset or by a moving piece of music. Sometimes it can be a moment of tragedy that creates the awareness. I remember when I was seventeen, a few months after my mother died, sitting in an empty Church and feeling a sense of love and comfort. In all these cases the person who has an experience like this is sure that the source is beyond the empirical world.

The second type is more dramatic. These are the experiences that are cultivated, through certain disciplines, by the mystics. They are found in all the major religions. Julian of Norwich (1342–1416) in Christianity, Rumi (1207–73) in Islam, Moses ben Jacob Cordovero (1522–70) in Judaism and Ramana Maharshi (1879–1950) in Hinduism. These people made it their life's work to connect with the divine. Both during their lifetime, but also through their writings, they have inspired countless followers by their wisdom and ethics.

The third type of religious experience is that sense of God grounded in a community. The Hebrew Bible documents the experience of God as encountered by the Jewish people. The New Testament documents the experience of God as encountered by Jews and Gentiles within the Church. Through rituals and practices, there are experiences that a community together enters into.

Now Richard Swinburne, the English philosopher, has argued convincingly that this witness to the transcendent should be trusted. Given we take so much on trust based on the reports of other people, it is not unreasonable to extend it to this realm. For example, I have never seen Mongolia, but I trust the reports of other people that it exists. He suggests two key principles for evaluating such experiences. The first is the principle of credulity (that the experiences are often caused by the object the person claims is the cause). Or as Richard Swinburne himself puts it: "I suggest that it is a principle of rationality that (in the absence of special considerations) if it seems (epistemically) to a subject that x is present, then probably x is present; what one seems to perceive is probably so."[35]

The second is the principle of testimony (that people should be trusted when they describe their experiences). Swinburne explains that this "component is the principle that (in the absence of special considerations) the experiences of others are (probably) as others report them."[36] Naturally there are occasions when these two principles do not operate: if I am taking LSD and claim to have seen an alien, then you are right to be skeptical. But with many of these religious experiences, the people are trustworthy, discriminating, and sophisticated. We would trust their reports of almost anything else. Swinburne's point is that there is no reason why this should not extend to God.

Globally and historically, the vast majority of people have had an experience of the transcendent. This should be treated as good evidence for belief. Granted the descriptions of the transcendent do vary, but that is not a decisive reason for denying that there is nothing transcendent causing the experience.

We turn then to the second pointer – the mystery of moral discourse. Consider a moral assertion: "I think I really ought to go to my son's performance at his elementary school." The odd word in that assertion is "ought." It quite clearly does not mean "want"; in fact one uses the word ought when implying that "I would rather go to lunch at the local bar, but . . ." So the moral obligation conflicts with one's desires. And it sounds as if there is an "external" pressure applying to me.

It is important that moral language has this external quality otherwise it is difficult to ensure that it is binding. If one decides that moral discourse is simply the result of culture, then it is difficult to see why it is binding. It is easy to reason thus: in a different culture, I would have different moral values. In a Nazi culture, my morality would include anti-Semitism; in a slave owning culture, slavery would be acceptable; and in a cannibal culture, it would be acceptable to eat people. Therefore if I create my own moral culture, then I am free from the widely accepted moral obligations, which are assumed by everyone else.

It is no coincidence that moral discourse arose in a religious culture. And although secular humanists are good at deciding to affirm basic moral values, it is difficult to see how the discourse is justified. And more importantly, the secular humanist has a major problem with those who want to challenge his or her moral values. Now of course, there is a danger here. Although it might be prudent to affirm religion as a basis for moral values, this is not an argument for the truth of religion. Just because Santa Claus is a good tool for encouraging children to behave well doesn't mean that Santa Claus exists.[37] A belief might be useful and still false.

Yet there is an argument here. Our moral instincts are very strong. When I condemn anti-Semitism, it does not feel simply a result of my East Coast, *New York Times* reading culture; it feels absolutely wrong. The obligations to care for family, strive to do good, and build communities of hope do not feel as if they are simply human constructs. Perhaps moral discourse does not simply depend on religion for intelligibility, but our moral intuitions are grounded in the transcendent. We feel so strongly because we are created in the Image of God. Granted this is not a decisive argument for belief, but it should be included as a pointer – a factor on the side of belief.

As with moral intuitions being grounded in the Image of God so it is with love. Although love takes many different forms, there is a type of love which tends to carry transcendent significance. For those committed to a naturalist narrative, the explanation for this type of love is reduced to either culture or biology. And of course it is possible that love is no more than a trick of the evolutionary process to encourage us to reproduce. However, for those of us who have had those moments when the only person in the world is the one who is loved, these reductionist accounts seem implausible.

The Christian alternative grounds the significance of love in the Trinity. We will look in more detail at the Trinity in chapter four. However, let us anticipate one of the key arguments. Christians are partly committed to the doctrine of the Trinity because we believe God is love. If God is love, the argument goes, then there must be the possibility of lovingness in the internal life of God himself or herself (and to avoid the gender problem, many advocates of progressive writing use the phrase "Godself"). In other words, within the oneness of God there is a dynamic interrelationality which enables the love of God to have meaning.

And given God knows, within the very life of God, the value of love, so God desires for a creation where more loving possibilities are realized. (Again we shall look at this in more detail in chapter four.) This is a key goal of creation. Now the argument is this: when we are granted the remarkable gift of love (as opposed to lust or just sex), we are discovering the reason for being.

When you have two contrasting explanations for a phenomenon, it is legitimate to ask which makes "more sense" of the phenomenon. Again, as a pointer, the suggestion I am making is that the Christian narrative makes more sense of the phenomenon than the naturalistic one.

With music and art, the suggestion is that it is a pointer to the transcendent. George Steiner (1929–) in his masterful essay *Real Presences* constructs the argument with considerable erudition and care. He states his thesis at the outset:

> It proposes that any coherent understanding of what language is and how language performs, that any coherent account of the capacity of human speech to communicate meaning and feeling is, in the final analysis, underwritten by the assumption of God's presence. I will put forward the argument that the experience of aesthetic meaning in particular, that of literature, of the arts, of musical form, infers the necessary possibility of this "real presence."[38]

For art, literature, and music to work, they must assume the reality of God; this is partly because it is the domain of the transcendent that art, literature, and music explore. Steiner's targets in this essay are all those tendencies in modern philosophy that deny any transcendent meaning. So logical positivism was a philosophical movement that insisted the only meaningful sentences are those which can be scientifically verified (if you can't touch, taste, see, hear, smell it, then you can't talk about it). Or deconstruction, which was formulated by Jacques Derrida (1930–2004), assumed that the cultural location of the text so submerges the meaning that we can never be sure what the meaning of the text is.

Steiner's response is to stress two aspects of the aesthetic experience. First the depths to which a piece of music or a famous work of art can reach. Steiner writes, "Entering into us, the painting, the sonata, the poem brings us into reach of our own nativity of consciousness. It does so at a depth inaccessible in any other way."[39] Granted this appreciation of great art requires cultivation. He stresses the need for great texts to be introduced to the child, and for the child's imagination to be allowed to grow. This is the key to human freedom: we discover options that are a key to human identity. Steiner warns: "If the child is left empty of texts in the fullest sense of the term, he will suffer an early death of the heart and of the imagination ... The waking of human freedom can also occur in the presence of pictures, of music. It is, in essence, a waking through the pulse of narrative as it beats in aesthetic form."[40]

The second aspect is that the act of creating great art is made possible because we are all creations. Steiner is here drawing attention to the genius that has the capacity to create *King Lear* or paint the *Mona Lisa*. Steiner writes:

> I can only put it this way (and every true poem, piece of music or painting says it better): there is aesthetic creation because there is creation ... I take the aesthetic act, the conceiving and bringing into being of that which, very precisely, could not have been conceived or brought into being, to be an *imitation*, a replication on its own scale, of the inaccessible first *fiat* (the "Big Bang" of the new cosmologies, before which there cannot be, in true Augustinian fashion, any "time," is no less a construed imperative and "boundary-condition" than is the narrative of creation in religion).[41]

The point is this: the miracle of Mozart's *Don Giovanni* (the capacity to create inspirational music from nothing) is a human echo of the divine achievement of creating the cosmos out of nothing.

These two aspects mean that the underlying disposition of the artist cannot share the constraints required by contemporary philosophical movements. Steiner explains:

> I have, before, cited some of those who know best: the poets, the artists. I have found no deconstructionist among them. I have found none who can, in conscience, accept the constraints on permissible discourse prescribed by logical atomism, logical positivism, scientific proof-values or, in a far more pervasive sense, by liberal skepticism ... D. H. Lawrence's is a summarizing statement: "I always feel as if I stood naked for the fire of Almighty God to go through me – and it's rather an awful feeling. One has to be so terribly religious to be an artist." And there is Yeats: "No man can create as did Shakespeare, Homer, Sophocles, who does not believe with all his blood and nerve, that man's soul is immortal." And quotation could continue. Wittily, Bertrand Russell asserted that God had simply given to man far too few indices of His existence for religious faith to be plausible. Yet this observation is, metaphysically, tone deaf. It leaves out the entire sphere of the poetic, be it metaphysical or aesthetic, it leaves out music and the arts, without which human life might indeed not be viable.[42]

Great art is born of faith. Great art also witnesses to faith. The problem with the atheist Bertrand Russell is that he had lost his spiritual sense that enabled him to see the presence of God in art.

For Steiner, this is a pointer. In fact, he talks about the wager, which we looked at in chapter one when we discussed Pascal. He will wager that the real presence that makes great music possible is indeed there. Steiner writes, "I am wagering, both in a Cartesian and a Pascalian vein, on the informing pressure of a real presence in the semantic markers which generate Oedipus the King or Madame Bovary; in the pigments or incisions which externalize Grünewald's Isenheim triptych or Brancusi's *Bird*; in the notes, crotchets, markings of tempo and volume which actualize Schubert's posthumous Quintet."[43] The evidence for the transcendent is all around us. We just need the eyes to see it.

Conclusion

Hidden in the creation are many pointers to the transcendent. As you sit and read this book right now, this moment of book reading is made possible by God. You are sitting in a stable universe. The electrons are behaving themselves: the universe is stable and consistent. It exists, thereby enabling you to exist. You are a connected person; you know the value of love; you believe that there are certain fundamental ways of behaving which are appropriate and other ways which are wrong. Even as you sit there, you have a sense of the fundamentals of morality. You think pedophilia is an evil and unequivocally condemn the Holocaust. There are certain pieces of music that can raise your soul to such an extent that you feel liberation. You have seen scenes of such beauty that your breath has been taken away. And perhaps, deep down, there have been moments when you have sensed the transcendent love around you. Perhaps when you were lonely and perturbed, there was a moment of comfort that, at the time, you found puzzling.

None of these things are spectacular; they are all normal. Yet they do need explanation. The theist has an explanation. This universe is intended. A loving being created a universe so that more loving opportunities might emerge. As a result of a long process of development (15 billion years), creatures have emerged on planet earth capable of giving and receiving love. The stable universe was always set up so that we would emerge: our sense of right and wrong is grounded in creation: and music and the beauty of the universe are intrinsic gifts.

It is possible that the order in the universe was a completely freak chance. Love might be just a trick of the evolutionary process to encourage us to reproduce. Music and morality might be just culturally conditioned, which in the process makes both dependent on human affirmation for meaning. All of this is possible.

But I want to suggest that perhaps in the court of law the case for belief might win. In my judgment, the evidence is overwhelming. However, there are plenty of skeptics who are less sure. There are also plenty of religious people who believe in God, but do not feel that there are strong arguments for their belief. However, for the purposes of this introduction to Christian doctrine, we are going to presume that we have a sufficient foundation to justify the next stage of our investigation. We have arrived at an entity who is creator and sustainer of everything that is. I have suggested that there is sufficient evidence from our creation for the existence of this reality. It beholds us to investigate further. This is our task in the next chapter.

QUESTIONS FOR REFLECTION AND DISCUSSION

1 Why do some arguments persuade some people and not others?
2 Do you think it is true that the arguments for faith are stronger than the arguments against faith?
3 Kant argued that all the traditional arguments for God depend on the Ontological Argument. What did he mean by this? Do you think it is true?
4 Are love, music, and beauty mysterious? Do they require an explanation? In what ways would God explain these things?
5 What is the Anthropic Principle? Do you think it is a modern version of the Design argument? What would David Hume say in response to the argument for God from the Anthropic Principle?

GLOSSARY

Anthropic principle: the discovery that the existence of life in this universe depends on a multitude of complex factors being precisely what they were

Contingent existence: a type of existence which could be otherwise

Deductive argument: the movement from true premises to a conclusion that inescapably follows

Deism: the belief in a creator God who then does not interfere with the world. Very popular in the seventeenth and eighteenth centuries in England. There are other versions of deism that include a belief in providence

Humanism: a term that has evolved to mean a belief in the importance of people which does not depend on religion

Inductive argument: the movement from true premises to a conclusion which in all probability is true

Natural theology: a theological method that starts with human reason and seeks to establish the existence of God through argument

Necessary existence: a complex notion, which has a variety of different meanings, all of which stress the impossibility of non-existence

Theism: a belief in a personal God

Notes

1 In both cases the original meanings of secular and humanism were less opposed to religion. However, the modern meaning sets secular humanism in opposition to religion.

2 See Paul Kurtz and Edwin Wilson, "Humanist manifesto II," in Ian Markham (ed.), *A World Religions Reader*, 2nd edition (Oxford: Blackwell, 2000), p. 43.

3 Ibid., p. 43.

4 I am not implying that the external world is as contestable as the existence of God. I am simply illustrating that even arguments in science make certain assumptions that cannot be proved.

5 Richard Swinburne, *The Existence of God* (Oxford: Clarendon Press, 1979).

6 Karl Barth, *Church Dogmatics* II, i (Edinburgh: T. & T. Clark, 1975), pp. 172ff.

7 Ibid., p. 168.

8 See Karl Rahner, *Foundations of Christian Faith* (New York: Seabury Press/Crossroad, 1976), p. 57.

9 Some of this material has been taken from my discussion of the Cosmological argument in my *Truth and Reality of God* (Edinburgh: T. & T. Clark, 1999), chapter 4. In that chapter I offer my own distinctive view of the cosmological argument, which is a version that moves beyond the second one considered in this chapter.

10 See W. L. Craig and Q. Smith, *Theism, Atheism, and Big Bang Cosmology* (Oxford: Clarendon Press, 1993), chapter 1.

11 Ibid., chapter 11.

12 See St Thomas Aquinas, *Summa Theologica*, translated by T. McDermott, vol. viii (London: Blackfriars, 1964), 1a, Question 46, Article 3, p. 79.

13 Craig and Smith, *Theism, Atheism, and Big Bang Cosmology*, p. 283.

14 J. Polkinghorne, *Science and Christian Belief* (London: SPCK, 1994), p. 73.

15 Leibniz as cited in W. L. Craig, *The Cosmological Argument from Plato to Leibniz* (London: Macmillan Press, 1980), p. 258.

16 Ibid., p. 274.

17 See David Hume, *Dialogues Concerning Natural Religion* (London: Hafner Press, 1948), pp. 59f.

18 See R. Swinburne, *The Existence of God* (Oxford: Clarendon Press, 1979), pp. 126f. Swinburne seems to opt for a very weak form of the cosmological argument. Owing to his difficulties with a necessary being, he cannot opt for Leibniz's position. So, instead, he suggests that it is just more likely that there is a God who decides to create a complex universe than that the universe is uncaused. The problem with this is it does depend on accepting his

quantification. This is the point that John Hick makes very effectively in his *An Interpretation of Religion* (Basingstoke: Macmillan, 1989), pp. 104–9.

19 J. C. A. Gaskin, *The Quest for Eternity* (Harmondsworth: Penguin, 1984), pp. 64–5.

20 David Hume made this point in part 9 of his *Dialogues Concerning Natural Religion*. An interesting variant on this criticism is found in Richard Gale's highly entertaining book *On the Nature and Existence of God* (Cambridge: Cambridge University Press, 1991). He thinks that the idea of an "unsurpassably great being" is extremely complex and problematic. He doubts whether a coherent account of God can be given.

21 It was Norman Malcolm in his famous article that introduced this distinction. Norman Malcolm, "Anselm's ontological argument," *Philosophical Review* 69 (1) (1960): 41–62.

22 Anselm, *Proslogian* http://www.fordham.edu/halsall/source/anselm.html.

23 This is the language of Alvin Plantinga who reformulated the argument using this language. See Alvin Plantinga, *The Nature of Necessity*, Oxford: Oxford University Press, 1974.

24 Anselm, *Proslogian* http://www.fordham.edu/halsall/source/anselm.html.

25 Malcolm, "Anselm's ontological argument."

26 Keith Ward, *Rational Theology and the Creativity of God* (Oxford: Blackwell, 1982), p. 31.

27 The *Dialogues* is a complex book with many arguments and sub-arguments. I have followed John Hick in treating these three objections as the main arguments found in Hume. For John Hick, see *Philosophy of Religion* (Englewood Cliffs, NJ: Prentice-Hall, 1963), pp. 25–6.

28 Paul Davies, *God and the New Physics* (London: Penguin, 1983), p. 179.

29 Ibid., p. 181.

30 John D. Barrow and Frank J. Tipler, *The Anthropic Cosmological Principle* (Oxford: Oxford University Press, 1988).

31 John Polkinghorne, *Reason and Reality* (London: SPCK 1991), p. 78.

32 Ibid., p. 78.

33 Ibid., p. 79.

34 Perhaps the majority of Christian theologians would disagree with my view. However, it is interesting to note that many Muslims are sympathetic to the project of natural theology and believe that the arguments for belief are overwhelmingly strong.

35 Richard Swinburne, *The Existence of God* (Oxford: Clarendon Press, 1979), p. 254.

36 Ibid., p. 272.

37 I am assuming that only adults are reading this book. If you are child, then I do apologize for suggesting that Santa Claus might not exist. Of course, it is possible that Santa does exist; the spirit of Christmas is real enough.

38 George Steiner, *Real Presences* (Chicago: University of Chicago Press, 1989), p. 3.

39 Ibid., p. 182.

40 Ibid., p. 191.

41 Ibid., p. 201.

42 Ibid., p. 228.

43 Ibid., p. 215.

Chapter 3
THE NATURE OF GOD

LEARNING OUTCOMES

By the end of this chapter you should be able to:

- understand the classical account of God
- appreciate the process alternative
- evaluate different approaches to Christian doctrine

STRUCTURE

- Alternative approaches to Christian doctrine – the Thomist approach, the Barthian approach, the Schleiermacherian approach, revisionist theologians, non-realism
- The concept of God in the Hebrew Bible
- The classical account of God
- The process challenge
- Between the two views

This book started by suggesting that we are shaped by the communities that we find ourselves in. If a person is interested in faith, then an appropriate decision is to find a community sympathetic to faith. In the last chapter, it was shown that a decision to join a community of faith is perfectly rational. If you treat the arguments as if you are in a court of law, then many of the traditional arguments are persuasive. Indeed in the light of continuing discoveries in modern cosmology, the arguments for "the transcendent" are very strong indeed.

We are now at the point when we need to unpack "the transcendent." What exactly is the transcendent like? How do we know whether there is just One God (monotheism) or Many gods (polytheism)? These are the questions, which we will discuss in this chapter.

However, before we can do this, this entire approach, which is loosely modeled on the approach of St Thomas Aquinas (hence a **Thomist approach**), has, in recent years, come under considerable attack. Before we can proceed, we need to explore at some length our theological methodology. It is necessary to take a look in detail at two major alternatives – the Barthian and Schleiermachian approaches.

Alternative Approaches to Christian Doctrine

In the last chapter, we looked at some of the arguments for and against natural theology. Many of the opponents of natural theology are also advocates for an approach to Christian doctrine, which starts very firmly with the Bible and the doctrine of the Trinity. We shall call this the **Barthian approach** as it is grounded in the work of Karl Barth. There are two arguments for this alternative approach.

First, unlike the Thomist approach, it does not attempt to arrive at a generalized theism that, supposedly, is universal. Daniel Migliore puts it this way:

> [A] Christian theology should not uncritically adopt these often general and inchoate notions about God and should certainly not attempt to make them normative. Christian faith and theology do not speak of God in a general and indefinite way; they speak of God concretely and specifically. Christians affirm their faith in God as the sovereign Lord of all creation who has done a new and gracious work in Jesus Christ and who continues to be active in the world through the power of the Spirit . . . In brief, Christians confess the triune identity of God.[1]

The point is that those who start with general arguments arrive at a very opaque concept of God. For Migliore, if we start with specific examples of God's action in Jesus, then we arrive at a much clearer (and explicitly Christian) account of God.

The second Barthian argument is that the whole Thomist project of natural theology is privileging a certain localized form of argument and reflection. So while the Barthian approach might privilege the New Testament text and the life, death, and resurrection of Jesus, the Thomist approach is simply privileging the Greek philosophical traditions. So Robert Jenson explains:

> [T]his body of theology was as historically particular as any other set of theological proposals: it comprised a part of the theology that Greek religious thinkers, pondering the revelations claimed for Homer and Parmenides, had provided for the cults of Mediterranean antiquity as it became religiously homogenous, the part that the church's fathers also found themselves able to affirm.[2]

Robert Jenson suggests that the genesis of natural theology is a certain type of argumentation, which becomes crucial during the Enlightenment. In a setting where arguments from authority were viewed with mistrust, Protestants had to establish the legitimacy of the Bible by providing a "natural" theology type argument. Some sort of "criterion" to justify the authority of the Bible was needed. Jenson then writes, "What in fact happened therewith was that the West's Mediterranean-pagan religious heritage – truly no more anchored in universal humanity than any other – was elevated to be judge of its biblical heritage."[3]

The main advantage of starting with the distinctive grammar of Christian doctrine (i.e. beginning with the Trinity) is that the content of faith is explicit right from the outset. But of course doctrine is then confined to the Christian insider.[4] For anyone outside the discourse, there is no obvious way in. The majority of the world is non-Christian: and it is important to take this pluralism seriously. The Thomist approach takes the semi-detached Christian and the secularist seriously. Inch by inch, the Thomist approach attempts to demonstrate that there are good reasons for participating in the Christian community.

Jenson's argument that the exercise of "finding reasons" is simply the privileging of the "West's Mediterranean-pagan religious heritage" is ingenious but unfair. As with every other discovery, the task of providing reasons for a metaphysical worldview has a history. Certain groups of people, living in a certain place, started doing it first. But this is equally true of logic or mathematics; it seems odd to say that taking the law of non-contradiction seriously privileges the thought of the pagan Aristotle over the Biblical heritage. Our Mediterranean pagans discovered the importance of justifying belief: there is a sense in which this approach should be privileged because it was a good discovery.

Jenson overstates the antagonism of the Biblical witness to this approach. It is true that we do not find any explicit philosophical arguments for faith in the Bible; there are, however, implicit arguments. St Paul writing in Romans 1 explains: "Ever since the creation of the world his invisible nature, namely, his eternal power and deity, has been clearly perceived in the things that have been made" (Romans 1:20). And the author of 1 Peter exhorts his readers to be "always prepared to make a defense to any one who calls you to account for the hope that is in you" (1 Peter 3:15). Add to all this, the many Psalms (see Psalms 19, 66:5–7, 89:5ff) that deduce the creator from the beauty of the creation, and we have a Biblical basis for the Thomist approach.

The major difficulty however with the Barthian approach is that it distorts our relations with Judaism. Jenson claims that "The church's trinitarianism is commonly thought to depart from Israel's interpretation of God. This is the exact contradictory of the truth."[5] For Jenson, the Trinity is in the Hebrew Bible.

Now it is true, as Jenson shows, that categories such as "son" (Israel is a "son" of God, although not sexually generated) and "Word" (the "Shekinah-phenomenon") are embedded in the Hebrew Bible.[6] And these categories proved very important for the subsequent development of Trinitarian theology. However, there is a significant difference between the claim that "the doctrine of the Trinity is compatible with the revelation of God in the Hebrew Bible" and the claim that "the doctrine is explicitly there."

Jenson understates the significance of Jesus. The Trinity is, in large part, a liturgical meditation on the significance of Jesus. Much is made of the distinction between the "**economic Trinity**" (the role that the different persons of the Trinity play in the work of salvation), and the "**immanent Trinity**" (a description of the inner-life of God). The truth is that the economic Trinity is a good description of how and why the doctrine emerged historically. And having arrived at the economic Trinity, we started to realize that this was not simply how God appears to us, but how God is in God's own inner-life. But more of this later in this chapter.

Given Judaism does not share our conviction that God has saved us through Jesus, it is distorting to impose the doctrine of the Trinity on Judaism. The Christian debt to Judaism was the discovery of monotheism. We share a theism. Our model of God then became more complicated as we reflected on our experience of God through Jesus. This more dynamic image of God is compatible with the Hebrew Scriptures but not explicitly required by them. For the modern day conversation with Judaism, it is

ECONOMIC AND IMMANENT TRINITY

This distinction is often used in the literature. The immanent Trinity is God in Godself = the life of God in eternity and outside creation. The economic Trinity is God as God is experienced in history, creation, and our lives.

F. D. E. SCHLEIERMACHER (1768–1834)

Often described as the "father of modern theology". His father and
grandfather were both clergymen. He was educated at a school organized
by the Moravian Brethren and later went to a Moravian theological seminary.
Later he studied theology at the University of Halle. After university he
served as a tutor in Berlin to an aristocratic family. When he was forty,
he became Pastor of the Trinity Church in Berlin, and later, Professor of
Theology at Halle. In 1808 he became Professor of Theology
at the University of Berlin.

---

important that we do not overstate the case. Therefore, despite the limitations and
loss of instant content, this chapter will explore the concept of theism before moving
to the concept of the Trinity. However, before doing this, we need to examine one
further alternative, which we shall call the **Schleiermacherian approach.**

Friedrich Daniel Ernst Schleiermacher is the founder of nineteenth-century liberal
theology. Heavily influenced by Immanuel Kant (1768–1834), Schleiermacher made
two key assumptions. First, the classical arguments for the existence of God are unhelpful. Schleiermacher writes, "[N]o obligation would arise for the system of doctrine to
prove the existence of God; that would be an entirely superfluous task. For since in
the Christian Church the God-consciousness should be developed in youth, proofs,
even if youth were capable of understanding them, could only produce an objective
consciousness, which is not the aim here, nor would it in any way generate piety . . .
Dogmatics must therefore presuppose intuitive certainty or faith; and thus, as far as
the God-consciousness in general is concerned, what it has to do is not to effect its
recognition but to explicate its content."[7] To defend faith, argued Schleiermacher,
we need to move away from reasons and stress instead "experience." This is what
produces piety and faith. Second, Schleiermacher assumes the Kantian account of
knowledge. For Kant, we do not know how things really are in reality. This is inaccessible because any attempted description of the world is a result of an experience
being interpreted by the mind. Our mind-interpreted sense of reality is the limit of
human knowledge – what Kant called the phenomenal world. So for Schleiermacher,
the universal awareness of God (our sense of dependence on God) is the heart of
religion. Doctrine is a result of reflection and interpretation of this basic experience.
Schleiermacher claims that "This account of the origins of dogmatic propositions, as
having arisen solely out of logically ordered reflection upon the immediate utterances
of the religious self-consciousness, finds its confirmation in the whole of history."[8] He

believes that experience, interpreted in community, makes sense of the whole history of religion, including the Scriptures.

Schleiermacher gave birth to a range of positions, some of which are closer to the Thomist approach and some are further away. Many revisionist theologians are heavily influenced by Schleiermacher.

In *Blessed Rage for Order*, David Tracy develops his revisionist approach to theology. For Tracy, the revisionist model is one grounded, albeit in a critical way, in the work of Paul Tillich (1886–1965). Tracy describes the approach thus:

> With the relative strengths and limitations of liberalism, orthodoxy, neo-orthodoxy, and radical theologies in mind, the revisionist theologian is committed to continuing the critical task of the classical liberals and modernists in a genuinely post-liberal situation. By that commitment, the revisionist will also try to rectify earlier theological limitations both in the light of the new resources made available by further historical, philosophical, and social scientific research and reflection and in the light of the legitimate concerns and accomplishments of the later neo-orthodox and radical theological alternatives. In short, the revisionist theologian is committed to what seems clearly to be the central task of contemporary Christian theology; the dramatic confrontation, the mutual illumination and corrections, the possible base reconciliation between the principal values, cognitive claims, and existential faiths of both a reinterpreted post-modern consciousness and a reinterpreted Christianity.[9]

So for Tracy it is an approach which takes our current situation seriously. Much as we might prefer to be living in a different time with different questions, we have to recognize where in fact we are. We need a theology, argues Tracy, that challenges both "secularism" and "supernaturalism." Revisionist theologians, explains Tracy,

> believe that neither secularism nor supernaturalism can adequately reflect or appropriately ensure our commitment to the final worthwhileness of the struggle for truth and honesty in our inquiry, and for justice and even agapic love in our individual and social practice.[10]

For Tracy, the commendable values of secularity (e.g. the equality of all persons and the evil of patriarchy) need to be sustained by a proper understanding of the Christian drama. For Tracy, the supernaturalism of the Christian tradition needs to engage and be modified by the insights offered by the modern world.

Paul Tillich is a key inspiration for revisionist theology. In the work of Tillich there is an important balancing act to maintain. One must respect the authorities of the tradition and at the same time engage constructively and imaginatively with the present. This is at the heart of his method of correlation. Tillich believed that the questions provoked by our time need to be "correlated" (i.e. put into dialogue with) the resources of our tradition. The more "conservative" revisionist theologians stress the importance of the authorities given to us from the Christian tradition; the more "liberal" revisionist theologians tend to stress the task of answering, imaginatively, the questions posed by the tradition.

At the more conservative end is Schubert Ogden (1928–): a Methodist who spent much of his career at Southern Methodist University in Texas. Ogden shares with Tracy the view that the task of theology involves the work of correlation. For Ogden, Christian witness needs to connect with human existence. However, he insists that this work of correlation is subject to two criteria: the first is appropriateness (i.e. the appropriateness to the normative Christian witness); and the second is credibility (the credibility of the idea as judged by the canons of "truth universally established with human existence").[11] Ogden's respect for the tradition points towards the "conservative end" of the spectrum amongst revisionist theologians. Ogden works on a similar canvas as Tracy: he shares a commitment to Process theology (which will be described later in the chapter) and affirms many of the insights from liberation theologians (theologians who stress the importance of justice in the construction of their theology). Although Ogden, methodologically, is at the conservative end of the spectrum, many of his conclusions are liberal. He has proposed what he calls a "revisionary Christology," where the task is to determine the meaning of Jesus for us.

Ogden's methodological opposite is Gordon Kaufman (1925–). However, before discussing Kaufman, I shall briefly mention the work of Peter C. Hodgson (1934–). In his *Winds of the Spirit: A Constructive Christian Theology*, Hodgson sets out the challenge of "constructive theology." The very term constructive theology embodies the revisionist task. Hodgson explains:

> [W]e can get carried away with intellectual systems, forgetting their limited, fragmentary, situation-dependent, heuristic character. This is where the word "constructive" has certain advantages over "systematic." ... In order to construct, we must deconstruct. But because of deconstruction, we must construct. Indeed, one of the challenges of a deconstructive age is to take up the constructive task afresh. Because of the destruction, waste, fragmentation, and loss that are all around us, we must engage in constructive acts in order to exist as humans as well as to live as Christians and think theologically. ... Finally, constructive activity is interpretative activity ... Constructive theology can also be likened to a work of fiction ... The theologian "invents" but not simply out of his or her subjective fantasy. Rather the inventions are based on multiple resources ranging from ancient texts to communally shared experiences and they elicit the root, radical dimension of these texts and experiences, namely a revelatory encounter with ultimate reality. Theological fiction has an experimental quality: One is invited to enter into its imaginative world, try out its construals, test and modify them in light of one's own experience. Good theology stands up against such tests; it proves its value, its veracity, in a community of discourse over space and time.[12]

This is a revealing description of the theological task, which is true for many revisionist theologians. First, we are in a context that needs an imaginative theology. Hodgson talks here about our deconstructive age. Elsewhere in *Winds of the Spirit*, he describes the challenge of postmodernism, the emancipatory quest (with our heightened sensitivity to suffering/oppression and recognition that this can change), the ecological quest, and the dialogical quest (the importance of dialogue between religions and beyond). Second, the basis of constructive theology is built on a particular analysis of how the experience of God shapes a community. Hodgson implies here a pre-textual experience "ultimate experience" which controls his theology. For Hodgson there are "root experiences or revelatory events that give rise to faith; the expressions of faith in language, texts, traditions; and the interpreters or believers who engage in both faith and practice in specific cultural contexts."[13] Like many revisionist theologians, one bypasses the Bible to get back to the authentic control on the modern theologian, which is the initial experience of the divine that gave birth to the Bible.

Now the result of this liberal methodology is a Trinitarian theology. With the three cultural quests (the emancipatory, the ecological, and the dialogical), Hodgson argues for a correlation[14] between "these quests and a triadic structure of divine life, namely *freedom*, *love*, and *wholeness*."[15] Hodgson explains:

> God is the One who creates out of love that which is radically different from yet deeply related to God, namely the world, and who liberates this world from its fallenness, fragmentation, and futility by drawing it into everlasting communion with God and empowering the endless struggle against evil. God is the One Who Loves in Freedom. God is not an isolated supreme being over against the world; rather, embodied by the world, incarnate in the shapes of Christ, God becomes a concrete, living relational God, "Spirit."[16]

The result, then, is that the language of the tradition is used to reconceive our understanding of God in such a way that enables humanity to face the challenges of living in the modern world.

So while Tracey, Ogden, and Hodgson are more conservative, the Mennonite theologian Gordon Kaufman (1925–) is more radical. Although Kaufman distances himself from some of the details of Schleiermacher's argument,[17] there are shared assumptions. For Kaufman, the task of theology must start with us. We do not have any clear or certain authorities; therefore it is an imaginative, constructive exercise.

Kaufman explains that there are four "fundamental dimensions" of his faith and piety that are assumed in his theological system. He writes:

> These are (a) my deep sense of the ultimate mystery of life; (b) my feeling of profound gratitude for the gift of humanness and the great diversity which it manifests; (c) my belief (with this diversity especially in mind) in the continuing importance of the central Christian

moral demand that we love and care for not only our neighbors but even our enemies; and (d) my conviction (closely connected with this last point) that the principal Christian symbols continue to provide a significant resource for the orientation of human life.[18]

Although Kaufman admits much of his theology is "agnostic,"[19] it is still rich with content. He wants to reinterpret the symbol "God" so that it is less oppressive (to the poor, marginalized, women) and yet still a demand on humanity. So God becomes "a norm or criterion or reality – what I call an 'ultimate point of reference' – in terms of which all else may be assessed and understood."[20] It is an ultimate point of reference which judges our values, hopes, and aspirations in this life. He is opposed to any dualism that sets God against this world or life against heaven or nature against the spirit.[21] Given all language is a human construct, we shouldn't be afraid about reinventing our concept of God so that it is more obviously life and justice affirming. The God symbol, explains Kaufman, "must be understood as a product of the human imagination."[22] This frees us up to think about an appropriate redefinition of the God symbol. Along with God, so Christology is revisited. He wants a wider Christology, where "Christ" brings "a new communal ethos in history."[23] And on ecclesiology (his view of the Church), Kaufman sees the churches as a "community of reconciliation and humanization."[24] All in all it is a remarkable and, in many respects, attractive vision of the Christian faith.

Kaufman is in the footsteps of others who have seen the logic of the Schleiermachian method. We are no longer confident about what is really out there: instead we are persons located in time – what Kaufman calls "biohistorical"[25] – who should create a faith that makes appropriate sense of and demands on our lives now. Schleiermacher would have understood Kaufman's theological enterprise.

There is much that is attractive about Schleiermacher. He was one of the first to recognize that a similar underlying religious disposition has given rise to the different religions of the world. Keith Ward commends Schleiermacher for his "new understanding of revelation, as rooted in privileged experience rather than in propositionally revealed truth" and his "new way of thinking about God in terms of the infinite, essentially expressed in and through the finite rather than in terms of the supremely self-sufficient purely actual being." Ward then writes:

> Schleiermacher was right to see, in his early work, that both these understandings open the field of possible revelation beyond the confines of the Christian tradition. It seems rather unlikely that just one religious teacher would have all inerrant experience of God, different in kind from any other – indeed, once inerrancy has been renounced in principle, it is implausible to take one teacher as having an exclusively correct apprehension of religious truth. And it seems rather unlikely that the infinite would only disclose its nature in one way and within one cultural tradition.[26]

The idea of allowing Christian theology to be shaped by other religious traditions will be developed further in chapter nine. Given what Christians believe about the nature of God, it is odd to believe that God didn't reveal something to the vast majority of cultures in the world, which are not Christian.

But there is a major danger with Schleiermacher, which Kaufman's theology demonstrates. His epistemology (the view of knowledge) can lead us to deny the possibility of truth. Christians want to claim that there really is a God; and therefore atheists and Buddhists (on this point) are mistaken. Granted the human mind plays a very important role in the knowing process. However, this should not be taken to imply that we have no knowledge of the way things are. When as a result of various observations, Copernicus (1473–1543) argued that it is more likely that the earth spins around the sun, rather than the sun moving around the earth, this was not simply his "mind's interpretation" of the data. This was closer to the way things really are. The Copernican cosmology was more accurate that the Ptolemaic cosmology, which Copernicus was challenging. Schleiermacher's epistemology runs the risk of separating our experience of God from the reality of God. Or as Colin Gunton puts it:

> The pit into which Schleiermacher fell was to accept the dogma canonized by Immanuel Kant that we do not experience things; rather, we shape the appearance of things into rational patterns which may or may not be true to reality. Even more insistent was Kant that there is nothing that can be called the knowledge of God, only an oblique positing of his existence on the basis of certain moral realities. The result was that the concept of experience that Schleiermacher developed in order to climb out of the pit dug by his enlightened predecessor was internal rather than external, a kind of inward human dynamic through which God was given, rather than the objective self-giving of God to and within the world.[27]

Gunton's two criticisms of Schleiermacher are well made. Gunton writes:

> The first objection is that it underplays the doctrine of creation, which assures us that at least the basis of our experience is reliable, because God has set the world on a sure foundation. Second – and this is the same point from a different perspective – Schleiermacher's is essentially a theology of the fallen intellect; or rather, it supposes that human thinkers are so stuck within their heads that the world – or God – is unable to break through them to shape and change the way they see things. A theology of experience more centered on particularities would want to say against this that although we are fallen creatures, and certainly often do fail to know things as they are, our experience can yet be and is from time to time redeemed.[28]

Schleiermacher is the start of an approach to theology that can lead to **non-realism** (i.e. all we have are our human interpretations of experience, which cannot be transcended

> ### NON-REALISM/REALISM
>
> Realism is the view that entities exist apart from our mind. In the medieval period there was a heated debate about universals (i.e. the qualities that link the particulars into a species or genus); in this setting realists opposed nominalism (i.e. the view that universal properties do not exist apart from the individual particulars). In modern philosophy, realists believe it is possible to describe reality and non-realists (sometimes called anti-realists) deny this.

or evaluated or judged by their approximation to reality).[29] Gunton insists that such an attitude to truth denies the doctrine of creation (the claim that God intended an ordered universe which provides reliable experiences). In addition it assumes that God cannot break through our experiences and reveal truths about ourselves.

Although it is tempting for a Christian theology, committed to generosity and revision, to build its edifice on the Schleiermachian approach, it is a temptation that must be resisted. We need truth in religion, especially those of us who identify with a liberal form of Christianity. Black theologians assume that racism is an unequivocal evil (it isn't simply their cultural view of white power); and feminist theologians assume that patriarchy is unequivocally wrong (feminism isn't simply another interpretation of reality to be put alongside every other interpretation of reality).

So both the Barthian approach and the Schleiermachian approach are unsatisfactory. This book is assuming a Thomist approach (in method, although as we shall see not always in content). Three assumptions are being made: first that truth in religion is possible; second, justice involves the recognition that certain culturally transcendent and objective values exist; and third, we can and should start with theism (and a concept of God in general) before moving to the specific doctrine of the Trinity. This will be explored in the next chapter.

It is then to the picture of God found in the Hebrew Bible that we turn next.

The Concept of God in the Hebrew Bible

The picture of God in the Hebrew Bible is very dynamic. Many of the images are anthropomorphic (i.e. projecting human features and characteristics onto God). G. B. Caird in his *The Language and Imagery of the Bible* writes, "[B]y far the greater proportion of the Biblical language which refers to God is anthropomorphic. At the simplest level God is said to have head, face, eyes, eyelids, ears, nostrils, mouth, voice, arm, hand, palm, fingers, foot, heart, bosom, bowels."[30] And when it comes to divine action and attitudes, Caird writes:

> God sees and hears, speaks and answers, calls and whistles, punishes and rewards, wounds and heals, opposes and supports, fights, preserves and rescues, guides and guards, makes and unmakes, plans and fulfills, appoints and sends. He displays love, pity, patience, generosity, justice, mercy, jealousy, anger, regret, hatred, pleasure, and scorn. He is potter, builder, farmer, shepherd, hero, warrior, doctor, judge, king, husband, and father.[31]

The great advantage of these anthropomorphic associations and images is that the God of the Hebrew Bible is both active and personal. God acts in creation and history. God shares with persons the capacity to decide, intend, require, and love. By the time of the sixth century BCE, a very elevated description of God is provided by the famous unknown prophet of the Babylonian exile, who writes:

> I am the LORD, and there is no other,
> beside me there is no God;
> I gird you, though you do not know me,
> that men may know, from the rising of the sun
> and from the west, that there is none beside me;
> I am the LORD, and there is no other.
> I form light and create darkness,
> I make weal and create woe,
> I am the LORD, who do all these things. (Isaiah 45:5–7)

The God of Israel is the God of the whole world. This God cares about the whole world and makes demands of everyone in this world. In addition, this God is ultimately responsible for everything that happens in the world; this God makes weal and creates woe. We have an uncompromising monotheism here. It is also a God who acts. The drama of the Hebrew Bible constructs a narrative of a God who takes a people from bondage to liberation. This was the God that the Early Church inherited from Judaism. As it engaged with Hellenistic thought (Greek culture), this monotheism was expressed with different words and concepts. And we find this best expressed in the thought of St Thomas Aquinas.

The Classical Account of God

Aquinas (1224–74) was trained as a good Augustinian Platonist. He learned his theology from the works of **Augustine of Hippo**. However, he also translated Aristotle (384–322 BCE). The result was a deeply creative synthesis.

When it comes to God, Aquinas shared with Augustine the key assumption: God is completely perfect. Given the concept of God is learned through worship, it is necessary that God is perfect. An imperfect God would not deserve the "ultimate worth" implied by worship. Perfection for Aquinas involved completeness, a wholeness, and a sense that nothing else is needed. It is a very static image of perfection. After some discussion of Aristotle, Aquinas writes:

> Now God is the first principle, not material, but in the order of efficient cause, which must be perfect. For just as matter, as such, is merely potential, an agent, as such, is in the state of actuality. Hence, the first active principle must needs be most actual, and therefore most perfect; for a thing is perfect in proportion to its state of actuality, because we call that perfect which lacks nothing of the mode of its perfection.[32]

Aquinas is here taking issue with the view that the cause of everything must be "simply potential and thus most imperfect."[33] Instead God as an efficient cause must be "most perfect."

Perfection is then combined with the doctrine of divine simplicity. At this point Aquinas cites, with approval, Augustine, who says that "God is truly and absolutely simple."[34] Simple here does not mean "unintelligent," but completely whole, without any parts. The reason why God is incorporeal (does not have a body) is because God is simple (he is not composite and therefore doesn't have different limbs).

From divine perfection and divine simplicity, we arrive at the logical corollaries, namely the immutability of God and the eternity of God.[35] On the immutability of God, Aquinas builds on Malachi 3:6 – "I am the Lord, and I change not" – and brings

AUGUSTINE OF HIPPO (354–430)

Augustine was born in Algeria (North Africa). His mother, Monica, was a Christian, while his father was a pagan. For much of his young adult life he was a Manichean (a strong dualist group that taught that light and darkness were in an ongoing conflict). It was while he was in Rome and Milan that he became a neoplatonist. He had a conversion experience in 386, was baptized in 387, became a priest in 391, and a bishop in 395. As was a common practice at the time, he had a concubine for much of his life, with whom he had one son. His output as a theologian was considerable; there is barely a question that Augustine did not consider, and everyone since has been forced to take his responses seriously.

together his arguments on perfection and simplicity. He provides three arguments. First, he repeats his argument that, as the first cause that changes everything else, God must be beyond change (an argument alluded to under divine simplicity). Second, everything that changes involves composition and given there is no composition in God, then God must be changeless. Here Aquinas explicitly refers back to the doctrine of divine simplicity. And third, Aquinas brings us back to God's perfection. He writes:

> But since God is infinite, comprehending in Himself all the plenitude of perfection of all being, He cannot acquire anything new, nor extend Himself to anything whereto He was not extended previously. Hence movement in no way belongs to Him. So, some of the ancients, constrained, as it were, by the truth, decided that the first principle was immovable.[36]

The perfection of God then entails, for Aquinas, the impossibility of all change. The assumption here is that change would entail either improvement or deterioration. Given that God is already the "plenitude of perfection of all being," it seems obvious that God cannot improve; and it would be impossible to conceive of God deteriorating; so Aquinas is driven to the doctrine of divine immutability. Immutability here is not simply a "consistency" of underlying character (the likely meaning of the Malachi verse that Aquinas cites, "I am the Lord and I change not"), but a complete impossibility of any change whatsoever. God cannot have additional knowledge or change of movement as a result of a divine action. So from perfection to divine immutability, and from divine immutability we are forced to timelessness. Time, at its simplest, is a measure of change. As God does not change at all, then there cannot be any time in God. Aquinas explains it thus:

> The idea of eternity follows immutability, as the idea of time follows movement . . . Hence, as God is supremely immutable, it supremely belongs to Him to be eternal. Nor is He eternal only; but He is His own eternity; whereas, no other being is its own duration, as no other is its own being. Now God is His own uniform being; and hence, as He is His own essence, so He is His own eternity.[37]

There are a host of well-known and endlessly discussed difficulties with this account of God. The hardest is the relationship of God to action: how can a changeless, timeless God create if God has no time in which to do so. Aquinas follows Augustine at this point. Augustine in the *Confessions* does concede that the question "what was God doing before the world was created?" seems a perfectly proper question. And so it is. When I make a cup of tea, there is a moment before, a moment during, and a moment after. To imagine the making of a cup of tea without any moments is simply unintelligible.

Augustine's famous solution to this dilemma was as follows. Augustine believed that time was the first entity that God created. And in the act of creation, God created all time – the beginning, middle, and end. In that one timeless action of creating all time, God also did all actions within creation (parting the Red Sea, raising the dead, ensuring the prayers of the Red Sox baseball fans are answered, and bringing about the end of the world). So God wasn't doing anything before the creation of the world because God hadn't yet created time in which things can be done.

Three features of this account of God should be noted. First, it definitely is not anthropomorphic. It is often said by critics that before the Enlightenment, Christians believed in a "big man sitting on a cloud in a three-tier universe." As is now clear, this criticism is not true. The classical account of God is totally unlike a "big man." If anything the opposite criticism has more validity, the classical account is very abstract and incomprehensible. Second, there is an appropriate emphasis on worship and perfection. It is through worship that we relate to God; and it is through worship that we think of God. It is important that this God we worship is worthy of ultimate worth. Third, it is heavily dependent on non-Christian thought. Augustine and Aquinas assumed that all truth belonged to God. And true insights found in non-Christian texts should be assimilated into Christian theology.

In these three respects the classical account should be commended. However, there are major difficulties with it; difficulties identified and described by a movement known as Process theology.

The Process Challenge

It was **A. N. Whitehead** who inspired Process theology. Whitehead was a mathematician who moved to Harvard to reflect on the philosophy of science. At the heart of White-head's philosophy was the recognition that the world had changed dramatically as a result of modern science – in particular the theory of evolution. Norman Pittenger notes, "The central conviction of American process-thought is that the evolutionary perspective must be taken with the utmost seriousness."[38] With the evolutionary perspective being followed by the New Physics (in particular Quantum physics), the Process theologians and philosophers believed it was important to modify our understanding of the world.

Whitehead took the lead. For Whitehead, everything is connected with everything else. He offered a complex and distinctive vocabulary to describe this interconnectedness. And a key theme emerged in his writing: change is not an imperfection. Dynamic creativity is not an inadequacy. For the classical account of God, change is a problem; for the Process theologians change is a condition for growth and development. John

A. N. WHITEHEAD (1861–1947)

Whitehead was a British philosopher. In his Cambridge period (1884–1910), he worked primarily on mathematics and logic. In his London period (1910–24), he worked on the philosophy of science and education. And finally in his Harvard period (1924 onwards) he developed his views on religion.

Cobb (one of the leading Process theologians) captures some of the difficulties with the classical account of God, when he writes:

> This concept derives from the Greeks, who maintained that "perfection" entailed complete "immutability," or lack of change. The notion of "impassibility" stressed that deity must be completely unaffected by any other reality and must lack all passion or emotional response. The notion that deity is the "Absolute" has meant that God is not really related to the world. The world is really related to God, in that the relation to God is constitutive of the world – an adequate description of the world requires reference to its dependence on God – but even the fact that there is a world is not constitutive of the reality of God. God is wholly independent of the world: the God-world relation is purely external to God. These three terms – unchangeable, passionless, and absolute – finally say the same thing, that the world contributes nothing to God, and that God's influence upon the world is in no way conditioned by divine responsiveness to unforeseen, self-determining activities of us worldly beings. Process theology denies the existence of this God. [39]

For Process theologians, God is connected to the world. The world does bring about changes in God. And the future is genuinely open; it is not determined.

For Process theology, the beauty of the world lies in his multi-faceted capacity to change. Marjorie Hewitt Suchocki describes reality as a "relational mode of existence." She explains:

> The process of integrating relationships produces reality. This process is dynamic, ever giving rise to new relations, new integrations, new realities. The terms "one," "many," and "creativity" become key terms for understanding this process. But relational reality is hardly exhausted by human existence. Process is not simply the prerogative of the human condition; process is fundamental to all reality. [40]

She uses the image of reality as a "dance." However, this interconnectedness also explains the ease with which we can damage and inflict pain on each other. When we are working constructively together, we can be a force for good; when we decide to inflict pain on each other, we can cause enormous damage. Our very closeness and mutual interconnection is both the force for good and for evil.

When it comes to the concept of God, Process theologians are much more sympathetic to **panentheism** (God and the world are identified together, but God is not reducible to the world). Instead of the classical model where God and the world are entirely independent, here God is much closer to the world. There are three elements to the Process account of God.

First, God is closely linked to the universe. For Process theology, God does not create *ex nihilo* (out of nothing). They reject a "cosmic dualism" that separates God from the world. Instead analogies are offered that stress the connection between God and the universe, for example, the world is God's body. For many feminist theologians, for example Sallie McFague,[41] this alternative model of God can free us from a patriarchal and environmentally exploitive view of God. Instead of God being entirely separate from the material and embodied, God is part of it. Instead of the world being used by humanity, it is sacred and part of God. Instead of women being identified with embodiment, God is embodied and matter has always been. Creation is a matter of forming. There is no creation *ex nihilo* (out of nothing).

Creation on this account becomes "forming" rather than being made "out of nothing." God shapes matter which is part of God into opportunities that enable life. A good way of seeing this is the growth of a life within the mother. Everything (including the fetus) is part of, and dependent on, the mother. However, the fetus is also independent and free (able to kick and move). So by analogy, human life is like the fetus; it is entirely dependent and part of God, yet free and independent.

Second, time and change are part of God's internal life. For the classical view, God does not change. If God does not change, then God does not empathize with our suffering because the act of empathy requires God to change from "not feeling" our pain to "feeling" our pain. Process theology finds this deeply objectionable. Time and change are part of God's internal life. So God is, technically, getting older, albeit given God has always existed and will always exist, this need not be a worry. God is "everlasting" (literally has always been and always will be). There is for God a before, during, and after. God creates the world, then redeems the world, and then will bring the world to an end.

PANENTHEISM

Panentheism is a version of pantheism. Pantheism identifies God and the world together (literally God-is-all-ism). Panentheism identifies God and the world together but acknowledges that God is "greater" than the world.

Third, the future is genuinely open. With the classical view, God has timeless knowledge of all time. However, this poses the obvious question so clearly stated by Nelson Pike: if God knows for certain how I am going to behave in the future, then in what sense can I do otherwise? Nelson Pike states the problem thus:

1   God's being omniscient implies that Jones mows his lawn on Saturday afternoon, then God believed at an earlier time that Jones would mow his lawn on Saturday afternoon.
2   Necessarily, all of God's beliefs are true.
3   No one has the power to make a contradiction true.
4   No one has the power to erase someone's past beliefs, that is, to bring it about that something believed in the past by someone was not believed in the past by that person.
5   No one has the power to erase someone's existence in the past, that is, to bring it about that someone who existed in the past did not exist in the past.
6   So if God believed that Jones would mow his lawn on Saturday afternoon, Jones can refrain from mowing his lawn only if one of the following alternatives is true:
    i   Jones has the power to make God's beliefs false;
    ii Jones has the power to erase God's past belief; or
    iii Jones has the power to erase God's past existence.
7   But alternative (i) is impossible. (from 2 and 3)
8   And alternative (ii) is impossible. (from 4)
9   And alternative (iii) is impossible. (from 5)
10 Therefore, if God believes that Jones will mow his lawn on Saturday afternoon, Jones does not have the power to refrain from mowing his lawn on Saturday afternoon, that is to say, Jones is not free.[42]

Process theologians concede this argument entirely. They turn the point around: instead of God knowing everything, God takes a genuine risk with Creation and allows humanity to become co-creators with God. Humanity shares with God the responsibility for the next segment of creation. It is a genuinely open future. We are co-creators of that future with God.

Process theology opened an important door. We have already noted how feminist theologians have used Process theology to challenge the patriarchy which, they believe, is embedded in the classical account. Building on the feminist theologians, several different liberationist theologies are emerging. Liberation theology developed in the late 1960s. Mainly Roman Catholic theologians in South America, inspired by Vatican II, argued that the heart of the Biblical message is about liberation from injustice to hope. One particular form of liberation theology is postcolonial theology.

Postcolonial analysis is an attempt to go "beyond the colonial in all its forms."[43] The analysis seeks to both understand and subvert the "colonial power,"[44] both in our politics and language. A postcolonial account of God, suggested by Mayra Rivera, revisits the ancient, yet neglected, image of God as Sophia, found in Proverbs. Here is an image endlessly contested: Biblical scholars argue that the origins of the image is "other." So with a home perhaps in a different culture and with numerous men finding the image problematic, Sophia is an ideal image for those working (and living) with postcolonial sensitivities. Rivera concludes:

> Unlike traditional models that imagine God's transcendence as over and against creation, the transcendence that Sophia represents is neither absent nor untouchable, but a challenging closeness that is always beyond grasp . . . She transcends our "world" not by being detached from it, but by opening the world to what it has not received, to what has been pushed outside – by crossing its borders. While exceeding theological constructions, her unforeseeable presence haunts theological certainties; it lurks as a "strange guardian in the margin," as though to keep us from idolatry.[45]

Those whose lives have been touched by colonialism recognize in this image an account of God that challenges the traditional image. The postcolonial account is one that questions the vested interests of those who want just one image to be the true and appropriate account. Process theology created an option that many liberationist theologies have seized.

Between the Two Views

In almost every area of theological discussion, someone has articulated an alternative that transcends the "either-or" of the current debate. Karl Barth, for example, has God simultaneously both inside and outside time. I shall look at the contemporary proponent Keith Ward.

Ward sets out a conundrum, which needs to be solved. He writes: "The demands of intelligibility require the existence of a necessary, immutable, eternal being. Creation seems to demand a contingent, temporal God, who interacts with creation and is, therefore, not self-sufficient."[46] Ward's point is that we need the classical God who is the creator of everything and therefore self-sufficient; yet we also need a Process God, who acts, loves and cares in time. So he solves this dilemma by advocating a "dynamic infinity." This, Ward explains, is "a move which requires the admission of potency and temporality in God, but which can be reconciled with a properly interpreted doctrine of eternity and necessity."[47]

The result is this: unlike classical theology, there is genuine freedom granted to humanity in the creation; however, unlike Process theology, God creates *ex nihilo* (out of nothing) and exists prior to, and is not dependent on, the creation. Ward explains that God:

> may be coherently conceived as dynamically infinite; as unlimited by any being which he himself does not creatively originate; as unlimited in his perfections by anything other than his own choices and their consequences, or by what is necessary to him, as the limitless potency of creative being, relating itself continually in new ways to its creatures. God is thus the absolutely originative creator, not the passive container of process philosophy; but the one who is uniquely and immutably self-existent, and is ontologically prior to all beings other than himself. But creatures, having been called into being, may have a proper autonomy of their own, in relation to which God may determine his nature in changing ways. He is the sole cause of an infinity of creative freedoms, not the predetermining tyrant of what has been called "monarchical theism." And free creatures may cooperate actively in the work of creation, seeking to achieve a community of all personal wills united in one society, and in conscious relation to the one all-sustaining God.[48]

Ward is challenging both accounts. The classical account is insufficient because it does not permit sufficient autonomy to the creation; the process account is insufficient because it does not recognize the independence of God from the creation.

A vision of this type is attractive. Naturally there are plenty of defenders of the classical and process accounts. However, Ward is not alone in wanting to take the best of both and weave them together.

Thus far, we have defended the legitimacy of talk of God and outlined an account of what is meant by God. The next stage is to look at the important doctrine of the Trinity.

QUESTIONS FOR REFLECTION AND DISCUSSION

1 What are the three main approaches to theological questions? Which one do you prefer?
2 Outline and explain the differences between classical theology and Process theology. Which approach do you prefer and why?
3 How do we know whether God is in time or outside time? Can we ever be sure which account of God is true?
4 Outline Schleiermacher's achievement. What is revisionist theology? To what extent is it legitimate to revise the truths of Christianity?

GLOSSARY

Correlation: the attempt to bring the questions posed by the living with the answers offered by the Christian tradition

Panentheism: a belief that God and the world are identified together, but God is more than the world

Postcolonialism: movements that take seriously the challenge of colonialism

Revisionism: the view that the theological task is to revise our understanding of the Christian drama in the light of justice issues, modern knowledge and insights from other faith traditions.

Notes

1 Daniel L. Migliore, *Faith Seeking Understanding. An Introduction to Christian Theology*, 2nd edition (Grand Rapids, MI: Eerdmans, 1991/2004), pp. 66–7.
2 Robert W. Jenson, *Systematic Theology*, vol. 1 (Oxford: Oxford University Press, 1997), p. 7.
3 Ibid., p. 8.
4 Jenson concedes this when he writes, "The church has a mission: to see to the speaking of the gospel . . . Theology is the reflection internal to the church's labor on this assignment." See ibid., p. 11.
5 Ibid., p. 63.
6 See ibid., pp. 77–8.
7 Friedrich Schleiermacher, *The Christian Faith*, edited by H. R. Mackintosh and J. S. Stewart (Edinburgh: T. & T. Clark, 1928), p. 136.
8 Ibid., p. 81.
9 Ibid., p. 32.
10 Ibid., p. 9.
11 Schubert M. Ogden, *On Theology* (Dallas, TX: Southern Methodist University Press, 1992), p. 3.
12 Peter C. Hodgson, *Winds of the Spirit: A Constructive Christian Theology* (Louisville, KY: Westminster John Knox Press, 1994), pp. 39–40.
13 Ibid., p. 31.
14 One should not be misled by the term "correlation" here. Although Hodgson does talk about a correlation between the three quests and the divine trinity, he has reservations about the Tillichian concept of correlation. He believes "it gives anthropology too dominating a role in theological construction." Ibid., p. 46.
15 Ibid., p. xi.
16 Ibid., pp. xi–xii.
17 For example, Kaufmann worries about any approach to Christian doctrine that emphasizes a particular essence. See Gordon D. Kaufman, *In the Face of Mystery: A Constructive Theology* (Cambridge, MA: Harvard University Press, 1993), p. 30.

18 Ibid., p. xii.

19 Ibid., p. xiii.

20 Ibid., p. 28.

21 Ibid., p. 326.

22 Ibid., p. 39.

23 Ibid., p. 396.

24 Ibid., p. 442.

25 Ibid., p. 125.

26 Keith Ward, "Comparative theology: the heritage of Schleiermacher" in J'annine Jobling and Ian Markham (ed.) *Theological Liberalism* (London: SPCK 2000), p. 65.

27 Colin Gunton, *The Christian Faith. An Introduction to Christian Doctrine* (Oxford: Blackwell, 2002), p. 176.

28 Ibid., p. 177.

29 For a sustained discussion of the realist and non-realist debate see Ian Markham, *Truth and the Reality of God* (Edinburgh: T. & T. Clark, 1999).

30 G. B. Caird, *The Language and Imagery of the Bible* (Philadelphia, PA: Westminster Press, 1980), p. 174.

31 Ibid., p. 175.

32 Thomas Aquinas, *Summa Theologica*, vol. 1, Part 1, Question 4, Article 1, p. 21 (Westminster, MD: Christian Classics, 1981).

33 Ibid., p. 21.

34 Ibid., Part 1, Question 3, Article 8, p. 19.

35 This summary of Aquinas is a reworking of my discussion of his concept of God in *A Theology of Engagement* (Oxford: Blackwell, 2003), p. 53.

36 Aquinas, *Summa Theologica*, Part 1, Question 9, Article 1, p. 38.

37 Ibid., Part 1, Question 10, Article 2, p. 41.

38 N. Pittenger, *God in Process* (London: SCM Press, 1967) p. 98.

39 John Cobb and David R. Griffin, *Process Theology* (Philadelphia: Westminster Press, 1976), pp. 8–10.

40 Marjorie Hewitt Suchocki, *God Christ Church: A Practical Guide to Process Theology* (New York, Crossroad, 1986), p. 10.

41 See Sallie McFague, *Models of God* (Philadelphia: Fortress Press, 1987).

42 Nelson Pike, "Divine omniscience and voluntary action" (1956). This version is taken from Craig, *The Only Wise God* (Grand Rapids, MI: Baker Book House, 1987).

43 Catherine Keller, Michael Nausner, and Mayra Rivera (eds.), *Postcolonial Theologies: Divinity and Empire* (St Louis, MO: Chalice Press, 2004), p. 7.

44 Ibid., p. 8.

45 Mayra Rivera, "God at the crossroad," in ibid., p. 202. Rivera quotes Gayatri Chakravorty Spivak.

46 Keith Ward, *Rational Theology and the Creativity of God* (Oxford: Blackwell, 1982), p. 3.

47 Ibid., p. 3.

48 Ibid., p. 231.

Chapter 4
THE
TRINITY

LEARNING OUTCOMES

By the end of this chapter you should be able to:

- understand the different sources that Christians use for theology
- appreciate the complex relation between the Bible and the doctrine of the Trinity
- understand what the Early Church tried to do in clarifying the doctrine
- know the three dangers that the doctrine of the Trinity sought to avoid
- appreciate contrasting ways in which the doctrine might be understood

STRUCTURE

- Sources for theology
- Biblical roots of the doctrine of the Trinity
- Development of the doctrine of the Trinity
- Three dangers in interpreting the Trinity
- Modern accounts of the Trinity
- Standing back
- Conclusion

In the first two chapters, the agnostic was a key conversation partner. In the third, Jews and Muslims would recognize the debates and have their own versions of the discussions. In this chapter, we become overtly Christian. We shift the focus from theism (the belief in a personal God) to the Christian doctrine of the Trinity.

As we make this shift, reason continues to be important. Thus far rationality (i.e. coherence, plausibility, and evidence) has been in conversation with the whole range of human experience (our sense of purpose, morality, love etc.), but now we need to apply reason to revelation (to the sense that God has disclosed the nature of God to humanity in the life of Jesus of Nazareth).

All religions depend on revelation. Here we are in the middle of creation. Puny little creatures cannot determine the ultimate nature of the universe without some help. As we noted earlier, Karl Barth is right on this point: we are either guessing what ultimate reality is or trusting a disclosure of that ultimate reality. For Muslims, that disclosure is the Qur'an; for Jews, the Torah; and for Christians, it is the life, death, and resurrection of Jesus Christ.

This raises an obvious question: how do we know which revelation is right? In chapter ten we shall look at the issue of religious diversity in some detail. However, for now, we return to an answer developed at the start of chapter one. Like all forms of human knowledge, we learn by living in community. If I am interested in astronomy, then I take a course or find an association that introduces me to astronomy: and the approach taken to the subject will be shaped by the teacher or association that I join. The same is true in religion: if you mix with Muslims, then you will discover the beauty and power of the Qur'an; if you mix with Christians, then you will encounter the remarkable claim that Jesus is the disclosure of God.

This is not to say that all communities are equally valid. Some are manifestly incoherent in their worldview; others are morally destructive. The truth is that some strands of Christianity are stronger (i.e. more coherent and more likely to generate virtue) than other strands within Christianity; and the same is true of most major religious traditions. We shall return to these topics and examine them in more detail. For now, we note that our decision to focus on the revelation of God in Christ is a decision that privileges the community of the Church. In one sense, we are stepping inside the circle and, once inside, will then allow the processes of moral and rational evaluation to affirm (or not) our decision to step inside the circle.

Naturally there are many arguments amongst Christians over precisely how we describe and evaluate the Christian revelation. So before we look at the Trinity, we are going to need to establish the sources that form the basis of our theological reflection.

MARTIN LUTHER (1483–1546)

The major impetus behind the Protestant reformation in Europe. He was born on November 10, 1483 in Eisleben (Germany). He studied at the University of Erfurt, where he distinguished himself as a student. In 1505, he became a monk and started teaching at the University of Wittenburg. He was appalled by the practice of selling "indulgences," so on October 31, 1517, he published the "95 theses," which ultimately led to his excommunication in 1521. Thanks to the protection of the German princes, he started a new movement known as Lutheranism. In 1525, he married and subsequently had six children. He died in 1546.

Sources

All Christians recognize that a primary source for theology is the Bible. For Roman Catholics, "God is the author of Sacred Scripture."[1] Although it should be interpreted through the "wise arrangement" of "Sacred Tradition, Sacred Scripture, and the Magisterium of the Church,"[2] there is no doubt that the Scriptures are given a central place in Roman Catholic theology. **Martin Luther**, the great Reformer, insisted that Scripture alone (*sola sciptura* – by Scripture alone) should be the authority.[3] All things must be judged by Scripture. Anything that is contradicted by Scripture is illegitimate.[4]

Today the branch of Christianity that makes the authority of the Bible central is the evangelical movement. A key text for the evangelical view of the Bible is 2 Timothy 3:16:

> All Scripture is inspired by God and profitable for teaching, for reproof, for correction, and for training in righteousness. (RSV)

The word "inspired" is literally, in the Greek, "God-breathed." From this a variety of different accounts of inspiration has emerged: verbal dictation (God dictates to the Biblical authors), verbal plenary inspiration (the Holy Spirit is an active agent in the selection of the actual words of Scripture, so the words become fully divine and fully human), concept inspiration (God inspires the concepts, while the Biblical authors pick the words) and partial inspiration (only parts of the Bible are inspired, others reflect human error and confusion).

While every theologian recognizes the importance of the Bible, it is the evangelicals who insist it is primary. At the other end of the spectrum, Roman Catholic theologians insist that the authority of the Bible resides alongside the authority of the Church. The primary reason for this is that it was the Church who decided which books became part of the Bible. It is worth remembering that Christians are continuing to disagree about which books make up the canon of Scripture: Roman Catholics recognize the Apocrypha (disputed books which were part of the Septuagint, which was the Greek translation of the Hebrew Bible), while Protestants do not. In addition, the emergence of the New Testament canon took many years and different lists have different books. The Muratorian Fragment (produced in about 170) mentions two of the three epistles of John and suggests that the Shepherd of Hermas is good to read in Church. At the very least, we have to concede the Church has a pivotal role in the selection of texts; but perhaps we should go further and say that "the mind of the Church" is an important source for theology.

For liberal Protestants, the sources of theology need to go beyond the Church and the Bible. **Paul Tillich** ranges very widely when he explains that the sources of systematic theology are "Bible, church history, history of religion and culture."[5] The Bible, explains Tillich, is the "original document about the events on which the Christian church is founded."[6] Church history matters because "every person who encounters a biblical text is guided in his religious understanding of it by the understanding of all previous generations."[7] And the history of religion and culture is crucial because of the impact on the interpreter of Scripture. Tillich explains that the spiritual life of the theologian is shaped by "language, poetry, philosophy, religion, etc., of the cultural tradition in which he has grown up and from which he takes some content in every moment of his life, in his theological work and also outside it."[8]

Underpinning Tillich's wide-ranging sources for the theologian are two considerations. The first is the historical inevitability of these sources being necessary. He makes much of the historical fact that we must take into account the gap between ourselves and the Bible; and correspondingly we cannot ignore the cultural influences that shape

PAUL TILLICH (1886–1965)

Tillich is one of the great twentieth-century theologians. Born in 1886 into a Lutheran home in Berlin, he rapidly rose to prominence. When the Nazis came to power, he fled Germany and moved to the United States. He worked for a time at the Union Theological Seminary in New York before moving to Harvard in 1955.

our interpretation. The second is theological. The God we worship is at work in every part of the world. And wherever truth is to be found, it is part of God's truth.

Many have followed Tillich's emphasis on a variety of sources. The Anglican theologian John Macquarrie (1919–) suggested that there are six formative factors in theology. He writes: "They are: experience, revelation, scripture, tradition, culture, reason."[9] Although Macquarrie insists that these factors are not all at the same level, he is firmly locating the Bible and tradition in the context of other factors that include practically everything else. For feminist theologians, it has been important to identify potential sources for theology which challenge the patriarchy of the tradition. Rosemary Radford Ruether talks about "usable tradition" (i.e. tradition that can still be used by feminists). She writes:

> I draw "usable tradition" from five areas of cultural tradition: (1) Scripture, both Hebrew and Christian (Old and New Testament); (2) marginalized or 'heretical' Christian traditions, such as Gnosticism, Montanism, Quakerism, Shakerism; (3) the primary theological themes of the dominant stream of classical Christian theology – Orthodox, Catholic, and Protestant; (4 non-Christian Near Eastern and Greco-Roman religion and philosophy; and (5) critical post-Christian worldviews such as liberalism, romanticism, and Marxism.[10]

The instinct to cast the net wide is sound. As we shall see, an insight underpinning the doctrine of the Trinity is that while Christians do believe that God was in Christ (i.e. the Son), we also believe that God is the creator and enabler of everything that is (i.e. the Father). Given God the Father is enabling everything that is, it is reasonable to assume that we can learn of God from a variety of sources. So in addition to the list of sources suggested by Tillich, Macquarrie, and Ruether, I believe it is important to add "the discoveries made by non-Christian religious traditions." People of faith, who earnestly seek the divine reality, should be privileged in the conversation.

This affirmation of a range of sources for Christian theology is partly grounded in the Christian doctrine of the Trinity. So it is now that we turn to this doctrine. What is it? And why should we believe it to be true?

Biblical Roots of the Doctrine of the Trinity

Towards the end of the Gospel of John, so-called Doubting Thomas wants proof of the resurrection. When Jesus appears offering him that proof, Thomas replies: "My Lord and my God!" (John 20:28) One tempting distraction, which must be resisted, is the whole debate about the historicity of these resurrection appearances. This is less important than the fact that there is a story circulating some sixty years after the life of Jesus that shows that Jesus is worshipped as God.

There are other passages in the New Testament that give Jesus a special status. Paul writing to the Church in Corinth some twenty years after the crucifixion explains that "no one can say 'Jesus is Lord' except by the Holy Spirit" (1 Corinthians 12:3). In Colossians, we read: "He [i.e. Jesus] is before all things, and in him all things hold together" (Colossians 1:17). And when Paul quotes a hymn in Philippians, we find the promise that "at the name of Jesus every knee should bow, in heaven and on earth and under the earth, and every tongue confess that Jesus Christ is Lord, to the glory of God the Father" (Philippians 2:10–11).

The fact is that Jesus was worshipped within years of the crucifixion. Given the Early Church also insisted that we worship "one God and Father of us all" (Ephesians 4:6), it was necessary to find some way to weave together the oneness of God with the reality of God being fully present in the life of Jesus of Nazareth.

Now what about the Holy Spirit? Sarah Coakley has argued that if one looks at Paul's account of prayer in Romans 8:9–30 and Galatians 4:4–7, one finds a "prayer-based trinitarian logic."[11] Prayer, for Paul, involves our incorporation into the love of God through Christ; and his description of this movement weaves together "God," "Christ," and "Spirit." Coakley is right to see all three members of the Trinity at work in prayer.

When it comes to the great Commission at the end of Matthew's Gospel, the Trinity is explicit: "And Jesus came and said to them, 'All authority in heaven and on earth has been given to me. Go therefore and make disciples of all nations, baptizing them in the name of the Father and of the Son and of the Holy Spirit, teaching them to observe all that I have commanded you'" (Matthew 28:18–20). Although the word "Trinity" is not found in the Bible, we do find both the idea and the reasons for the doctrine.

Development of the Doctrine of the Trinity

All Christians agree that worship can only be given to God. We have already noted those passages in the New Testament where Jesus seems to be accorded a special status alongside God. These trends continue beyond the New Testament. The so-called second letter of Clement, which was written in approximately 140, starts: "Brethren, we ought so to think of our Lord Jesus Christ as of God, as of the judge of quick and dead."[12] If we are supposed to think of Jesus as God and yet at the same time there is only one God, then some sort of formulation that protects diversity within unity is needed.

At the start of the fourth century, **Arius** argued that Jesus should be seen as the first, preeminent created creature; "there was a time," argued Arius, "when he [Jesus] was

ARIUS (*c.* 250–*c.* 336)

We suspect that Arius was probably a Libyan. According to tradition he was ordained deacon by Bishop Peter of Alexandria, who subsequently had to excommunicate him. He was a popular preacher and famous for his personal discipline. He attracted considerable support for his teaching of subordinationism (i.e. the view that the Son is not equal to the Father). His views provoked the council of Nicaea, at which they were condemned. In Constantinople, he died rather tragically on the streets.

ATHANASIUS (296–373)

Athanasius was also from Alexandria and was the main opponent of Arius. He was born in 296 or perhaps 298 and died in 373. He was probably from a wealthy family, which provided him with an excellent education. In 328, he became the Bishop of Alexandria, where he continued to provoke the ire of virtually everyone. He was the primary theological inspiration behind the theology of Nicaea in 325 and Constantinople in 381. He was the first theologian to list the 27 books which became the New Testament canon.

not." His opponent was **Athanasius**, who later became the patriarch of Alexandria. He argued that you cannot worship a semi-divine Christ and God; this denies monotheism. The Roman Emperor Constantine, fearful of the divisions in his empire, insisted that a council was needed to resolve this argument. So in 325 in Nicaea, some 300 bishops convened. The concluding statement, which became the basis of our Nicene Creed, stated that the Son was not "of similar substance" (*homoiousios*) but "of the same substance" (*homoousios*) with the Father. So it is not sufficient to say that Christ is similar to the Father, but that Christ is identical to the Father. Arianism was declared a heresy.

Although the mainstream Church was agreed about the divinity of the three persons (Father, Son, and Holy Spirit), there were still unanswered questions. And two contrasting responses emerged: the Church in the east (Greek) suggested a way forward that contrasted quite markedly with the response from the Church in the west (Latin).

It was the **Cappadocian Fathers** who saw God as three particular persons (*hypostases*) in one essence (*ousia*). In much the same way as individuals all share the essence of

CAPPADOCIAN FATHERS

Cappadocian Fathers is a term that describes two brothers and a close friend, who all came to prominence almost reluctantly. The two brothers were Basil the Great (c. 330–379), and Gregory of Nyssa (330–395). Basil was a hermit before becoming the Bishop of Caesarea; Gregory was a monk before becoming the Bishop of Nyssa. Their close friend was Gregory of Nazianzus (329–389) who was also a monk who became Bishop of Jasima and later Bishop of Constantinople.

TERTULLIAN (160–220)

Tertullian came from Carthage and was born in about 160 and died in 220. Trained as a lawyer, he then became a priest. He was the author of numerous works, in which he defends the Catholic faith against a variety of heresies. He wrote in Latin.

humanity, so the three persons of the Trinity all share the essence of divinity. Now of course, unlike humans, there is perfect unity amongst the persons of the disembodied triune God. To use terminology that came later in eastern theology, there is "mutual interpenetration" (*perichoresis*) in the Trinity; this means that each member of the Trinity participates in the work of the other members of the Trinity. There is a "community of being" in the Godhead. So, to oversimplify and generalize a little, the eastern Church tended to stress the difference between persons while the western Church developed models of the Trinity that stress the unity amongst the persons.

It was **Tertullian**, writing in about 200, who used the language *persona* and *substantia*. *Substantia* simply means substance. *Persona* has connotations from the theater and means a "mask." This created an image of the Trinity that stressed unity. There is one substance that has different masks (appears to us in different ways). The Trinity describes the one God who plays different roles.

One key expression of these differences in approach to the Trinity emerged over the relationship of the Holy Spirit to the Father and Son. For the eastern Church, it was clear that the Spirit in terms of status is analogous to the Son. So given the Bible talks of the "Son" being "begotten" of the Father, so we should talk of the "Spirit" proceeding from the Father. However, the western Church was thinking of the Spirit in a relational way – the Spirit was the love that bound the Father and the Son together. So they added to the creed the words "and the Son" (the *filioque* clause); this meant that the Spirit proceeded from the Father and the Son. The eastern Church disagreed theologically with this terminology and, anyway, strongly disapproved of words being added to the creed. As a result it split from the western Church in 1054.

Both models have their dangers: for the eastern Church, the emphasis on the distinct persons could lead to the heresy of tritheism (the view that there are three gods); for the western Church, the emphasis on the unity could lead to modalism (the three persons are simply three different modes of the one God). In addition the eastern Church believes that there is a danger of subordinationism (a denial of the equality of the three persons) in the western view of the Holy Spirit. It is to these three dangers that we turn to next.

Three Dangers in Interpreting the Trinity

The first danger is Tritheism. This is an explicit denial of monotheism. This is the belief that the "Father," "Son," and "Holy Spirit" are independent and separate entities. The Mormons (i.e. the Church of Jesus Christ of Latter Day Saints) come closest to Tritheism. They affirm that the Godhead is made up of the Father (who has a physical body), Jesus Christ (who is also Jehovah), and the Holy Ghost. These three are separate beings, but work in complete harmony of purpose. Daniel Migliore explains the problem with Tritheism is that it "flatly contradicts the command of the Old Testament and of Jesus to love God, the one and only Lord, with all one's heart, soul, mind, and strength (Mark 12:30). How can the object of Christian trust, loyalty, and worship be three different Gods?"[13] Migliore's point here is sound. To be able to ascribe ultimate worth to God (the meaning of worship), the entity needs to deserve the "ultimate." If there are different entities making up the Godhead, and they are all demanding worship, then we cannot have any confidence we are really worshipping a being worthy of ultimate worth. If there are many divine entities, then which one really is the greatest? Given that certain divine beings are responsible for certain areas, there are all the complexities of "spheres of responsibility" and therefore "degrees of power." The logic of worship in many religious traditions (Hinduism as well as the Abrahamic traditions) is monotheism.

The second danger is modalism. It was Sabellius (fl. 215),[14] who was excommunicated by Pope St Calixtus I in 220 for teaching modalistic monarchianism (namely, God was unknowable and that the Christ is simply a mode of God). Modalism can take different forms. Alistair McGrath distinguishes helpfully between "chronological modalism" and "functional modalism."[15] Chronological modalism uses the language of the Trinity to describe the different ways in which God operates across the centuries. So in the Hebrew Bible, it is God the Father operating; in the Gospels, it is God the Son who appears as savior; and the Holy Spirit comes at Pentecost to guide the Church. Functional modalism talks of the Trinity as having different roles. So, for example, the Father might be the creator and sustainer; the Son is the savior and revealer; and the Spirit is the sanctifier and enabler.

The key difficulty with modalism is whether these masks are reliable indicators of the nature of the one true eternal God. We need to know what God is like; but, for Sabellius, the eternal nature of the one true immutable God is not changed by these modes of God's activity. So we cannot be sure whether Jesus really shows us what God is like.

The third danger is subordinationism. This is the denial of the equality of the three persons of the Trinity. At its most extreme, there is God the Father (the one true God) and two lesser divinities (on some accounts – creatures). The attraction for the pre-modern mind was that this protected God from being contaminated by matter and change. The hierarchy enables God to relate to the world without actually having any contact with the world.

Again the problem with subordinationism is that we need to know that Christ is really God. Given Christ is the revealer of God, we need to be sure that Christ is really showing us what God is like. This needs Christ to be identical with God.

Modern Accounts of the Trinity

Sensitive to the three dangers outlined above, it is now necessary to look at two modern accounts of the Trinity. Different accounts of the Trinity abound. However, two in particular are representative of two very contrasting approaches. These are the Anglican theologian John Macquarrie (1919–) and the German theologian Jürgen Moltmann (1926–).

John Macquarrie starts by endorsing the view of Ian Ramsey (1915–72) that trinitarian language is both coherent and important. The purpose of the language is not to describe – in a rather indecent way – the inner life of God, but to provide rules for the legitimate talk of our experience of God. Macquarrie puts it like this:

> It is not an objective language, describing a fact laid out for our dispassionate inspection, whether with or without a high-powered telescope. It is a language rooted in existence, in the community's experience of the approach of God. At the same time, it is a language that tries to express an insight into the mystery of God. It has the mixed character that we have seen to belong to all theological language and which we express by the term "existential-ontological."[16]

Our experience has given birth to a sense of God which recognizes God in a variety of different forms. Macquarrie acknowledges that these forms might be found in the Hebrew Bible, but he is also appropriately nervous about imputing to the holy text of Judaism a fully blown Trinitarian theology. Nevertheless Macquarrie insists: "the doctrine of the Trinity safeguards a dynamic as opposed to a static understanding of God."[17] Drawing on the insights of existentialist philosophy, Macquarrie suggests the following account of the three persons. For the Father, Macquarrie writes:

> The Father may be called "primordial" Being. This expression is meant to point to the ultimate act or energy or letting-be, the condition that there should be anything what-soever, the source not only of whatever is but of all possibilities of being.[18]

This primordial Being could be abstract and remote. So it is important to understand the Father in relation to the Son and vice versa. For the Son, explains Macquarrie:

> We shall call "expressive" Being. The energy of the primordial Being is poured out through expressive Being and gives rise to the world of particular beings, having an intelligible structure and disposed in space and time.[19]

It is interesting to note that Macquarrie is making the role in creation central to his description of the Son. In this way he safeguards himself against the modalist heresy: he is not leaving the Father to be the creator and the son to be the redeemer. Instead the Son expresses God both in creation and in the world of humanity. The Holy Spirit is described as "unitive" Being, which involves the following:

> It is in the "unity of the Holy Ghost" that the Church in her liturgy ascribes glory to the Father and the Son, and more generally, it is the function of the Spirit to maintain, strengthen and, where need be, restore the unity of Beings with the beings, a unity which is constantly threatened.[20]

Macquarrie is stressing the unity of God; yet he also recognizes the value of Trinitarian language. And using terminology grounded in modern philosophy, he suggests an account of the Trinity that explains (and, he hopes, illuminates) the purpose of the language.

Jürgen Moltmann develops his account of the Trinity in *The Trinity and the Kingdom: The Doctrine of God*. He is representative of a major trend in modern theology com-mitted to a "social Trinity."[21] He starts by complaining that too much theology has been written assuming a certain inflexible account of God's unity. Instead we need to start with the Biblical witness and then think through an account of God's unity. So, explains Moltmann, his intent is "to start with the special Christian tradition of the history of Jesus the Son, and from that to develop a historical doctrine of the Trinity."[22] His point is that when one reads the New Testament text closely, one can see a dynamic interplay between the Father and the Son (in particular) but also with the Spirit. This dynamic interplay needs to be taken much more seriously.

So when it comes to his interpretation of the Trinity, Moltmann stresses the inter-relationships within the Trinity. The Father should not be understood as a remote, austere entity that rules the world, but instead as that which eternally begets the Son. Moltmann writes:

> [I]n the Christian understanding of God the Father, what is meant is not "the Father of the Universe," but simply and exclusively "the Father of the Son" Jesus Christ. It is solely the Father of Jesus Christ whom we believe and acknowledge created the world ... If God is the Father of this Son Jesus Christ, and if he is only "our Father" for his Son's sake, then we can also only call him "Abba," beloved Father, in the spirit of free sonship.[23]

So unlike Macquarrie, the Trinity is not defined in terms of role, but in terms of relationships. And as we understand the relationships within the Trinity, so we understand how we should relate to God.

Moltmann's treatment of the Son is similar: the emphasis is on the relationship with the Father. Given it is the eternal Son who becomes human and dies, he emphasizes the difference in relation. He explains:

> The love of the Father for the Son, and the love of the Son for the Father are not the same – are not even congruent – simply because they are differently constituted. They do not stand in an equal reciprocal relationship to one another. The Father loves the Son with an engendering, fatherly love. The Son loves the Father with a responsive, self-giving love ... [T]he Son's sacrifice of boundless love on Golgotha is from eternity already included in the exchange of the essential, the consubstantial love which constitutes the divine life of the Trinity. The fact that the Son dies on the cross, delivering himself up to that death, is part of the eternal obedience which he renders to the Father in his whole being through the Spirit, whom he receives from the Father.[24]

For Moltmann, the answer to the question – why was it the Son who came and died and not some other member of the Trinity? – is embedded in the nature of the relationship between the Father and the Son.

Traditionally, the Spirit has always been associated with breath. In the resurrection appearance in John 20, Jesus "breathed" on the apostles and said to them "Receive the Holy Spirit" (John 20:22). Moltmann develops this when he links the Spirit with the Son. He writes:

> [T]he inner coherence immediately becomes perceptible when we understand the Son as *the Word* (Logos). The Father utters his Eternal Word in the eternal breathing out of his Spirit. There is no Word without the Spirit, and no Spirit without the Word.[25]

The point is that in the same way humans cannot have words without breath, so we cannot have the Word of God (the Son) without the breath (of the Spirit). Both proceed from the Father (so on this point Moltmann agrees with the eastern Church).

Now Moltmann believes that a very different politics will emerge from this understanding of God. The logic of monotheism, argues Moltmann, is monarchism.[26] The purpose of this social account of the Trinity is to challenge this monarchism. Moltmann writes:

> The doctrine of the Trinity which evolves out of the surmounting of monotheism for Christ's sake, must therefore also overcome this monarchism, which legitimates dependency, helplessness and servitude. This doctrine of the Trinity must be developed as the true theological doctrine of freedom.[27]

Now there is a problem here. The implication is that Islamic and Jewish accounts of God are less likely to support a politics of freedom. Leaving aside the semi-offensive nature of that suggestion (and the dangers of contributing to anti-Semitism and Islamophobia), there is no empirical evidence for the idea that Trinitarian regimes are freedom friendly. Now Moltmann has no wish to offend Muslims and Jews. Nevertheless Moltmann does push for a model of God which he believes we should reflect in our human communities. As an inspiration for Christians, this may work: as a requirement for any theology of political freedom, this is more problematic.

These are two very different accounts of the Trinity. In Macquarrie the unity of God is central; for Moltmann the dynamic interrelationships are central.

Standing Back

From the outside, it looks like the Trinity is a quaint mathematical sum that has gone wrong. So perhaps at this point it is worth reminding ourselves why the Trinity is so important for Christians. Let us start with epistemology (our theory of knowledge). We started the chapter recognizing that we need some sort of revelation if we are going to talk about God beyond mere generalities. The distinctive Christian claim is that the Word of God (*logos* – in Greek) is Jesus. In the life, death, and resurrection of Jesus we can see God.[28] Karl Barth had it right when he suggested that the Bible (because it is the source for all we know about Jesus)[29] becomes the Word of God when it witnesses to the Word which is Jesus. The point of all this is that when someone asks me the question: "how do I know that God is loving and not unpleasant?", my reply is that I know because this is the witness found in the disclosure of God in Jesus of Nazareth. Granted this witness is found in the Hebrew Bible and elsewhere in other faith traditions, but the Christian form of the message is found in the Logos, which is Christ. So given the Christian claim that to have some knowledge of God depends on Jesus being God, an account of how this is possible is clearly essential. Related to this, the primary purpose of the doctrine of the Trinity is to explain the range and variety of divine action. Ironically the doctrine is intended to protect monotheism.

It is interesting to note how both Orthodox Jews and Observant Muslims talk about the eternal nature of both the Torah (for Jews) and Qur'an (for Muslims). The Word of God in both traditions is eternal, which presumably means the Word coexists with God in eternity past. Now Christians, partly because of a deep commitment to monotheism, were not content to leave the Word of God (which is Christ the Son) running parallel with the creator in eternity past, but felt obliged to think through the precise relation that makes it possible to believe in the Eternal Word and at the same time in one creator God.

The Jesuit theologian Thomas Michel is right to talk about the Trinity as "radical monotheism."[30] The problem with the social trinity of Moltmann is that it hints at almost anthropomorphic intrigues within the divine life. John Macquarrie cautions:

> [T]he so-called "social analogy" for elucidating the Trinity is unsatisfactory. On that view, "person" is taken in something like its modern sense, and the Trinity is understood as like a society of persons. Even when we make every allowance for the fact that a person is constituted through his relations to other persons, such a model goes too far in the direction of "dividing the substance."[31]

Keith Ward, commenting on David Brown's form of the "social trinity," explains: "This is very much like a form of polytheism; indeed, a rather cozy and harmonious polytheism."[32] This definitely will not do: Christians believe in one God. And the purpose of the doctrine of the Trinity is to safeguard that one God.

Both Karl Barth and Karl Rahner have suggested we need to find an alternative to "person." Barth suggested "modes of being";[33] Rahner wanted "distinct modes of subsisting."[34] The picture we need is of God working in a variety of ways. Each of these ways completely represents God. Many potential mistakes occur because we are working with the classical model of God. Robert Jenson points out that classical assumptions about time meant that: "The Son and the Spirit had to be, like other late-antique saviors, in such fashion divine as to mediate our access from time to timeless full deity."[35] A pre-modern modalism (as advocated by Sabellius) left us with an unknowable timeless God, set apart from creation, who appeared with various masks. This was rightly condemned. The modes of God in Sabellius' theology are not really God.

One reason, then, why the instincts of Process theology (appropriately modified) are sound is that it makes a Trinitarian theology easier to expound. The Incarnation (that Jesus was completely God and completely human) witnesses to the truth that God and the world are connected together. When we think about God, we are thinking about a God who is dynamic and active. God creates and sustains (and in this mode it is primarily, but by no means exclusively, the work of the Father); God reveals and redeems (again primarily the work of the Son); and God unites, heals, and transforms (again primarily the work of the Spirit). Given that God is not simply revealed in the life of Jesus but also in creation (then we properly talk of the Son involved in creation, even though this is primarily the work of the Father). Given that God has disclosed truths about God which are found in other faith traditions, we properly expect to encounter the Son in other religions, even though this is primarily the work of the Spirit. There is endless movement between the three modes of being.

Thomas Michel concludes his thought-provoking article by comparing Islamic and Christian accounts of God. He writes:

> If the Islamic vocation in our world remains that of witnessing to God's true oneness and challenging any conceptualizations or formulations that would diminish or deny that Unity, the Christian vocation is to bear witness that this one and same God is radically close to humankind, has become part of our changeable human history, and unceasingly lives and acts at the heart of the cosmos. One might say that Muslims approach the Divine with the basic question, "Who?" and the answer of Islamic faith is "Allah, the One God." Christians agree and then ask a second question, "How?" and the answer of Christian faith is "in three essential modes of Divine presence."[36]

One advantage of this emphasis on the Trinity as descriptive of three modes of divine presence is that it does free the Church up to rethink the terminology. The language of Father and Son is irredeemably male. It is also misleading. Save for an appropriate emphasis on the personal qualities of God, it creates a very anthropomorphic image of God. For this reason many feminists are suggesting we revisit the terminology. Some use the language *Creator*, *Redeemer*, and *Sustainer*, while David Cunningham has suggested *Source*, *Wellspring*, and *Living Water*.[37] It is important that we recognize the personal dimension of the language; nevertheless it is helpful that we use different images from time to time. God is beyond gender; the alternative language draws attention to that fact. And as we work with different images, so we appreciate the insights underpinning this remarkable doctrine.

Conclusion

As we noted at the start of the chapter we are now moving to a different level. We have stepped inside the Christian circle. We are trusting that in the life of Jesus we can see God. We are therefore seeking to understand the relationship of the revelation of God to God the creator. This is the work of the Trinity. We have examined the history of the doctrine. I have defended an account of the Trinity that stresses the unity of God who operates in three contrasting modes.

QUESTIONS FOR REFLECTION AND DISCUSSION

1 Do you agree that we need to trust some sort of revelation if we are going to claim to know anything about God? How do we decide which revelation is right?
2 How would an evangelical respond to the list of sources suggested by Rosemary Radford Reuther?
3 What are the three dangers we can slip into when talking about the Trinity? Why are they dangers?
4 What is the "social Trinity"? Why is it popular? What are the attractions and the problems with the account?
5 In what sense does the doctrine of the Trinity protect monotheism?

GLOSSARY

Epistemology: the science of knowing
Monotheism: a belief in one God
Polytheism: a belief in many gods
Subordinationism: the heresy that the Son is less important (subordinate) to the Father
Tritheism: a belief that there is no fundamental unity to God; instead there are three divine persons

Notes

1 *The Catechism of the Catholic Church* (Mahwah, NJ: Paulist Press, 1994), p. 31.
2 Ibid., p. 29.

3   Although this was Luther's line, he did hold that the key theme of Scripture was "justification by faith" and that those books in the Bible which did not develop this theme are less important than those which do. Paul Tillich helpfully identifies this criterion as the norm of systematic theology: all traditions, explains Tillich, have a norm. See Paul Tillich, *Systematic Theology*, vol. 1 (London: Nisbet and Co. 1953), pp. 54f.

4   Luther also talked about *adiaphora* (literally things that do not make a difference). He applied this to all those things that were neither required nor proscribed by Scripture.

5   Tillich, *Systematic Theology*, vol. 1, p. 45.

6   Ibid., p. 40.

7   Ibid., p. 42.

8   Ibid., p. 44.

9   John Macquarrie, *Principles of Christian Theology*, revised edition (London: SCM Press, 1977), p. 4.

10 Rosemary Radford Ruether, *Sexism and God-talk: Towards a Feminist Theology* (Boston: Beacon Press, 1993), pp. 21–2.

11 Sarah Coakley, "Why three? Some further reflections on the origins of the doctrine of the trinity," in Sarah Coakley and David A. Pailin (eds.) *The Making and Remaking of Christian Doctrine: Essays in Honor of Maurice Wiles* (Oxford: Clarendon Press, 1993), pp. 29–56.

12 "2 Clement (so called)" in Charles H. Hoole (trans), *Apostolic Fathers*, available at http://www.earlychristianwritings.com/text/2clement-hoole.html.

13 Daniel L. Migliore, *Faith Seeking Understanding: An Introduction to Christian Theology*, 2nd edition (Grand Rapids, MI: Eerdmans, 2004), p. 71.

14 Just for clarification, the abbreviation *fl.* is for the Latin word *floruit* which means "flourished." It is an abbreviation used by historians, when the birth and death are not known.

15 See Alister E. McGrath, *Christian Theology: An Introduction*, 3rd edition (Oxford: Blackwell, 2001), pp. 328–9.

16 Macquarrie, *Principles of Christian Theology*, p. 191.

17 Ibid., p. 197.

18 Ibid., p. 199.

19 Ibid., p. 199.

20 Ibid., p. 201.

21 Other examples include David Brown, *The Divine Trinity* (London: Duckworth, 1985) and Richard Swinburne, *The Christian God* (Oxford: Clarendon Press, 1994).

22 Jürgen Moltmann, *The Trinity and the Kingdom: The Doctrine of God* (San Francisco: Harper and Row, 1981), p. 19.

23 Ibid., p. 163.

24 Ibid., p. 168.

25 Ibid., p. 170.

26 Ibid., p. 191.

27 Ibid., p. 192.

28 Recognizing this truth can illuminate many related matters. For example, in the Christian-Muslim dialogue, one commonplace mistake is to assume that the Bible is the equivalent of the Qur'an. The problem with this is that while the Qur'an reads as the "Word of God"

(after all each sura is introduced with a declaration that the words that follow are indeed from God), the Bible does not. In addition the Bible teaches that the Word of God is Jesus (see John 1:1). A better way of viewing the relation of authorities in Christianity and the Qur'an is to see the life, death, and resurrection of Jesus as the equivalent to the Qur'an and the Bible as the equivalent of the Hadith.

29 Much as I enjoy the extra-canonical Gospels, the Early Church was right not to include them in the canon. The so-called Gnostic Gospels are clearly second century and are therefore less reliable as history and often contain a very problematic theological worldview.

30 Thomas Michel, SJ, "The trinity as radical monotheism," available at http://puffin.creighton. edu/jesuit/dialogue/documents/articles/michel_radical_monotheism.htm.

31 Macquarrie, *Principles of Christian Theology*, p. 194.

32 Keith Ward, *Religion and Creation* (Oxford: Clarendon Press, 1996), p. 322.

33 Karl Barth, *Church Dogmatics* I/1, 2nd edition, translated G. W. Bromiley (Edinburgh: T. & T. Clark, 1975), p. 355.

34 Karl Rahner, *The Trinity*, translated Joseph Donceel (New York: Crossroad, 1977), pp. 103–15.

35 Robert Jenson, *Systematic Theology*, vol. 1 (Oxford: Oxford University Press, 1997), p. 95.

36 Thomas Michel, "The trinity as radical monotheism."

37 See David Cunningham, "What do we mean by 'God'?" in William Placher (ed.) *Essentials of Christian Theology* (Louisville, KY: WJK, 2003), pp. 86–7.

Chapter 5
THE PROBLEM OF EVIL AND SUFFERING

LEARNING OUTCOMES

By the end of the chapter you should be able to:

- understand the difference between coherence and evidentialist accounts of the problem
- appreciate some of the main theodicies
- understand why the author believes that Christian doctrine is primarily a response to the problem of evil

---

STRUCTURE

- The reason why suffering and evil are a problem
- The inadequacy of the traditional responses
- Ivan's question and critique
- Doctrine as the Christian response

Watching the television news can be difficult. News broadcasters have no option but to focus on the tragic: the normal and routine isn't "new" and therefore isn't "newsworthy"; good news is dull; so tragedy dominates the headlines. A famine in Africa; a family unable to escape a burning house; a serial killer taking another innocent life; the child abused by those who should protect her; the Tsunami that destroys entire communities; the hurricane that takes out New Orleans; and finally the political paralysis at the heart of Government. Everyone suffers.

The fact is that suffering touches every human life. It is probably true that we suffer more than we are happy. One strength of Buddhism is that it places the reality of suffering front and center. The Four Noble Truths are all about the challenge of suffering and the need to find strategies to cope. The heart of Buddhism is the discovery by the Buddha that if we cultivate certain underlying dispositions, in which we see everything for what it really is, then the power of things to make us suffer disappears. Buddhism can be seen as a religion which is a response to suffering. One argument of this book is that Christianity is misunderstood unless one sees that it too places suffering front and center. Indeed every chapter that follows this one can be seen as the Christian response to the reality of evil and suffering. The claim that the world is created and that humanity lives in awkward tension with the divine (the next chapter) is part of that response. Later chapters, which explore God becoming human and bringing out the possibility of redemption, are also part of the Christian response to suffering and evil.

Now most books on doctrine treat the problem of evil as a dilemma one arrives at after everything else is sorted out. It is, in terms of space, relatively trivial. Daniel L. Migliore in *Faith Seeking Understanding* discusses the problem of evil in the chapter on providence.[1] Robert Jenson offers a four-page chapter on "the character of creation."[2] And Alister McGrath's popular *Christian Theology: An Introduction* also opts for four pages in a chapter dedicated to the "Doctrine of God."[3] The structure of a book is often an indicator of an argument.[4] For most theologians, the problem of suffering is just that – a difficult problem. I am arguing that although we have sufficient reasons to believe in the existence of God, there is no satisfactory explanation or justification of evil.[5] Instead all of Christian doctrine is a response to evil and suffering – from creation, through Incarnation, through atonement to our theology beyond the grave.

The Reason Why Suffering and Evil Are a Problem

The God revealed in Judaism and inherited by Christians and Muslims is one. The great commandment that requires us to "love the LORD your God with all your heart, and with all your soul, and with all your might" starts with the declaration: "Hear, O Israel: The LORD our God is one LORD" (Deuteronomy 6:4). The point of this declaration is that there is nothing besides God: there are no other competing forces that make it difficult for God to operate. Indeed we worship this God because we are confident that God is in control. Some Christians are tempted by the view that perhaps God "cannot" do anything about evil and suffering. If they mean by this that God cannot do the logically impossible (e.g. create round squares), then that is true. But if they mean God is not all-powerful, then there is a problem.

Jews, Christians, and Muslims did not arbitrarily alight on the doctrine of omnipotence (which means all-powerful) because they just liked the idea. Instead omnipotence is embedded deep in the logic of worship. We worship God as creator: this is a basic truth. So, at the very least, God must be powerful enough to do that work. However, worship also entails a confidence that God will triumph. I cannot "give ultimate worth to" (the literal meaning of worship) a God who might lose at some time in the future. Put the idea that God must be powerful enough to create a world together with the idea that God cannot lose in the future and we find ourselves compelled to, at least, a version of omnipotence. To stop short of omnipotence and say that God is jolly powerful but not all-powerful provokes the question – so how powerful exactly is God? There is a simplicity in the logic that God's power is not simply great (great enough to create and sufficient for us to be confident that God will triumph) but all-powerful (i.e. God is able to do all logically possible tasks which God is able to do).[6]

As with power, so it is with knowledge and love. God is not just bright (brighter than Einstein) but knows everything it is logically possible for God to know. And God is not just loving, more loving than Mother Teresa of Calcutta, but God is all-loving. There is a simplicity in that we are not trying to work out where God's power, knowledge or love stops. And with such an account of God, the logic and implications of worship are safeguarded because we can be sure that the Being to whom we are giving absolute worth really is worthy of that worship.

So our conundrum with the problem of evil and suffering arises. President Truman had a sign on his desk that stated "The Buck Stops Here." If that was true for President Truman, then how much truer it must be for God. Everything is ultimately determined by God. The prophet of the Babylonian exile even acknowledges God as the author of evil: he writes, "I am the LORD, and there is no other. I form light and create darkness, I make weal and create woe, I am the LORD, who do all these things" (Isaiah 45:7). God might have many reasons for the creation; but let us not evade the implications of monotheism by turning God into a bystander slightly surprised that there is suffering and evil in the world.

In the philosophy of religion, it is customary to distinguish between the coherence form of the problem and the evidential form. The coherence form stresses that it is incoherent (self-contradictory) to postulate a God with the traditional attributes creating a world with evil and suffering. So put simply and in its classical form, the problem can be stated thus:

1 If God is all-powerful, then God must be able to abolish evil and suffering.
2 If God is all-loving, then God must wish to abolish evil and suffering.
3 But evil and suffering exists, therefore God cannot be all-powerful and all-loving.

It was Alvin Plantinga who pointed out that this form of the problem has a major and insurmountable problem with it. It assumes that every conceivable reason why a God with these attributes might allow evil and suffering has been shown to be invalid. The problem for the atheist is that this is very difficult to show. Not only would the traditional theodicies (theodicy means an attempt to justify God's actions) have been shown to be inadequate, but also every other conceivable theodicy including those which haven't been thought about yet. Obviously this is an impossible task. So most skeptics (who want to use the problem of evil against theists) concede that incoherence is difficult to prove and move instead to the evidential form of the argument.

The evidential form does not make the grandiose claim that theism is logically impossible and therefore incoherent. Instead it argues that theism is very unlikely to be true given the reality of evil and suffering in the world. As the term "evidential" suggests, the problem of evil is seen as decisive evidence against the existence of God. One way to think about the argument is this. Imagine for a moment that you are God (omniscient, omnipotent, and perfectly good) and you are creating the world: is this the best you could come up with – a world with serial killers, earthquakes, and hurricanes? And if not, then it must be conceded that it is very unlikely that God is responsible for this world.

The Inadequacy of the Traditional Responses

It is not possible to discuss every theodicy in the literature. Christians have had centuries to arrive at various sophisticated responses to the problem. Most theodicies tend to a version of the "end is justified by the means" argument. The end of freedom, for example, entails the means of the possibility of evil. The end of character development (e.g. patience) requires the means of problem and pain to get there. Given, the argument goes, God wanted certain ends, God had no choice but to permit, at the very least, the possibility (and probably the actuality) of evil and suffering.

To make this discussion manageable, I shall focus on two theodicies. The first is the free will defense; the second is the "greater goods" (sometimes called the Irenaean) theodicy. I shall show that neither are particularly successful. And by successful, I mean that having engaged with the theodicy, we remain left with a deep sense of unease – a sense that the explanation does not meet the full force of the tragedy in our world.

We start then with the free will defense. Forms of this argument are found in a variety of places from Augustine of Hippo to the contemporary philosopher of religion Alvin Plantinga.[7] This argument is part of virtually every attempt to explain why evil and suffering exists. It starts with the assumption that the goal of creation is to have creatures who are able to have a loving relationship with each other and with God. Love cannot be programmed or compelled. Although I am able to set my computer on start up to announce "I love you," I know that this is not true love. True loves requires freedom – a freedom to hurt, disagree, and hate. And love is precious precisely because true love includes this possibility. As one trusts every parent knows, one of the finest moments in the world is when a child turns and says "I love you Daddy and Mommy." It is precisely because a child has the capacity to dislike and hate that the sentence is so extraordinary. So the free will defense goes like this: God desires a creation where there is love. Love requires freedom. Given love is a desirable end, then freedom is a necessary condition. However, freedom entails the possibility of evil. This possibility was realized (and is realized every day) by humans exercising their freedom for evil ends.

Now although all this might be true, is it sufficient to explain the sheer range of evil and suffering in the world? The first thing to note is that it doesn't explain natural disasters (such as earthquakes) or illness and death. Some postulate that even illness and death are due to the human or angelic exercise of freedom. This is implied by Augustine[8] in the *City of God*, when he explains that angels divide into one of two types:

> One of these companies enjoys God, the other swells with pride; to one is said, "Adore him, all you angels of his"; while the chief of the other company says, "I will give you all these things, if you bow down and worship me." The one company burns with holy love of God; the other smoulders with the foul desire for its own exaltation. . . . The one enjoys tranquility in the bright radiance of devotion; the other rages in the dark shadows of desire. The one brings merciful aid, or just punishment, in obedience to God's bidding; the other seethes with the lust to subdue and to injure, at the behest of its own arrogance. The one serves the good purposes of God, striving to give full effect to the desire to help; the other is restrained by God's power, to prevent their fulfilling the desire to harm.[9]

For Augustine, the free will defense includes angels. The Devil and demons are a result of the exercise of free will. Augustine puts it thus: "These are the two societies of angels, contrasted and opposed; the one good by nature and rightly directed by choice, the other good by nature but perverted by choice."[10] And these fallen angels are responsible for much of the chaos and misery in this world. Alvin Plantinga follows this line when he attributes much natural evil to the activity of the Devil. However, there are problems here: to assume that the Devil is behind an earthquake is to assume that an earthquake is a malfunction in the earth's structure. But an earthquake is the inevitable outcome of the movement of the oceanic and continental plates, which make up the earth's crust. The earthquake is a symptom of how the earth is made: to attribute this to the Devil is to make the Devil the creator.

Second, the free will defense seems to conflict with the Christian doctrine of heaven. Heaven is a state where love combines with a pain-free existence. If such an existence is logically possible, then why not bring it about in the first place? J. L. Mackie, the atheist philosopher, makes the point that given it is logically possible for a good person to freely choose the good repeatedly, then it must be logically possible for God to create humanity in such a way that they repeatedly freely choose the good.[11] In other words, why did not God simply create lots of really good people (for example, lots of Mother Teresas) who repeatedly freely choose the good? Brian Hebblethwaite and others object that we cannot be free and be caused to be good[12]: the achievement of Mother Teresa is precisely that she chose to do the right thing. And as for creating heaven at the outset, the problem here is that we need the earthly stage to prepare us for heaven.

Although Hebblethwaite might have a point, there is still a mystery about why God endowed us with the range of choices that we have. David Hume in *Dialogues Concerning Natural Religion*[13] suggested that God could have reduced much human suffering by making us twice as industrious. Now, of course, doubling our capacity to work would benefit both the virtuous (who can then do more good) but also the wicked (who can do more harm). However, Hume does have a point. God could have made us agents with superheroic, telepathic powers. In such a universe we would have moral choices to make about our enhanced moral powers (whether to use such powers in a constructive or destructive way). Conversely God could have made us all with "special needs"; and in such a universe the types and forms of evil and suffering that we could inflict on each other would be reduced. It is also, incidentally, a universe which would continue to include love and freedom. Clearly God did make a call that humans should have the strength and intelligence to organize an Auschwitz: it is not at all obvious that this needed to be the case for a universe in which there is freedom and love.

As I have already noted, the free will defense might be true or at least have some truth embedded within it. But I suggest as one thinks about it, one is still left with a sense of disquiet. The truth is that it is not necessary for the existence of human freedom that a child is abused by a parent or that a woman is gang raped. Given this thought, it is difficult to continue to bow the knee to the creator and acknowledge God's loving concern for us all.

The so-called Irenaean theodicy does not fare any better. **John Hick** in his rightly acclaimed classic *Evil and the God of Love* argues for an Irenaean, rather than Augustinian, theodicy. For Augustine, we are placed into a perfect setting that humans spoil by sinning; for Irenaeus (*c.* 130–*c.* 202) we are placed into a challenging setting through which we move from the Image of God (our fundamental nature as creatures of intelligence) to the likeness of God (the state where the human is perfected by the action of the Holy Spirit). Hick develops the contrast between Augustine and Irenaeus thus:

> There is . . . to be found in Irenaeus the outline of an approach to the problem of evil which stands in important respects in contrast to the Augustinian type of theodicy. Instead of a doctrine that man was created finitely perfect and then incomprehensively destroyed his own perfection and plunged into sin and misery, Irenaeus suggests that man was created as an imperfect, immature creature who was to undergo moral development and growth and finally be brought to the perfection intended for him by his Maker. Instead of the fall of Adam being presented, as in the Augustinian tradition, as an utterly malignant and catastrophic event, completely disrupting God's plan, Irenaeus pictures it as something that occurred in the childhood of the race, an understandable lapse due to weakness and immaturity rather than an adult crime full of malice and pregnant with perpetual guilt. And instead of the Augustinian view of life's trials as a divine punishment for Adam's sin, Irenaeus sees our world of mingled good and evil as a divinely appointed environment for man's development towards the perfection that represents the fulfillment of God's good purpose for him.[14]

With this contrast established, Hick then develops the Irenaean theodicy in an interesting and imaginative way. God desires a world which is a vale of soulmaking – a setting in which we move from immaturity into maturity. The setting is a stable one, in which humans can exercise their freedom and learn to interact with each other. There is an appropriate "epistemic distance" between us and God: God is not so overwhelmingly obvious that we would not dare to develop our character and autonomy. With the challenge of coping with tragedy and pain, we develop character. John Hick is pointing to an experience which – fortunately – is often recognized by people who suffer. It arises when a person is forced to cope with some tragedy (job loss or divorce) and then in retrospect decides "it was all for the good." A person, for example, loses her job and in the moment of despair discovers resources "deep" inside to transform the situation.

JOHN HICK (1922–)

Contemporary British theologian who was born in 1922. After an evangelical conversion, he specialized in the philosophy of religion, with a particular interest in interfaith. After lecturing at the University of Birmingham, he moved to Claremont Graduate School in the United States. He is best known for his Gifford Lectures called *An Interpretation of Religion*.

Yet a problem remains. Again it was David Hume who identified the problem. Hume writes:

> The winds are requisite to convey the vapours along the surface of the globe, and to assist men in navigation: But how often, rising up to tempests and hurricanes, do they become pernicious? Rains are necessary to nourish all the plants and animals of the earth; But how often are they defective? How often excessive? Health is requisite to all life and vegetation; but is not always found in due proposition. On the mixture and secretion of the humors and juices of the body depend the health and prosperity of the animal; But the parts perform not regularly their proper function.[15]

The problem Hume identifies is that some wind and some sunshine are essential. One might add a little excessive wind and sunshine can be a learning moment. But a hurricane that destroys lives and homes and a drought that destroys crops and leads to starvation are not learning moments but moments that lead to despair. The Jewish Holocaust was not a character building opportunity but a wicked, cruel, unspeakable horror. A child abused and tortured by a pedophile before being killed is not an opportunity for growth, but a deep evil. An earthquake that killed over 80,000 people was not an opportunity for us to give, but an inconsolable devastation that will haunt generations of people to come.

The suffering of the world is too much. Both the free will defense and the Irenaean theodicy collapse in the face of the extent of human tragedy. We are left with a deep unease. We cannot work out why God allows evil and suffering. At the most basic level: We are forced simply to accept that God does allow it and that God must have reasons which we can never know.

Ivan's Question and Critique

All of this comes together in the widely discussed chapter of **Fyodor Dostoyevsky's** novel *The Brothers Karamazov*. This great novel of three sons – Dmitry (an army officer), Ivan (the skeptic writer), and Alyosha (a novice) – is a remarkable insight into Dostoyevsky's Russia of 1870. For our purposes, the relevant passage is Ivan's discussion with Alyosha. The two brothers are meeting at an inn; and the conversation turns to religion, love, and evil. Ivan explains to Alyosha why he finds faith all so difficult.

In the chapter "Rebellion," Ivan documents the suffering of children, who are innocent and have not yet "eaten the apple."[16] In each case it is tragic and moving: one illustration will suffice for our purposes.

I've collected a great deal of facts about Russian children, Alyosha. A father and mother, "most respectable people of high social position, of good education and breeding," hated their little five-year-old daughter . . . This poor five-year-old girl was subjected to every possible torture by those educated parents. They beat her, birched her, kicked her, without themselves knowing why, till her body was covered with bruises; at last they reached the height of refinement; they shut her up all night, in the cold and frost, in the privy and because she didn't ask to get up at night (as though a child of five, sleeping its angelic, sound sleep, could be trained at her age to ask for such a thing), they smeared her face with excrement and made her eat it, and it was her mother, her mother who made her! And that mother could sleep at night, hearing the groans of the poor child locked up in that vile place! Do you realize what it means when a little creature like that, who's quite unable to understand what is happening to her, beats her little aching chest in that vile place, in the dark and cold, with her tiny fist and weeps searing, unresentful and gentle tears to "dear, kind God" to protect her? Can you understand why all this absurd and horrible business is so necessary and has been brought to pass?[17]

The narrative culminates in Ivan's absolute refusal to accept that any "justification" is acceptable for such tragedy. The suffering of that five-year-old child is too high a price to pay for cosmic harmony beyond the grave or as a necessary condition for human freedom. Ivan finds creation morally obscene. He explains:

"Besides, too high a price has been placed on harmony. We cannot afford to pay so much for admission. And therefore I hasten to return my ticket of admission. And indeed, if I am an honest man, I'm bound to hand it back as soon as possible. This I am doing. It is not God that I do not accept Alyosha. I merely most respectfully return him the ticket."

"This is rebellion," Alyosha said softly, dropping his eyes.

"Rebellion? I'm sorry to hear you say that," Ivan said with feeling. "One can't go on living in a state of rebellion, and I want to live. Tell me frankly, I appeal to you – answer me: imagine that it is you yourself who are erecting the edifice of human destiny with

FYODOR DOSTOYEVSKY (1821–81)

Fyodor Michaelovitch Dostoyevsky was a gifted Russian novelist. He spent much of his life in trouble with the authorities: he was actually sentenced to death, after being arrested for fermenting revolution in 1849. Although the death sentence was never carried out (instead he spent four years doing hard labor in Siberia), he lived life aware of the challenge of death. During his lifetime, he was best known as a journalist.

the aim of making men happy in the end, of giving them peace and contentment at last, but that to do that it is absolutely necessary, and indeed quite inevitable, to torture to death only one tiny creature, the little girl who beat her breast with her little fist, and to found the edifice on her unavenged tears – would you consent to be the architect on those conditions? Tell me and do not lie!"

"No, I wouldn't," Alyosha said softly.[18]

For Ivan, the problem is not God (the idea of God might be possible) but the creation. Ivan rejects completely and categorically all attempts at a means-ends theodicy: for Ivan the end of freedom or character building cannot justify the means of the suffering of children. Ivan rejects the cosmic experiment where such means are used to such ends – "It is not God that I do not accept Alyosha. I merely most respectfully return him the ticket." Ivan wants out of this experiment: the values of the project are fundamentally immoral.

Ivan has been described as a "protest atheist."[19] It is a protest that this world is not worthy of a good God. If Ivan was put in a position where he had to make the same decision as God – to allow a child to be abused by her parents for the sake of human freedom and happiness in the eschaton (at the end of the age), then Ivan would have decided against creation. The price is just too high.

Ivan captures our sense of unease. Even if the traditional theodicies are true, there is still a sense of heart-wrenching tragedy that makes it almost blasphemous to believe them. Is God really calculating that character building is worth a Tsunami? Is God's inactivity at Auschwitz really a decision to protect the virtue of human freedom and the right to exercise that freedom for wickedness? If a human being had the power to do something about the Tsunami or Auschwitz and decided that inactivity was appropriate because it leads to some desirable end, then we would judge that human being very harshly. So why are our expectations of God less than our expectations of each other?

These are difficult questions. And it is the argument of this book that the response (I dare not say "answers") to these questions is the entire character and formulation of Christian doctrine.

Doctrine as the Christian Response

It is interesting that there is no theodicy in the Bible. Although the Bible documents page after page the entire range of human suffering, nowhere do we find the "free will defense" or an "Irenaean theodicy." The most detailed exploration of suffering in the Bible is to be found in the elegant poetry of the book of Job. Job, so the story goes, is tested by God. He loses everything. Job's friends, Eliphaz, Bildad, and Zophar, suggest the traditional theodicy: suffering is a result of sin. So Job must have sinned. Later Elihu stresses the way in which suffering can transform us. Finally, after extensive pleading, God delivers the answer out of the whirlwind. And it is an extraordinary answer: God asks Job various questions, all of which make clear that God is the creator and Job a mere puny entity within the creation. So God says:

> Where were you when I laid the foundation of the earth?
> Tell me, if you have understanding.
> Who determined its measurements – surely you know!
> Or who stretched the line upon it? (Job 38:4–5)

And so it goes on. In a remarkable set of questions put by God to Job (which strangely neglects the creation of humanity), God makes the point that the creator is not obliged to provide answers to the questions that people asked. Job responds:

> Then Job answered the LORD:
> "I know that thou canst do all things,
> and that no purpose of thine can be thwarted.
> 'Who is this that hides counsel without knowledge?'
> Therefore I have uttered what I did not understand,
> things too wonderful for me, which I did not know.
> 'Hear, and I will speak; I will question you; and you will declare to me.'
> I had heard of thee by the hearing of the ear,
> but now my eye sees thee;
> therefore I despise myself,
> and repent in dust and ashes." (Job 42:1–7)

Job repents of the temerity of daring to ask questions. However frustrating it might seem, God is not going to explain to us why the innocent suffer. The Biblical witness agrees that there is innocent suffering; indeed the Biblical witness documents all forms of suffering from natural disasters to despicable acts of human evil. But we are not given to know precisely why this is so.

Yet there is a narrative, which we will explore in the rest of this book, that is a response to the reality of evil and suffering. First, we need to understand how humans are both capable of goodness and at other times agents of wickedness. The theological explanation is grounded in the doctrines of the creation and the Fall. Our goodness is made possible by the fact we are all created in the Image of God; our propensities for wickedness arise due to our struggle for autonomy (traditionally called the "Fall"). Second, we need to appreciate that the God we worship has disclosed his nature in the life of Jesus of Nazareth. This is the doctrine of the Incarnation. In addition to seeing in that life the priority of love, we also see how it was necessary for God to die at the hands of God's creation. This is conceptually difficult and confusing: yet this is the central claim of Christianity. Ultimately the Christian response to Ivan is to point to the person that we believe was God hanging and dying on the cross. Theologically we learn from this that God knows what suffering is and that it is an inescapable part of the creation. But we also learn that this death has made it possible for our relationship with each other and God to be transformed. And this is the third aspect, the doctrine of the atonement calls us to allow God to transform our lives so that love becomes the dominant theme. Through the pivotal movement of repentance, the action of God in Christ gives God the authority to forgive those moments when egoism, selfishness, and hatred dominate, thereby affording an opportunity to live open to the transforming power of God's love. In other words, an important part of Christian response to evil and suffering is that we accept the invitation of God to allow grace to overcome our propensity to evil and allow love to then dominate. Fourth, our struggle for transformation is not an isolated challenge, but should take place within a mutually-supporting community. This is where our ecclesiology (view of the Church) comes in. The Church is not simply another organization, but an agent of divine transformation. The Church is not just an hour on Sunday morning, but a Spirit-led community that is called to transform individuals and the world. Fifth,our eschatological hope (eschatology means "doctrines about the end") invites us to place the struggles of human existence into an appropriate context. This life is not it. This does not mean that we are promised "pie in the sky," but we are invited to place this moment of human existence into the context of eternity. So as individuals we will die; and as a planet and a species, our time on earth will come to an end. These realities invite us to participate in the promise of an ultimate reconciliation in the cosmos between the injustice suffered and the love promised.

This sketch will require much more detail. And this will follow in the rest of the book. However, the point, I trust, is clear. The entire schema of Christian doctrine should and can be interpreted as a response to the problem of evil and suffering. We are not invited to solve at a theoretical level the problem of theodicy; instead we are invited into the life of the Church to interpret the challenge of suffering in the light of a God who is involved and who is inviting us to live transformed lives. In much the same way that Buddhism has the problem of evil and suffering front and center, so Christianity is the same.

QUESTIONS OF REFLECTION AND DISCUSSION

1 Do you agree that evil and suffering is a major challenge to belief?
2 Can you think of any other theodicies, which are not considered in this chapter?
3 Would you agree with Ivan that a world where certain ends are justified by evil and suffering is immoral?
4 In what ways does Buddhism help us cope with suffering?
5 Do you agree that Christian doctrine is in part a response to the problem of evil and suffering in the world?

GLOSSARY

Epistemic distance: the distance which is necessary to enable humanity not to be overwhelmed by the presence of God

Evidential form of the problem of evil: the claim that the problem of evil does not necessarily demonstrate that theism is incoherent, but it does point to the idea that theism is unlikely to be true

Omnipotence: the doctrine that God is all-powerful

Omniscience: the doctrine that God is all-knowing

Theodicy: an attempt to justify why God allows evil and suffering in the creation

Notes

1 See Daniel L. Migliore, *Faith Seeking Understanding* (Grand Rapids, MI: Eerdmans, 2004), pp. 117–38. To give Migliore his due credit, the discussion is substantial and appropriately serious. The only weakness in my view is that it does not give theodicy a sufficiently central place in Christian doctrine.

2 See Robert Jenson, *Systematic Theology*, vol. 2, *The Works of God* (Oxford: Oxford University Press, 1999), pp. 20–4.

3 See Alister McGrath, *Christian Theology: An Introduction* (Oxford: Blackwell, 2001), pp. 292–5.

4 Steward Sutherland made a similar point, although his concern was the account of God. For Sutherland see *God, Jesus and Belief* (Oxford: Blackwell, 1984).

5 The ways in which a natural theology can assist us with theodicy was ably made by R. Douglas Geivett, *Evil and Evidence for God* (Philadelphia: Temple University Press, 1993).

6   There is a significant literature on omnipotence. With this definition I am following the scholarly consensus. See, for example, Richard Swinburne, *The Coherence of Theism* (Oxford: Clarendon Press, 1977) and Keith Ward, *Rational Theology and the Creativity of God* (Oxford: Blackwell, 1982).

7   There is some disagreement over the extent to which the free will defense is found in Augustine. It is John Hick in his classic *Evil and the God of Love* (London: Collins, 1968) who argues that this is the case. Hick writes: "Augustine attributes all evil, both moral and natural, directly or indirectly to the wrong choices of free rational beings" (p. 65). Alvin Plantinga's argument is found in a variety of places: for a good summary see Alvin Plantinga, "The Free Will Defence" in William Rowe and William Wainwright (eds.) *Philosophy of Religion: Selected Readings* (New York: Harcourt Brace Jovanovich, 1973), pp. 217–30.

8   Augustine's response to the problem of evil is very complex. He assumes that "evil" is ultimately the "absence of good." Much like dark is the absence of light. Evil is ultimately "unreal."

9   St Augustine, *City of God* (Harmondsworth: Penguin, 1984), Book XI, chapter 33, p. 468.

10 Ibid., p. 469.

11 For J. L. Mackie see *The Miracle of Theism* (Oxford: Clarendon, 1982), pp. 162–76.

12 Brian Hebblethwaite, 'The Problem of Evil' in G. Wainwright (ed.), *Keeping the Faith* (Philadelphia: Fortress Press, 1988).

13 See David Hume, *Dialogues Concerning Natural Religion*, ed. H. D. Aiken (London: Hafner Press, 1948), part 11. This paragraph is a summary of my argument set out in "Hume revisited: A problem with the Free Will Defence," *Modern Theology*, 7 (3) (1991): 281–90.

14 Hick, *Evil and the God of Love*, pp. 220–1.

15 Hume, *Dialogues Concerning Natural Religion*, part XI.

16 Fyodor Dostoyevsky, *The Brothers Karamazov* (Harmondsworth: Penguin Books, 1958, reissued in one volume, 1982), p. 283.

17 Ibid., pp. 282–3.

18 Ibid., pp. 287–8.

19 See for example the very helpful study by Kenneth Surin, *Theology and the Problem of Evil* (Oxford: Blackwell, 1986), p. 101. My debt to this book has not simply shaped this chapter, but also my entire emphasis on the problem of evil at the heart of any good systematic theology.

Chapter 6
CREATION AND THE SIGNIFICANCE OF HUMANITY

LEARNING OUTCOMES

By the end of this chapter you should be able to:

- understand the differences between three different readings of Genesis 1–3: fundamentalist, Augustinian, and ecofeminist (Anne Primavesi)
- appreciate the scientific narrative and understand the theory of evolution
- recognize different ways in which the Fall narrative can be interpreted

STRUCTURE

- The scientific narrative
- The Biblical narrative
- Reconciling different narratives
- The Fall
- Standing back

It is now time to start developing the Christian response to the reality of suffering and pain. The first stage is to draw on certain key "myths" (stories that capture truth in a way that is non-historical) embedded in the Christian drama. As Susan Nieman observes: "When one begins to seek an explanation, one can end in anything from myth, like the Fall, to metaphysics, like Hegel's *Phenomenology*."[1] One way of coping with suffering is to postulate a Fall. In this chapter, we look at three key claims that Christians want to make in the face of evil and suffering. The first is that this universe home is a creation (i.e. intended by God, not a random purposeless entity); the second is that each person is special (made in the Image of God); and the third is that because we are human we are in a perpetual struggle with the creator, with each other, and with the environment around us (i.e. we are fallen).

To get to these points, we shall compare the modern scientific narrative with the Biblical narrative. When it comes to the Biblical narrative, we examine three contrasting readings of that text. The first is a fundamentalist narrative – one which stresses the historical nature of the Biblical narrative. The second is the Augustinian narrative – perhaps the preeminent orthodox reading of the text. The third, by way of stark contrast, is the narrative of the ecofeminist; for this, I draw on the writings of Anne Primavesi. In the concluding section of this chapter, I shall draw the threads together and by using the work of Paul Tillich provide an account of the Biblical narrative that can be reconciled with the scientific narrative. We start then with the scientific narrative.

The Scientific Narrative

13,700,000,000 years ago, the universe started and in the first ten-thousandth of a second, so much happened. The universe emerged from a spatial order that boiled and then blew apart. At that point, the universe was just made up of quarks, gluons, and leptons. But as those moments came to an end, protons, neutrons, and electrons were forming and slowly gravity became a significant fact. A battle emerged between the desire of the universe to expand and the force of gravity that wanted the universe to collapse on itself. After about a billion years, galaxies and stars started to form. Within these stars, nuclear reactions occurred which gave birth to various elements including iron. Ten billion years later some of those stars started to die. Carbon – the crucial condition for life – started inside those stars. We are all, as Carl Sagan used to say, made of "star dust."

Other stars and planets were born. On at least one of these planets (and probably others) the factors that created life coincided. About a billion years after the start of the Earth, in ways that we don't entirely understand, some molecules emerged that were able to replicate themselves. Genetic code arrived: the earth's atmosphere started to contain oxygen and photosynthesis evolved, putting in place the crucial means by which the sun's energy can be trapped by living plants for survival.

Life is a relatively recent arrival in the universe. 700 million years ago worms and jelly fish were in control. 350 million years ago, insects, ferns, and amphibians emerged. Mammals arrived just 200 million years ago. 70 million years ago, the dinosaurs mysteriously died out. Australopithecus Lucy (so named because when she was discovered by Donald Johanson on November 24, 1974, the archaeological team was playing the Beatles track "Lucy in the sky with diamonds") walked erect 3.5 million years ago. Primitive *homo sapiens* appeared 300,000 years ago. And recognizable humanity is only 40,000 years old.

The Biblical Narrative

The majestic opening of Genesis 1 is a clear theological affirmation of God's control. "In the beginning God created the heavens and the earth." Unlike other ancient myths, there is no struggle with recalcitrant matter or a battle with a cosmic evil opponent. Instead, here we have *creatio ex nihilo* (creation out of nothing).[2] Prior to the creation there was God and nothing else.

In the opening chapter of Genesis (known by scholars as the P account, which was almost certainly written after the Fall of Israel in 722 BCE) the creation comes about through the spoken word of God. God speaks and light appears. This is followed by the seas and dry land, vegetation, day and night, birds and fish, animals, and finally on the sixth day God creates humanity. The author writes:

> Then God said, "Let us make humankind in our image, according to our likeness; and let them have dominion over the fish of the sea, and over the birds of the air, and over the cattle, and over all the wild animals of the earth, and over every creeping thing that creeps upon the earth." (Genesis 2:6)

Humanity is created in the Image of God; the next verse explains that God created "male and female." Both men and women are created in the Image of God. Having been created, we are also invited to have "dominion" over the rest of creation. This has been controversial: for some environmentalists, this text has been deeply damaging. It has cultivated a human superiority which is indifferent to the fate of animals and the environment.

Starting at Genesis 2:4b, we find a different style and tone. Scholars attribute it to the J/E traditions – earlier traditions that were probably written down in 1200 BCE.

The order of creation is different: humanity is created before the plants. The location is Eden. God gives one command: he forbids humanity to eat from the "tree of the knowledge of good and evil." Woman, who is created from the rib of the man, talks to the serpent, who persuades her to disobey God. This is the Fall, which brings about banishment from the garden.

Now this text can be read in a variety of different ways. Indeed the reading I have just given is heavily influenced by modern scholarship. This is one of several ways in which the text can be read. We shall now look briefly at three alternative readings of the text.

The first is the **fundamentalist** reading. Fundamentalists are Christians committed to an inerrant Bible (a Bible without error in any respect – including scientific and historical claims). It was **Archbishop Ussher** who did the sums. By comparing the different calendars and weaving the results with the Authorized version of the Bible, Ussher demonstrated that creation took place on Sunday 23 October 4004 BCE. Ussher is assuming that the purpose of the text is to provide a straightforward history. God created the universe in seven days (each day being twenty-four hours). Adam and Eve are historical figures. Into this perfect setting these two humans are placed. Although they had access to the entire garden, they exercised the sin of pride. They were led astray by Satan (who in the garden took the form of a serpent) into believing that humans were entitled to be "like God" (Genesis 3:5). At this point, sin and death entered into the world.

The second is the Augustinian reading. Now many fundamentalists would credit Augustine for their reading of the text. Although there are significant similarities, there are also major differences. Augustine does not invest strongly in the historicity of the Genesis narrative: indeed his primary mode of Biblical interpretation is allegorical. For him the Genesis story forms part of a cosmic journey from eternity past to the end of the time in which he documents how the city of God gets mingled in with the city of wickedness, sin, and hatred.

FUNDAMENTALISM

A post-World War One movement that developed in the United States and wanted to call Christians back to the basics (the fundamentals). This movement proved to be a significant influence on evangelical Protestantism, which places considerable emphasis on the inerrancy of Scripture, a literal return of Christ, and the incompatibility of Christianity with evolution.

> **ARCHBISHOP USSHER (1581–1656)**
>
> James Ussher was born in 1581 in Armagh, Ireland. Educated at Trinity College, Dublin, he had a distinguished career both as a Churchman and a scholar. Spending much of his time in England, he became well known for his capacity to extend Christian friendship to a wide circle. He died in 1656.

Yet it is important that everything wicked in creation is not the fault of God. So God creates a completely perfect world; a world that Augustine stresses is good. Augustine writes:

> "God saw that it was good." This statement, applied to all his works, can only signify the approval of work done with the true artist's skill, which here is the Wisdom of God.[3]

Everything God does is good. In this way Augustine prepares us for the human responsibility for sin. For into this perfect world, humanity is placed. There is no sin, suffering, or death. All of this is due to the Fall.

A major question for Augustine is: What was the Garden like before the Fall? A particular preoccupation is whether sexual activity is due to the Fall or not. So he poses the question thus:

> A question then arises which demands discussion and resolution, with the help of the Lord God of Truth. If sensual desire arose in the disobedient bodies of the first human beings as a result of the sin of disobedience, when they had been forsaken by divine grace, if, in the consequence, they opened their eyes to their own nakedness, that is, they observed it with anxious curiosity, and if they covered up their shameful parts because an excitement, which resisted voluntary control, made them ashamed – if this is true, how would they have produced children if they had remained without sin, in the state in which they were created?[4]

Part of the purpose of the exercise is to determine whether certain activities are part of God's holy divinely created order or an aspect of the disordered sinful world. So he needs to establish whether Adam and Eve would have had sex in the garden prior to the Fall. For reasons that are not entirely clear, he determines that they did not have sex prior to the Fall because there "wasn't time." But then he invites us to go on a speculative exercise. He determines that sex would have occurred. But it would have been "passionless" sex: the male organ would be completely under the control of the male reason.[5] In addition, the woman would have remained a virgin. For Augustine, there is sex in the garden, but it is without the passion that we have in this fallen world.

Turning then to the first sin, Augustine firmly blames free will. The serpent is a fallen angel. Augustine believes that Isaiah 14 describes the Devil "in the figurative person of the Babylonian emperor"[6] falling from heaven. The Devil persuades the woman, who in turn persuades Adam – her spouse – and together they embark on an act of disobedience. Augustine writes:

> They were alone together, two human beings, a married pair; and we cannot believe that the man was led astray to transgress God's law because he believed that the woman spoke the truth, but that he fell in with her suggestions because they were so closely bound in partnership. In fact, the Apostle was not off the mark when he said, "It was not Adam, but Eve, who was seduced," for what he meant was that Eve accepted the serpent's statement as the truth, while Adam refused to be separated from his only companion, even if it involved sharing her sin . . . They were not both deceived by credulity; but were taken captive by their sin and entangled in the snares of the Devil.[7]

For Augustine, Eve is worse than Adam. Eve is the one who believes the Devil, while Adam simply stands in solidarity with his wife. However, the consequence was disobedience, followed by the greater sin of pride.[8] Sin had entered the world: and with that sin all forms of evil and death.

One last aspect of the Augustinian account needs to be mentioned: the Genesis narrative is also responsible for the problem of original sin. So for Augustine unbaptised babies go to hell, or as he puts it:

> Therefore if even infants, as the true faith holds, are born sinners, not on their own account, but in virtue of their origin (and hence we acknowledge the necessity for them of the grace of remission of sins) then it follows that just as they are sinners, they are recognized as breakers of the Law which was given in paradise . . . Thus the process of birth rightly brings perdition on the infant because of the original sin by which God's covenant was first broken, unless the rebirth sets him free.[9]

For Augustine, a baby is getting the just consequences of being born into sin. A baby mysteriously participates in the sin of Adam and by virtue of that act is justly condemned to hell.

This, then, is the Augustinian reading. It is a text that explains the origin of sin. For Augustine, God is the generous creator who simply made one request: do not eat of certain trees. But Eve, persuaded by the Devil, seduces Adam into the sin of disobedience, rapidly followed by the sin of pride. As a consequence all manner of evil befalls the world: everything from lust to original sin can be traced back to this moment.

The third reading is from the ecofeminist Anne Primavesi. For Primavesi the traditional reading has been deeply destructive: Eve has been turned into a villain which
has justified misogyny and patriarchy. However, she suspects there are other ways to
read the text. She starts by noting that the words "fall" and "sin" are not actually found
in Genesis 1–3. A clue, she implies, that this text might not be about a fall at all. The
opening chapter of Genesis establishes both the equality of the genders and that there
is the feminine in God: the text reads: "So God created humankind in his image, in
the image of God he created them; male and female he created them" (Genesis 1:27).
This is the context for the second creation story.

Here God is more like a potter developing a creation in process. The creation of
the male is firmly linked to the world; there is a deliberate Hebrew word play – God
creates an "earthling (or human) of clods from the earth (or humus)." There is no
hierarchical male, lording it over woman and the rest of creation. Instead the male
shares with the rest of the created order the same substance and spirit. The image of
God in the text is odd. God permits Adam and Eve to enjoy the garden save for the
tree of the knowledge of good and evil. The text seems to suggest that God wants
Adam and Eve to live in perpetual immaturity – like children who never grow up. In
fact, suggests Primavesi, God comes out of the text rather badly. She writes:

> God appears as a rather benevolent, albeit tyrannical male parent, kind enough to give
> his children life, a cosy existence and suitable playmates. In return he demands total
> obedience from them, under constant supervision. They are denied basic human liber-
> ties: the knowledge of good and evil and freedom of choice. God secures their obedience
> by threats.[10]

For Primavesi, it is clear that in the disagreement between the serpent and God,
God does not tell the truth. Both the serpent and God describe the consequences of
eating the fruit from the tree of knowledge of good and evil. (She notes in passing
that elsewhere in the Hebrew Bible knowledge of good and evil is a virtue; God, for
example, praises Solomon who asks that he may "discern between good and evil"; 1
Kings 3:9.) So "the LORD God commanded the man, 'You may freely eat of every tree
of the garden; but of the tree of the knowledge of good and evil you shall not eat, for
in the day that you eat of it you shall die" (Genesis 2:16–17). So the punishment is
"death" on the day the fruit is eaten. Now the serpent disagrees: the text reads: "But
the serpent said to the woman, 'You will not die; for God knows that when you eat of
it your eyes will be opened, and you will be like God, knowing good and evil" (Genesis
3:4–5). And at the end of chapter three, God says: "See, the man has become like one
of us, knowing good and evil; and now, he might reach out his hand and take also
from the tree of life, and eat, and live for ever" (Genesis 3:22). To Primavesi, it is
clear. God is insisting on moral immaturity and makes a threat to keep humanity in

that place. The serpent explains to Eve that humanity will not die, but instead have a moral awareness like God. And at the end of the chapter, God seems to concede that humanity has a moral awareness.

For Primavesi, the two most misunderstood characters in the story are the serpent and woman. She correctly points out that nowhere in the text is the serpent identified as the Devil. Instead the serpent is introduced as "shrewd." It is almost as if the serpent is representative of nature, with whom woman takes the initiative and enters into dialogue. On this reading the woman is the hero. She is the one who takes the initiative and risk and enters into dialogue with the wisest of animals. Primavesi writes:

> There is no suggestion of inferiority to the man in the way she behaves. She opens the conversation with the serpent on behalf of both of them, judges for herself that the fruit is good to eat, to get insight from, and takes the initiative in eating it. She receives insight into the nature of good and evil, shares it with man, and he accepts it from her. Are the consequences of this so terrible for them? God admits that after eating the fruit all that differentiates him from them is eternal existence. According to the prologue, similarity to God was bestowed on male and female from the beginning. In the garden story it is won from God through the woman's action. The human race has won self-awareness and the ability to exercise judgment and discretion. It has leaped irreversibly into maturity and independence.[11]

For Primavesi, this is not a fall. It is a growing up. Naturally the text captures all the ambiguity of such "growing up." As every child learns there is a beauty in the security of being young; but the time comes when a child is forced to become an adult and live with all the complexity that brings. For Primavesi, this is the drama lived out in this text.

These are three very contrasting readings. Along with the scientific narrative, we need to start to disentangle the most appropriate way to understand these texts.

Reconciling Different Narratives

Theology recognizes truth wherever it is found as part of God's truth. So let us start by acknowledging the imperative of recognizing the truth within the scientific narrative and therefore the problems with the fundamentalist reading. Genesis 1–3 should not be treated as a crude history. Although a more "poetic reading" is commonplace after **Charles Darwin**, you do find similar readings before Darwin. **Origen** was adamant that a literal tree of "good and evil" was sheer nonsense: and **Kierkegaard** writing twenty or so years before Darwin insisted that Genesis should be read as metaphor. Indeed there is something rather tragic about turning Genesis 1 into a rather odd history.

CHARLES DARWIN (1809–82)

An Englishman, who became the leading scientist of the nineteenth century. Having studied medicine and theology, he pursued his interests in geology and biology. He was appointed to travel with the crew of the *Beagle* on a tour of South America. It was as a result of this trip that he accumulated sufficient data to support the hypothesis of evolution. In 1859, he published *The Origin of Species*. The text caused considerable controversy. He stood by his views; and they slowly attracted widespread acceptance by the academic community. He became increasingly agnostic towards the end of his life.

ORIGEN (185–254)

Church Father who was born in 185 CE in Alexandria, Egypt. He read widely and as a result was a very innovative theologian. It was when he moved to Caesarea that he became famous; but towards the end of his life, he was caught up in a period of persecution of the Church. Many of his views were very controversial; as a result, few of his writings have survived, save through the descriptions of his critics.

SØREN KIERKEGAARD (1831–55)

Kierkegaard was a gifted and creative philosopher who spent almost his entire life in Copenhagen, in Denmark. A son of Lutheran parents, he struggled to find happiness. He was engaged in 1841 to Regina Olsen, but decided that marriage was inappropriate. In a series of books, of which the first appeared in 1843, he offered a highly distinctive account of God and the self, which had a significant impact on subsequent existentialist philosophy (especially Martin Heidegger), and later, on Karl Barth.

When each stage of the creation is ushered in by God speaking, one shouldn't try and think of a rather large mouth speaking, but of the way in which words are the expression of the mind, and so the creation reflects the mind of God. It is intended as poetic (or if you prefer, myth): it describes in a metaphorical way the dependence of the world upon the creator.

In addition, the historical reliability of Genesis 1 had already been undermined by the breakdown in the Hebrew cosmology. The Genesis passage assumes a three-tier universe: with a flat earth, heaven up in the sky, and hell down below. It talks about the creation of a firmament (or better a vault) to separate the waters. Some waters are up above the sky which come down as rain and others are down below the ground. The sun is not a source of light, but simply a major light in the sky that serves as a sign for festivals. By the time Darwin came along we already knew that this cosmology was not true. The Biblical record treated as history had already been falsified. It is tempting to leave my rebuttal of fundamentalism at this point, but given that Charles Darwin remains a significant issue amongst Christians, let us look at the life and work of Darwin in more detail.

Darwin did not set out to challenge religion. Indeed the opposite is true. As a younger man, he thought very seriously about going into the Church. He shared the Victorian obsession with botany, for here it was believed that God's care could be clearly seen. The beauty and order of the world, the miracle of the eye, and the designing skill involved in a butterfly's wing: all were clear evidence for the creator. **William Paley** in 1802 published a classic entitled *Natural Theology: Evidences of the Existence and Attributes of the Deity Collected from the Appearances of Nature* which pointed to all these intricacies as clear evidence for the creator. At that time, Paley's Design Argument was required reading for all students at the University of Cambridge in England.

Darwin did not invent the theory of evolution. The ideas were first expressed by the ancient Greeks; and earlier on in the nineteenth century R. Chambers had written a book called *Vestiges of the Natural History of Creation*,[12] which suggested an evolutionary origin for life on earth. However, the problem with Chambers was the

WILLIAM PALEY (1743–1805)

Paley was born in 1743 in England. A gifted churchman and academic. After taking a degree from Christ's College, University of Cambridge, he was elected Fellow at Cambridge in 1766. In 1794, he wrote the book *Views of the Evidences of Christianity*, which became very popular. This was followed in 1802 with his last book *Natural Theology*, which elegantly stated the Design Argument.

lack of scientific evidence; the difference with Darwin was that he offered considerable evidence for his account, evidence that he had found when he was employed as the research scientist on the ship called the *Beagle*.

The *Beagle* travelled for five years around South America, the Galapagos Islands and Australia. It was while on this trip that Darwin found himself with certain problems. First, he noticed that as the ship travelled southwards, certain closely allied animals seemed to replace one another. Second, he was puzzled by the close structural relationship between extinct fossil species and living animals. And third, when he got to the Galapagos Islands the locals could distinguish between a finch from each of the islands. There were very slight, but significant and noticeable, variations which depended on which island the finch came from. Locals could do the same with the giant tortoise. Building on the geological work of Charles Lyell (*Principles of Geology*, published in 1830[13]), Darwin started to construct the argument that became his book, *The Origin of Species*.[14] He suggested the principle of "natural selection" (i.e. the preservation by the environment of especially well-adapted variations). In other words, from generation to generation many random variations emerge within each species. Some of these variations are better suited to survival and thus advance the species. The fittest of these species survive, becoming the basis of all subsequent generations.

Finding a publisher for his book was not easy. Indeed one publisher suggested that a book on pigeons would be much more popular. However, in 1859, *The Origin of Species* was published. The book was a model of scientific sensitivity. Darwin very carefully documents his evidence for his hypothesis. He never overstates his evidence. He admits that there are significant problems with the geological record. For at the time when Darwin was writing, there was no complete geological example of the development of a species; now we have several, the best known being the horse. It is a book which is not afraid to document both the evidence and the problems.

One hundred and fifty years further on, we are now able to see things a little more clearly. The basic shape of Darwin's hypothesis has survived critical scrutiny. There is no scientist of repute working in a British university who would quarrel with the main outline. The main difference is that we are now clearer as to the mechanism: we have discovered that the main player in the development of life is DNA mutation. Arthur Peacocke sums up neo-Darwinian evolution in two ideas: "all organisms past, present, and future, descend from earlier living systems, the first of which arose spontaneously; and species are derived from one another by natural selection of the best procreators."[15] In other words, life on planet Earth is linked together; subsequent species emerged from earlier ones, and in particular humanity is related to apes. As a scientific hypothesis, this has been established beyond all reasonable doubt.

It is important therefore that Christians accept the basics of the scientific narrative. To insist that young thoughtful Americans must choose between an increasingly well-documented theory that makes sense of the data or belief in God is to serve the interests of atheism. We should also resist versions of creationism such as "Intelligent Design." This is the view that at certain points in the story, a particular divine action is needed. So, for example, divine action is postulated to explain the emergence of life from inanimate matter or the development of humans from animals. Unfortunately, this sounds like the discredited "God of the gaps". God is slowly pushed out as scientific knowledge advances: God as creator is confined to the bits that we are currently ignorant about. In a hundred years time, we might find that there are fewer mysteries, so God will be needed even less.

However, Christians do want to say that the evolutionary story is only part of the story. John Polkinghorne – former Professor of Mathematical Physics at the University of Cambridge – argues that the spiritual openness of humans requires explanation that transcends the purely biological.[16] Polkinghorne believes that to make sense of the increasing complexity of the evolutionary process, particularly in respect of the brain, requires explanations of a different level. It is not just a biological process, but a divine one too.

Overall, Christians should talk about Genesis the way the Church has always talked about Genesis. Although it is true that many Christians saw the text as affirming a particular scientific model (which, incidentally, is always bound to be partial and modified by developments in ideas), this was always secondary to the truth of Genesis as a timeless statement of God's activity. So Genesis 1, which describes the creation, is not simply a statement about the past, but a statement about God's ongoing activity. The universe is always dependent on God, and God continues to work within the creation to bring about the purposes of love. Genesis 2 and 3 (which we will consider in more detail in a moment) capture the contemporary human attempts to thwart the love of God. It does not describe an idyllic state at the start, but our constant inability to be perfect. This understanding of the tradition leaves the Christian free to affirm both the truth of the Genesis stories and the scientific account of human origins.

The Fall

Once we see Genesis 1 has a timeless assertion of the truth that everything is created and sustained by God, we then have the essential clue to interpreting Genesis 2 and 3. Genesis 2 and 3 are a timeless description of the human predicament. The differences between the Augustinian and the Feminist readings are less important once one recognizes that this narrative is not crude history. The truth about the narrative is that humans are inevitably exercising their freedom in ways that create tension with the rest of creation and God; it is both a growing up and a fall. Indeed as every child learns, growth leads to autonomy and autonomy often leads to tension. This is the point of Genesis 2 and 3.

The scientific narrative does not permit an idyllic moment in history when there is no sin, suffering, or death in the world. The growing consensus in paleoanthropology (study of human origins) is that we emerged from Africa, with a mind that gave us a significant advantage over other animals. Our evolution assumes the processes of birth and death; and in the struggle for survival we were fortunate.

Since the beginning, humans have always been struggling with the creator. Our capacity to think, which is a crucial part of the *imago dei* (Image of God), makes the quest for moral awareness and autonomy inevitable. Furthermore, moral awareness and autonomy are essential aspects of being a free human. It is inevitable: our freedom will be exercised to shape who we are.

Therefore Primavesi's reading is easier to reconcile with the science: as part of the growing up process the human shapes his or her autonomy by seeking to discern good from evil in tension with our creator. However, Augustine is still right to talk about a fall. This inevitable reaction against the creator is still an assertion of human sin which needs to be contrasted against the good creation.

An analogy at this point may help. The delight of small children is their innocence. And as a child moves into adulthood, through that stressful period of adolescence and the teenage years, there will inevitably be tensions between the child and the parents. There will be arguments, slammed doors, and endless pushing of the parental limits. These tensions are both an inevitable part of growing up and, at the same time, acts of disobedience. So both Primavesi and Augustine are right: it is not "either or," but "both and." Humans are like rebellious teenagers: we are both striving for maturity and at the same time in rebellion against our creator.

Now at this point, it might be objected: If the Fall is an inevitable part of growing into humanity, then to what extent is it fair to "blame" humanity? Paul Tillich, who I think is the theologian who most successfully weaves together the science with the inevitability of the Fall, recognizes the legitimacy of this question, when he writes:

> The tragic universality of existence, the element of destiny in human freedom, and the symbol of the "fallen world" naturally raise the question as to whether sin is made onto-logically necessary instead of a matter of personal responsibility and guilt.[17]

The phrase "ontologically necessary" requires some explanation. Tillich is conceding that the Fall is inevitable on a variety of levels: it is inevitable by virtue of existing; it is inevitable because we will – to use his phrase – move from "dreaming innocence" to "aroused freedom" in a desire to exercise our freedom; and it is inevitable because scientifically we know there was never an idyllic state. So Tillich asks himself, perhaps the Fall is "ontologically necessary" – that is, the Fall is necessary for being – for existence.

Having asked himself the question, he then provides the answer. He writes:

Creation and the Fall coincide in so far as there is no point in time and space in which created goodness was actualized and had existence. . . . He who excludes the idea of a historical stage of essential goodness should not try to escape the consequence. This is even more obvious if one applies the symbol of creation to the whole temporal process. If God creates here and now, everything he has created participates in the transition from essence to existence. He creates the newborn child; but, if created, it falls into the state of existential estrangement. This is the point of coincidence of creation and the Fall. But it is not a logical coincidence; for the child, upon growing into maturity, affirms the state of estrangement in acts of freedom which imply responsibility and guilt. Creation is good in its essential character. If actualized, it falls into universal estrangement through freedom and destiny.[18]

For Tillich the point of Genesis 1 to 3 is that logically, although not historically, there are two truths which need to be affirmed. The first is that everything is created and sustained by God and is good. The second is that as part of the process of growing up and exercising our God-given freedom we live in tension with God. Although these two events coincided (and continue to coincide every day with every single person), logically we can and should disentangle them. The creating, sustaining, and goodness of the creation are truths which are logically prior to our growth and rebellion against the creator. We would not be able to grow and rebel against the creator unless God had enabled us to exist. And our existence is good, while our inevitable growth and rebellion is harder to cope with.

Thus far, I have argued that the insights of Primavesi need to be reconciled with the assumptions of Augustine. We are handling both an inevitable growth and a fall. Furthermore, Augustine is right to insist we need to talk about sin. But what is sin? Paul Tillich, once again, is helpful here. He draws on the classical description: sin involves unbelief, concupiscence (which traditionally means lust but has associations with any "strong desire"), and hubris (pride). Tillich explains that unbelief "means the act or state in which man in the totality of his being turns away from God. In his essential self-realization he turns towards himself and his world and loses his essential unity with the ground of his being and his world."[19] Concupiscence is "the unlimited desire to draw the whole of reality into one's self."[20] And hubris is "the self-elevation of man into the sphere of the divine."[21]

The point is this: when exercising the gift of freedom, there are significant dangers. We start to assume that we can live without God (without recognizing the truth of Genesis 1 that we are created and sustained by God); we exercise our desire and seek to make everything serve our desires; and we start to imagine that we are much more important than we are – indeed we start to think of ourselves as God. Although it is important not to overstate the teenager analogy, it is a little like the teenager who so discovers the power of self-assertion that he or she decides that there is no need for parents!

Throughout this chapter we are trying to hold together the growth image and the Fall image. However, a further complication is the whole doctrine of original sin.[22] Many Christians today find the doctrine of original sin puzzling. What exactly is the mechanism that leads to the disease of sin to pass down the generations? Why should I be blamed by birth for the sins of prehistoric forbears? Once again Paul Tillich is helpful when he writes:

> [T]heology should reinterpret the doctrine of original sin by showing man's existential self-estrangement and by using the helpful existentialist analyses of the human predicament. In doing so, it must develop a realistic doctrine of man, in which the ethical and the tragic element in his self-estrangement are balanced. It may well be that such a task demands the definite removal from the theological vocabulary of terms like "original sin" or "hereditary sin" and their replacement by a description of the interpenetration of the moral and tragic elements in the human situation. The empirical basis for such a description has become quite extensive in our period. Analytic psychology, as well as analytic sociology, has shown how destiny and freedom, tragedy and responsibility, are interwoven in every human being from early childhood on and in all social and political groups in the history of mankind.[23]

Tillich is right. The point of the doctrine is that it describes the ways in which our social and psychological lives make it so difficult for us to realize the purposes that the creator desires for us. We find it all so complicated. And this is a universal predicament.

Standing Back

Let us now bring together our reflections on this topic in the light of our theme about the Christian drama being a response to evil and suffering. There are five main insights learned from the Christian narrative about our response to evil and suffering.

The first and main insight is that we live in a world created and enabled by a being who is loving and good. The world around is intended: it is not pointless or accidental. It continues to be because God desires that it continues to be. And in those moments when we face the futile and tragic nature of so much suffering, the Christian is forbidden to lapse into despair because we know that God is there. In addition, the creator saw that everything was "good." In certain religions, matter is a problem. In Christianity, God made matter and declares firmly, it is good.

The second insight is that humans are made in the Image of God. This brings with it part of our struggle. The image does not mean that God is anthropomorphic (literally has a human body), but rather that humans have the capacity to think, evaluate, and reflect morally. Unlike other forms of life (a carrot or a spider), there is a capacity for reflection which exacerbates the problem of evil and suffering. However, for most of us, given a choice between being an unreflective pig or a struggling reflective human, we would opt for the latter. It comes with a price: but the price is worth paying.

The third insight is that all people are part of the family of humanity. Regardless of whether or not, as a matter of evolutionary history, humanity had one origin does not change the theological truth that all people are connected. In the history of ideas protogenesis is very important. Christians should and can affirm our kinship. However banal it might sound, we need to learn to live together as a family.

The fourth insight is that the inevitable exercise of our freedom leads to tension with the creator. Part of being human is that we exercise this freedom. And in so doing we create significant problems for ourselves. To have humans we must have evil; it is inescapable. In the chapter on evil and suffering we speculated that God could have surely created humans that would have been so much nicer. The drama of Genesis 2 and 3 is that this is not possible: humans were always going to grow up.

The fifth insight is that embedded in the remarkable gift of being human is also the great temptation. We are special in the creation. And this truth pushes us to imagine that we are really all that matters in the creation. It is because we are remarkable that we start to imagine that the creator does not exist (unbelief); it is because we are remarkable that we start to assume that everything should serve our desire (concupiscence); and it is because we are remarkable that we start to imagine that we are really the center of the universe and creators of our own destiny (hubris). This is the Fall. Herein lies the great irony, these temptations are a result of the remarkable creation. It is because God created humanity in God's image that we start to imagine that there is no creator and we can take the place of God.

This is not an explanation for evil. It is intended to be a description of why it is inevitable. It is inevitable because God decided we were worth creating. As we shall see in later chapters, this came at a great cost both to us and to the divine disclosure of God, which is Jesus. But more of that in the next chapter.

QUESTIONS FOR REFLECTION AND DISCUSSION

- Before you started reading this chapter, what was your interpretation of Genesis 1–3? To what extent, if any, has it changed?
- Do you think creation is compatible with evolution?
- Do you think there was a historic fall from a state of perfection to sin and death? If so, then do you think there was a moment before that when there was no death in all creation?
- Of the three accounts of the Fall, which one do you prefer?
- Identify at least one criticism of Paul Tillich's account of the Fall

GLOSSARY

Empirical: the emphasis on the data collected from sense experience (what we see, touch, taste, hear, and smell)

God of the gaps: the view that God explains those aspects of creation that science cannot explain

Hereditary sin: the view that original sin is inherited and transmitted from generation to generation

Misogyny: the hatred of women

Myth: various meanings. At the popular level it is the idea of a story which is untrue; at the more technical level, it is a story whose truth might be found in the poetry rather than the history

Original sin: the view that all humanity is born in a state of alienation from God

Patriarchy: the rule of men

Notes

1 Susan Neiman, *Evil in Modern Thought: An Alternative History of Philosophy, with a new preface* (Princeton, NJ, and Oxford: Princeton University Press, 2004), p. 5.

2 When we looked at Process theology, we noted that some of those do not accept the doctrine of *creatio ex nihilo*. It is important to note that some commentators of the Hebrew Bible suspect that the doctrine is not found in Genesis 1. Catherine Keller makes the idea that creation came from chaos a central part of her theology. In *The Face of the Deep: A Theology of Becoming*, she writes, "Among biblical scholars there has existed on this matter a near, if nervous, consensus for decades. The Bible knows only of the divine formation of the world out of a chaotic something: not *creatio ex nihilo*, but *ex nihilo nihil fit* (from nothing comes nothing), the common sense of the ancient world" (London and New York: Routledge, 2003), p. 3.

3 St Augustine, *City of God*, translated Henry Bettenson, introduction by John O'Meara (London: Penguin, 1984), XI, 21, p. 451.

4 Ibid., XII, 24, p. 546.

5 Ibid., XIV, 26, p. 591.

6 Ibid., XI, 16, p. 447.

7 Ibid., XIV, 13, p. 570.

8 Ibid., XIV, 15, p. 574.

9 Ibid., XVI, 28, p. 689.

10 Anne Primavesi, *From Apocalypse to Genesis* (Kent: Burns and Oates, 1991), p. 234.

11 Ibid., p. 233.

12 Robert Chambers, *Vestiges of the Natural History of Creation*, with an introduction by Alexander Ireland (London and Edinburgh: W. and R. Chambers, 1884).

13 Charles Lyell, *Principles of Geology* (New York: D. Appleton and Co., 1960).
14 Charles Darwin, *The Origin of Species* (London: Penguin, 1968). (The introduction by J. W. Burrow is especially helpful.)
15 Arthur Peacocke, *Theology for a Scientific Age* (London: SCM Press, 1993), enlarged edition, p. 56.
16 John Polkinghorne, *Science and Christian Belief* (London: SPCK, 1994), pp. 16f.
17 Paul Tillich, *Systematic Theology*, vol. ii (Chicago: University of Chicago Press, 1957), p. 43.
18 Ibid., p. 44.
19 Ibid., p. 47.
20 Ibid., p. 52.
21 Ibid., p. 50.
22 Amongst modern theologians there is a variety of different ways to interpreting this doctrine. One popular distinction is between "original sin" and "hereditary sin." Some theologians see the doctrine of original sin illustrating the capacity of humankind collectively to sin.
23 Ibid., pp. 38–9.

chapter 7
GOD
INCARNATE

LEARNING OUTCOMES

By the end of this chapter you should be able to:

- understand the reasons why Christians want to claim that Jesus is God Incarnate
- appreciate the issues amongst New Testament scholars about the Incarnation
- appreciate the complexity of the debates and arguments over the Incarnation in the Early Church
- understand an account of the Incarnation which attempts to be coherent and grounded in the New Testament

STRUCTURE

- Reasons for the doctrine of the Incarnation
- New Testament witness
- Sorting it out in the Early Church
- Making sense of the Incarnation today

In the previous chapter we were preoccupied with the problem of how to reconcile a God of love with the suffering of the created order. We saw that although we have hints why God permits such suffering, a total explanation evades us. Yet Christians make the striking claim that although we can't know "why" God permits suffering, we do know that God cares. We know this because God Almighty undertook the journey to Calvary. The God we worship knows what it is to suffer. And the God who had to permit evil and suffering in the creation had to face the consequences by suffering on the cross. It is a remarkable idea, but Christians believe that the creator of the Universe was killed by creatures which the creator created.

This is of course a striking claim. It is not surprising that Jews and Muslims have problems with this idea. After all, the God set of attributes (omniscience, omnipotence, omnipresence) don't easily coexist with the human set of attributes (finite, limited in knowledge and power). And along with the problem of the coherence of the idea, there are many New Testament scholars who do not believe that the historical Jesus would agree with the claim that he was the incarnation of God.

Reasons for the Doctrine of the Incarnation

There are Christians who want to move beyond the Incarnation. In 1977 seven distinguished theologians in a collection of essays called *The Myth of God Incarnate*[1] set out the main arguments against the Incarnation. For John Hick, the distinctive doctrine of the Incarnation was a problem for the Christian relationship with other religions. For Leslie Houlden, the plurality of different Christologies needed to be taken more seriously and the Council of **Chalcedon** in 451 CE should not be privileged as the only acceptable Christology. For Michael Goulder and Francis Young, the evidence of the New Testament does not point towards the Incarnation. Let it be added, these are strong arguments, which need to be taken seriously. For many contributors to the *Myth*, it was the Chalcedonian form of the Incarnation, which they found problematic. A lower or functional Christology, where Jesus perhaps *shows* us God rather than *is* God, might be acceptable. However, for the *Myth* contributors, Chalcedon was simply incoherent and too far away from the New Testament.

So it is worth pausing, before we embark on our sustained discussion of the Incarnation, to decide whether we would lose anything if Christianity became non-incarnational, or perhaps opted for a simpler Christology. There are, I suggest, three reasons why the Incarnation, which insists Jesus really is identical with God, is important.

The first has already been placed front and central. The doctrine of the Incarnation is a key aspect of the Christian response to the problem of evil. Brian Hebblethwaite is right to insist that:

> One of its [the doctrine of the Incarnation] most profound claims is that God in Christ subjected *himself* to the world's evil at its most harsh and cruel, and by so doing both revealed his love and accepted responsibility for the suffering entailed by the creation of an organic self-reproducing world of sentient and free persons. There is a profoundly moral insight here. The divine love and forgiveness are shown most clearly in the lengths to which our God is prepared to go to win the love of the loveless "that they might lovely be." These things cannot be done through a representative.[2]

In the last chapter we felt the force of the problem of evil and suffering. However, if Jesus is simply a person who shows us what God is like, then we no longer have God taking responsibility for the suffering and evil in the creation. For an adequate response to theodicy, we need God to be in Jesus – in a distinctive and unique way.

The second reason is that the doctrine of the Incarnation is central to our understanding of revelation. As we saw in an earlier chapter, for Christians, the Word of God is Jesus. In the life, death, and resurrection, we see God. It is important that somewhere there is a claim to knowledge of God. Here we are, puny little entities in this vast cosmos. Skeptics are right to complain that it seems very implausible to claim that we know what God is like, unless we have some sort of revelation from God. No revelation will tell us everything about God. God is, of course, enormously complicated – well beyond human understanding. But we do need some basic knowledge about what God is like. We need to know that God is loving rather than evil. We need to know that God is interested in humanity. We need some hint about what God has planned in the life to come. For Muslims and Jews, it is the text of Scripture which provides these answers. The Qur'an for Muslims and the Torah for Jews are the Word of God. For Christians, the Word is the Eternal Word which completely interpenetrates the life of Jesus of Nazareth.

As Christians, we are in the business of reading a life – a life, which was very enigmatic. Our definitive disclosure of what God is like is a poor young man from Nazareth, who took enormous risks as he reached out to include the marginalized – especially women, the poor, and the reviled. He found himself a victim of power – finally dying as a common criminal at the hands of the occupying power. Yet remarkably, the movement he inspired believed that death was not able to hold him. Reports of his resurrection started to circulate and so the Church was born.

CHALCEDON

The location of the 4th council of the Church. Chalcedon is in Asia Minor, north of Constantinople. Emperor Marcian called the meeting.

So what do we know about God? In what ways does this operate as a revelation of God? In these ways, as we read the life we can determine that God is on the side of those who are least fortunate. We can know that the love of God is willing to go to any length for the sake of humanity. We can know that in our moments of despair, God promises to create hope. And Christians are also required to treat this life as authoritative. We should imitate the "words and deeds" of Jesus of Nazareth.[3] Unlike Islam, the Christian "word of God" is a life, which is harder to interpret. It is a major reason why Christianity is inherently liberal and open. Our challenge is to meditate on that life, within the context of worship and prayer, to discern what God is like and what God requires of us.

As we saw in an earlier chapter, it is the revealing "mode" of God which is disclosed in the life, death, and resurrection of Jesus. So it is not sufficient to simply believe that Jesus was a prophet of God – to whom the Word of God had been given. The Word of God belongs to God (words are part of a person's identity). For Jesus to be the Word of God, we need Jesus to be identical with God.

The third reason is soteriological. Soteriology is the "study of salvation." As we shall see in the chapter on the atonement, Christians believe that God has made it possible for humanity to be forgiven by God's action in Christ. It is sufficient, for now, to note that Christians, from the beginning, recognized the importance of God being in Christ to bring about our salvation.

New Testament Witness

It was C. S. Lewis who made famous the "mad, bad, or God" argument. In *Mere Christianity*, he points out one option that makes no sense is that Jesus is simply a good man.

> I am trying here to prevent anyone saying the really foolish thing that most people say about Him. "I'm ready to accept Jesus as a great moral teacher, but I don't accept His claim to be God." That is the one thing we must not say. A man who was merely a man and said the sort of things Jesus said would not be a great moral teacher. He would either be a lunatic – on a level with the man who says he is a poached egg – or else he would be the Devil of Hell. You must make a choice. Either this man was, and is, the Son of God or else a madman or something worse.[4]

For Lewis, others have argued for the Incarnation in the following way.[5] Starting with the assumption that Jesus made the claim to be God, they argued that this is either true or crazy or evil. Given the Jesus of the New Testament does not appear crazy or evil, the argument leaves us with one option: Jesus must be God.

For most New Testament scholars, the key problem is the assumption of Incarnation. It is not obvious that Jesus claimed to be God. The problem is the source. Although it is true that one finds an explicit assumption of Incarnation in the Gospel of John, it is less obvious in the rest of the New Testament. The term "Son of God" is found in the Hebrew Bible and refers to the "righteous person," which suggests to most scholars that this is the intended meaning for Jesus and his contemporaries. Our problem is that we tend to bring certain assumptions to the text, which are a result of the Councils of the Church. Therefore we find it difficult to interpret Jesus in his original Jewish context. Overcoming this problem is the challenge behind the quest for the historical Jesus.

The historical Jesus debate has been raging for over a hundred years. Albert Schweitzer's classic *Quest of the Historical Jesus* was published in 1906,[6] and started the modern debate. Larry Hurtado provides a summary of some of the main options emerging in the debate, when he writes:

> However one prefers to characterize Jesus' public persona and how he was perceived by contemporaries (e.g. prophet, messianic claimant, exorcist/healer, holy man/Hasid, shaman, magician, teacher/rabbi, sage, peasant spinner of tales, clever wordsmith, revolutionary, establishment critic, friend of social outcasts, a liberal Jew ahead of his time), and whatever one posits as Jesus' message and intention (e.g., to found a new religion/ religious movement, to reform Judaism, to call for national repentance of Israel, to announce God's eschatological kingdom, to promote the overthrow of Roman colonialism in Jewish Palestine, to encourage new patterns of social interaction, to articulate a more carefree lifestyle), it is clear that he quickly became a figure of some notoriety and controversy.[7]

Although there are many options, there is a growing consensus that primarily Jesus should be interpreted as a Jewish apocalyptic prophet. Apocalypticism is the view that God has revealed (revealing is the meaning of apocalypse) the secrets about the end of the world. It assumes a world where the evil forces are in control and that a divine action will bring about the reign of God. Bart Ehrman helpfully summarizes:

> According to the apocalypticists, God will eventually make right all that has gone so badly wrong. He will once again manifest his sovereignty by saving the world from the evil that now runs so rampant. Many apocalypticists were especially concerned about God's chosen people – the nation of Israel – and were intent to show that despite Israel's suffering, God has not abandoned them. He will send a deliverer who will overthrow the enemies of his people and set up a kingdom here on earth, to be ruled by his special emissary, the messiah. Other apocalypticists had a more cosmic view, thinking that not just Israel but the entire world is in the throes of the forces of evil, and that God will send not just an earthly king (the messiah) but a cosmic judge of the whole earth.

This one will destroy the Devil and all his minions, and bring in a paradisal world, the Kingdom of God, in which there will be no more pain and suffering of any kind. God himself will rule supreme.[8]

If one locates Jesus in this context operating with these assumptions, then we find ourselves with the following picture. Jesus sees himself as an agent, who is ushering in the end of the age. He was preaching a literal kingdom of God (reign of God), where the forces of wickedness will be overthrown, and a new set of values will dominate the community. Bart Ehrman summarizes thus:

Jesus' proclamation in our earliest surviving sources is about this coming Kingdom and the need for people to prepare for it. It will be an actual kingdom, here on earth, where people will lead joyous lives under the governance of God. It will be a kingdom brought from heaven by a cosmic judge, whom Jesus mysteriously calls "the Son of Man." . . . This Son of Man will come in judgment on the earth, bringing destruction upon those who have opposed God and salvation for those who have obeyed him. Indeed, anyone who adheres to the teaching of Jesus himself will be saved when this Son of Man arrives.[9]

We have a Jesus, then, who believed that a divine action was going to bring about the end of the world. There are two problems with this picture for traditional Christianity: First, Jesus does not claim to be God; and second, Jesus was mistaken – the world did not end.

We will revisit this apocalyptic theme in the teaching of Jesus in the last chapter of this book. It is undoubtedly a major part of the teaching of Jesus, which Christians must take seriously. However, for now, the question is this: does this Jewish apocalyptic prophet capture the entirety of Jesus from the earliest sources?

I want to suggest that the apocalyptic prophet, although important, is indeed a partial picture. Jesus is an apocalyptic prophet and more. It is worth remembering when we read the New Testament that the earliest sections are the letters of Paul. They come before the Gospel stories. The apocalyptic strand is still very much there: Paul clearly expected the world to end during his lifetime (see 1 Thessalonians 4:13–18). However, there is another aspect which is equally, if not more, dominant: We have a Jesus who is being worshipped and adored as God.

We have Larry Hurtado to thank for a major study on "devotion to Jesus in earliest Christianity." As one reads the New Testament, the affirmation "Jesus is Lord" pulsates throughout the text. So many passages are a celebration of Jesus (see for example, Colossians 1:15–20, Acts 2:36, and Philippians 2:1–11). Hurtado shows that this devotion to Jesus did not emerge gradually but exploded on to the scene. Hurtado writes:

Christians were proclaiming and worshipping Jesus, indeed, living and dying for his sake, well before the doctrinal/creedal developments of the second century . . . Moreover, devotion to Jesus as divine erupted suddenly and quickly, not gradually and late, among first-century circles of followers. More specifically, the origins lie in Jewish Christian circles of the earliest years.[10]

The sudden eruption, coupled with its home amongst Jewish monotheism, is clear evidence of the remarkable impact that the totality of Jesus' life, death, and resurrection had on the first Christians. Here we have Jews who, at considerable personal cost, believe in one God yet want to pray to and worship Jesus.

The point is that we do not simply have a Jewish prophet who preached the imminent end of the world. We also have a life that inspired followers to worship him. There was in the clarity of expectation, the celebration of love, and the commitment to the outcast, a witness that subsequent generations felt was worthy of worship. This is the important seed that slowly grows into the doctrines of the Incarnation and Trinity. For a Jewish monotheist, you cannot worship two Gods. If you are worshipping Jesus, then you must be worshipping the one God. The question is: how can this be? And it is this question that preoccupies the Early Church.

Sorting It Out in the Early Church

Early Christians were not stupid. The idea of the one God becoming human was a difficult one to sort out. It is not surprising that it took several centuries of thought, argument, and division to formulate exactly what Christians believed. It is a complex idea. One tool used in these debates is the concept of heresy. Now, for many, the category of heresy is problematic. This is partly because the concept was used as a political tool by those in power to crush those with whom they disagreed. Furthermore heretics were often given a very hard time. It is tempting therefore to simply reject the concept. However, Colin Gunton is right to point out that the concept of heresy is necessary. Gunton writes:

About heresy it must be said, first, that as a theological concept it refers to those teachings, internal to Christianity, which are judged so to distort the faith from within that it ceases to be authentically Christian. It is therefore indispensable in theological discussion because the gospel claims to be true and its truth therefore requires defence against teaching judged to be false.[11]

As the Church tried to determine precisely what Christians believed had been discovered in the life, death, and resurrection of Jesus, the concept of heresy played an important role. And in the chapter on the Trinity, we looked at the arguments between Arius and Athanasius at the Council of Nicaea in 325 CE, where the views of Arius were declared heretical. And that is the place to begin in this section.

Arius had argued that Jesus was a creature, created in eternity past. Athanasius insisted this was wrong. And at the Council convened by the **Emperor Constantine**, Athanasius won. The subsequent creed, commonly called the Nicene Creed,[12] affirms the following about Jesus:

> We believe in one Lord, Jesus Christ,
> the only Son of God,
> eternally begotten of the Father,
> God from God, Light from Light,
> true God from true God,
> begotten, not made,
> of one Being [*homoousios*] with the Father.[13]

Jesus is "of the same substance" as the Father. The divinity of Jesus is entrenched as part of Christian orthodoxy. However, this still leaves plenty of questions as to how the divinity relates to the humanity. And this became the key set of questions for the Church.

The Church sought to avoid two extremes. The first is docetism (from the Greek – to seem). A docetic Christology plays down the humanity of Christ; the humanity of Jesus was only an appearance. The primary mode of description is the divinity of Jesus. The second is adoptionism[14] (sometimes called Ebionism – after the early Jewish-Christian movement which started in the second century and operated through to the fifth). This position tends to play down the divinity of Jesus. So for example, this position might see Jesus as simply a prophet of God, whom God adopts with the honorific title of "son."

EMPEROR CONSTANTINE (*c.* 285–337)

Flavius Valerius Constantinus was born in Naissus in Serbia. When Constantine went to war against Maxentius, who had far greater numbers, he had a vision that promised him success if he fought in the name of Christ. At the bridge of the Tiber (the Milvian Bridge) Maxentius was resoundingly defeated. From this moment, Christians who had been systematically persecuted in the Roman Empire, were now in control. Christianity became the official religion of the Roman Empire.

As the Church struggled with these questions, two contrasting approaches emerged. One emerged in Alexandria in Egypt; the other, in Antioch, Cappadocia – now part of Turkey. The Alexandrian school argued for a "Word-flesh" Christology, while Antioch insisted on a "Word-human being" Christology.[15] For the Alexandrians, the second person of the Trinity (the Eternal Word) replaces the human mind of Christ. The Alexandrians were sympathetic to Apollinaris of Laodicea (310–90), who argued that Jesus was literally the mind of God located in a human body.

The problem with Apollinarianism was that a divine head and a human body does not sound like a complete human being. The Council held in Constantinople in 381 declared Apollinarianism heretical: Christian theology needs Jesus to be a complete human being. Apollinarianism was a continuing temptation, with the Monophysites taking up their mantle during much of the fourth century.

For the Antiochian school, Jesus was completely human. And the second person of the Trinity was "indwelling" a human person. This meant that there were two natures (a human one and a divine one) in one person. This was intended to safe-guard the humanity of Christ. Nestorius (c. 386–c. 451) who became the Patriarch of Constantinople believed that there were two persons in Christ and therefore challenged the growing piety around the Virgin Mary. He insisted that it was wrong to call her "mother of God" (in Greek, *Theotokos*: literally, God-bearer), because she was simply the mother of the human nature. Cyril, the patriarch of the rival center Alexandria (375–444) thought this outrageous. He continued to argue against the Antiochian school wanting to stress the importance of there being one person in Christ (even if he, reluctantly, conceded the need to talk about "two natures").

It was this argument that went to the Council of Chalcedon, which was held in 451 CE. The final text is a carefully worded compromise. It reads:

> Therefore, following the holy Fathers, we all with one accord teach men to acknowledge one and the same Son, our Lord Jesus Christ, at once complete in Godhead and complete in manhood, truly God and truly man, consisting also of a reasonable soul and body; of one substance (*homoousious*) with the Father as regards his Godhead, and at the same time of one substance with us as regards his manhood; like us in all respects, apart from sin; as regards his Godhead, begotten of the Father before the ages, but yet as regards his manhood begotten, for us men and for our salvation, of Mary the Virgin, the God-bearer (*Theotokos*); one and the same Christ, Son, Lord, Only-begotten, recognized in two natures, without confusion, without change, without division, without separation; the distinction of natures being in no way annulled by the union, but rather the characteristics of each nature being preserved and coming together to form one person and subsistence, not as parted or separated into two persons, but one and the same Son and Only-begotten God the Word, Lord Jesus Christ; even as the prophets from earliest times spoke of him, and our Lord Jesus Christ himself taught us, and the creed of the Fathers has handed down to us.[16]

This Chalcedonian definition (it is not a creed) seeks to hold together the insights of Alexandria and Antioch. The phrase "truly God and truly man" is a reaffirmation of Nicaea – this puts docetic and Arian views of Jesus outside the realm of legitimate Christological discourse. The phrase "consisting also of a reasonable soul and body" means that Jesus has a human soul and body, thereby taking issue with the Apollinarians. The phrase "Mary the Virgin, the God-bearer" disagrees with Nestorius.

Although Chalcedon was widely accepted, there were opponents. Even today the Egyptian Coptic Orthodox Church continues to reject Chalcedon, believing a form of Monophysitism (Christ had one nature) is more appropriate. However, the majority of Christians did follow Chalcedon. The goal of Chalcedon was to sketch out the boundaries of legitimate talk about Christ. Chalcedon says that to protect our experience of Christ we cannot ever imply that he is anything less than completely human, nor can we say that he is anything less than completely divine and that the inner life of Jesus is a unity. The language of Chalcedon, to use St Augustine's phrase, provides a "fence around a mystery."

Making Sense of the Incarnation Today

Chalcedon largely got it right. To protect the experience of God disclosed in Christ, Christians need to believe that Jesus is completely human and yet, simultaneously, completely divine. We need to exclude any discourse that implies that Jesus is less than fully human and fully divine. As a theodicy, revelation, and a mechanism of salvation, we must be able to say that Jesus was really a person – as we are. But we also must be able to say that Jesus was really God – the creator of the universe.

Lots of problems with the Incarnation are caused by an insufficiently dynamic model of identity. What does it mean for Jesus to be identical with God? If one operates with Leibniz's law of identity, then we rapidly run into problems. In what is called the indiscernibility of identicals by philosophers, the view emerged that for two things to be identical they must have all properties in common. With God and Jesus the problems are obvious: God is transcendent and omnipotent; Jesus is finite and limited. It is clear that they cannot be identical.

However, if we work with a more dynamic model of identity, then it might be possible to see how God and Jesus can be identical. One can arrive at a more dynamic model of identity if one thinks of the way in which a five-year-old child grows into a forty-year-old adult. There is a unique connection between the child and the subsequent adult. They are identical, despite the numerous differences, because there is a unique continuity that connects the youth with the grown up.

The doctrine of the Trinity helps us with the challenge of making sense of the Incarnation. It is not necessary for Christians to believe that all of God is incarnate in Christ. Although Jesus is "all God," it is not true that all of God is in Jesus. If we did believe that all of God is in Jesus, then we would have no one sustaining the universe when Jesus was dying on the cross. It is the second person of the Trinity who is present in Jesus. The second person of the Trinity is of course inseparable from the other members of the Godhead, but that does not preclude the possibility of talking about a distinctive mode of God's being in Jesus. The doctrine of the Incarnation involves the Eternal Word (the revealing, disclosing aspect of God) being completely and uniquely present in the life, death, and resurrection of Jesus. Jesus, then, is identical with God in this way: the Eternal Word completely permeates the humanity of Jesus. This is done not in a way that eradicates the humanity, but uses the humanity to disclose and reveal God.

As we read the New Testament, we have sufficient clues to know that it took some time for Jesus to realize that in his mind there were two poles – a human pole and a divine pole. It is clear from the Gospels that Jesus was human: He wept and was hungry, tired, and exhausted by the crowds. It is also clear from the Gospels that Jesus knew he had a close relationship with God: He was intimate with his heavenly Father. The doctrine of the Incarnation does not require that Jesus knew who he was. Brian Hebblethwaite makes the point well when he writes:

> As a human being, he shared a first-century Jewish, Palestinian, perspective. In all probability, he was unaware of who, ultimately speaking, he really was. As a human being, he was probably conscious only of a closeness to God, his heavenly Father, of the powerful and compelling inspiration of the Spirit, and of an unquestionable authority to speak and act for God among his fellow Jews. He shared many of the demonological categories of the day, regarding what we call epilepsy or schizophrenia as possession. And he shared much of the apocalyptic framework of first-century Judaism, even to the extent of expecting the "end" within the lifetime of his disciples.[17]

Hebblethwaite is advocating a "kenotic" Christology. Such a Christology admits that the second person of the Trinity – the Eternal Word – "sets aside" or "empties" or "limits" the divine attributes to enable the Son to become human. However, the Eternal Word is speaking when Jesus teaches us about the love and demands of God. And the Eternal Word is at work when, out of love for humanity, Jesus is willing to go to the cross and die.

God was in Christ. This is the distinctive claim that Christians want to make. Although easy to misunderstand, we can provide an account of the Incarnation, which is true to the evidence of the New Testament and, at the same time, is coherent and plausible.

QUESTIONS FOR REFLECTION AND DISCUSSION

1 Is it logical or appropriate for a monotheist to believe that a human is God?
2 If Jesus is God, then Jesus must be omniscient. Discuss.
3 Do you think Jesus believed that He was divine?
4 If Jesus had got married and had children, then Jesus could not have been the incarnation of God. Discuss.
5 In what way is a Christian theodicy helped by the Incarnation?

GLOSSARY

Adoptionism: the view that at some point in Jesus' life, God "adopted" him as a son (some say at baptism, others say at the resurrection)

Apocalypticism: expectations about the "end of the age"

Apollinarianism: the view that Jesus was not completely human

Docetism: the view that Christ was not actually human, but simply appeared to be

Eschatology: the study of views about the "end of the age"

Heresy: a view condemned by the Church as incompatible with the truth believed to be orthodox

Incarnation: the claim that God was in a human person. In Christian doctrine it involves the claim that Jesus was both completely God and completely human

Kenotic: the view that when God became human, God "emptied" himself of his divine attributes

Monophysitism: the view that in Christ there was just a single nature, not a dual nature

Soteriology: the study of "salvation"

Notes

1 John Hick (ed.), *The Myth of God Incarnate* (London: SCM Press, 1977).
2 Brian Hebblethwaite, *The Incarnation: Collected Essays in Christology* (Cambridge: Cambridge University Press, 1987), p. 5.
3 I am enormously grateful to the work of Richard Burridge, who argues that if one takes the genre of the Gospels seriously one can see that the purpose of the Gospels is to invite us to imitate Christ. See his forthcoming book, *Imitating Christ* (Grand Rapids, MI: Eerdmans, 2007).

4 C. S. Lewis, *Mere Christianity* (San Francisco: HarperSanFrancisco, 2001), p. 52.

5 See for example Josh McDowell, *Evidence Demands a Verdict* (San Bernardino, CA: Campus Crusade for Christ International, 1972).

6 See Albert Schweitzer, *The Quest of the Historical Jesus: A Critical Study of Its Progress from Reimarus to Wrede* (New York: Macmillan, 1978).

7 Larry W. Hurtado, *Lord Jesus Christ: Devotion to Jesus in Earliest Christianity* (Grand Rapids, MI: Eerdmans, 2003), p. 55.

8 Bart D. Ehrman, *Peter, Paul, and Mary Magdalene: The Followers of Jesus in History and Legend* (Oxford: Oxford University Press, 2006), p. 29. This section of Ehrman's book is a good summary of an argument he makes in full in *Jesus: Apocalyptic Prophet of the New Millennium* (Oxford: Oxford University Press, 1999).

9 Ibid., pp. 29–30.

10 Hurtado, *Lord Jesus Christ*, p. 650.

11 Colin E. Gunton, *The Christian Faith: An Introduction to Christian Doctrine* (Oxford: Blackwell, 2002), p. 86.

12 Technically it is the "Niceno-Constantinopolitan" creed because the doctrine of the Holy Spirit was expanded at the Council of Constantinople in 381.

13 *The Book of Common Prayer* (New York: Church Publishing Inc., 1979). According to the use of the Episcopal Church.

14 Identifying the right term for this extreme is difficult. There are forms of adoptionism which are very sophisticated and do admit a degree of divinity (properly understood).

15 These distinctions are commonplace in the literature. See, for example, Daniel Migliore, *Faith Seeking Understanding: An Introduction to Christian Theology*, 2nd edition (Grand Rapids, MI: Eerdmans, 2004), pp. 170–1.

16 This text is available in numerous sources. This is taken from Henry Bettenson and Chris Maunder, *Documents of the Christian Church*, 3rd edition (Oxford: Oxford University Press, 1999), pp. 51–2.

17 Brian Hebblethwaite, *The Essence of Christianity* (London: SPCK, 1996), p. 91.

chapter 8
DYING TO SIN, LIVING TO REDEMPTION

LEARNING OUTCOMES

By the end of the chapter you should be able to:

- understand the different theories of the atonement
- appreciate why many Christians find such theories difficult to affirm
- understand why the author believes that atonement and forgiveness need to be linked

STRUCTURE

- Biblical roots of atonement
- Different theories
- Christ as sacrifice
- Christ who pays the debt
- Christ as victor
- Christ as moral example
- Problems with atonement
- Moral authority and forgiveness

One very practical response to the problem of evil is this: "we should all stop sinning." Granted there would still be natural suffering, but a world where people are not finding imaginative ways to hurt each other would make a massive difference. One problem is that people seem to find it difficult to live a life focused on others. It is easier to be selfish and preoccupied with our ego. To transcend our immediate world of self-interest is so difficult. Exhortations to individuals to "try harder to be good" just do not persuade.

At the heart of the Christian narrative is a dramatic claim. Christianity is not a religion that simply exhorts people to live changed lives; instead, Christians believe that God has provided the resources to make transformed lives possible. Somehow and in some way, when Jesus died on the cross he created the possibility of a transformed relationship with God.

Many millions of Christians have been inspired by the idea that "it is not what we do, it is what God has already done for us." The great reformer Martin Luther (1483–1546) made this idea the key to his theology. After years of struggling to please God by being exceptionally observant in his prayers and at confession, he was suddenly liberated by Paul's letter to the Romans. The good news is that we are not required to try to meet God's standards but simply accept the offer of "grace" (the undeserved merit and favor of God) made possible in Christ. But all this poses a question: what is the connection between Jesus dying on the cross and my sinful activity 2000 years later? This is the doctrine of the atonement (which literally means at-one-ment) – a doctrine which is firmly rooted in the New Testament. This is where our analysis will start.

Biblical Roots of Atonement

Whereas scholars argue over the extent to which the Incarnation is found in the New Testament, the idea that Jesus has saved humanity is a key and central theme. In the Gospel of Mark, we find the image of ransom occurring: "For the Son of Man came not to be served but to serve, and to give his life a ransom for many" (Mark 10:45). The image here seems to be suggesting that the life given by Jesus buys release for others from captivity.

In Romans 5, the Apostle Paul explains: "But God shows his love for us in that while we were yet sinners Christ died for us" (Romans 5:8). And later by way of explanation, he writes, "Then as one man's trespass led to condemnation for all men, so one man's act of righteousness leads to acquittal and life for all men" (Romans 5:18). Paul is developing a second Adam Christology (see also 1 Corinthians 15:45). Where Adam had sinned, Jesus was obedient. So Adam brings judgment on the world, where Jesus brings life.

Elsewhere in Paul a different image is at work. He writes: "For our sake he made him to be sin who knew no sin, so that in him we might become the righteousness of God" (2 Corinthians 5:21). Here we have the seeds of a "vicarious atonement" – an atonement on behalf of humanity. The sinless Jesus became sin to enable the rest of us to know the righteousness of God.

Perhaps the most pervasive image in the New Testament is "sacrifice." The author of the book of Hebrews explains:

> And every priest stands day after day at his service, offering again and again the same sacrifices that can never take away sins. But when Christ had offered for all time a single sacrifice for sins, "he sat down at the right hand of God," and since then has been waiting "until his enemies would be made a footstool for his feet." (Hebrews 10:11–13)

The practice in the Hebrew Bible of the annual blood sacrifice to atone for sins has been replaced by the one decisive sacrifice by Jesus. These sacrifices prior to the death of Jesus "foreshadow" or "anticipate" the effective and decisive sacrifice made possible by Jesus giving his life for humanity.

These different images all occur in the New Testament. The ransom image sits alongside the second Adam, both of which sit alongside the vicarious atonement and sacrifice: At no point did the Church officially endorse one particular account of the atonement.

Different Theories

The challenge for the Church is to explain how the death of Jesus two thousand years ago makes a difference to individuals living today. Many of the theories pick up a particular Biblical image and develop that image in a distinctive way. I shall now examine four different theories.

Christ as Sacrifice

The sacrifice model is very popular amongst the Church Fathers. One typical and clear representative is St Augustine of Hippo. In *The City of God*, the motif of sacrifice is central in his account of the atonement. Augustine's account is very nuanced; so we shall examine it with some care. "True sacrifices," explains Augustine, "are acts of compassion, whether towards ourselves or towards our neighbors, when they are directed towards God."[1] Here Augustine sets up the parameters for his discussion: sacrifices are given to God and they are acts of compassion.

He acknowledges his debt to the Jewish tradition. Even here, Augustine explains, it is important to see that sacrifice matters because of what it points towards. Augustine writes, "[T]he visible sacrifice is the sacrament, the sacred sign, of the invisible sacrifice."[2] So a sacrifice always was a symbol of the life given to God. This explains the paradox of God both desiring sacrifice yet despising sacrifices, which is found repeatedly in the Psalms and the prophets. Augustine explains:

> When he says that God does not want sacrifices he means that he does not want them in the way supposed by the fools, namely for his own gratification. For if he had not wished the sacrifices he desires (and there is only one, the heart bruised and humbled in the sorrow of penitence) to be signified by those sacrifices which he was supposed to long for as if they gave him pleasure, then he would not have prescribed their offering in the old Law. And the reason why they had to be changed, at the fitting and predestined time, was to prevent the belief that those things were objects to desire to God himself, or at least were acceptable gifts from us to him, and to make us realize that what God required was that which they signified.[3]

For Augustine, the animal sacrifices offered in the Temple were intended to be symbolic – a symbol of the necessity to repent for our wickedness before our creator. However, humanity, in its stupidity, was starting to imagine that God enjoyed the animal sacrifice as an end in itself. So it became necessary for God to change the system.

At this point we come to Jesus. Jesus is unique: as both completely God and completely human. Augustine writes, "In respect of his divinity he is always equal to the Father, and by his humanity he became like us."[4] By virtue of his unique status, Jesus becomes the definitive and perfect sacrifice because Jesus is both the recipient of the sacrifice and the giver of the sacrifice. Or as Augustine puts it:

> Hence it is that the true Mediator (in so far as he "took the form of a servant" and was thus made "the mediator between God and mankind, the man Christ Jesus") receives the sacrifice "in the form of God," in union with the Father, with whom he is one God. And yet "in the form of a servant" he preferred to be himself the sacrifice than to receive it, to prevent anyone from supposing that sacrifice, even in this circumstance, should be offered to any created being. Thus he is both the priest, himself making the offering, and the oblation. This is the reality, and he intended the daily sacrifice of the Church to be the sacramental symbol for this; for the Church, being the body of which he is the head, learns to offer itself through him. This is the true sacrifice.[5]

For Augustine, Jesus as God receives the sacrifice, yet Jesus also gives the sacrifice. Gone forever is the idea that God requires a sacrifice of animals. Instead the symbol has been replaced with God, and Godself provides the definitive model. Even God gives – out of compassion (which returns us to Augustine's definition of sacrifice) – of Godself which God then graciously receives.

Although there are other accounts in the tradition, which develop sacrifice in terms of the necessity of a blood sacrifice for sin, Augustine's account is much more careful. For Augustine, there is a remarkable circle of God sacrificing God to God. In this way, we need to learn how to offer ourselves as a sacrifice to God – to offer ourselves as an act of compassion to God.

Christ Who Pays the Debt

Perhaps the most famous account of the atonement comes from Anselm of Canterbury (1033–1109). A key idea here is that Jesus takes upon himself the punishment that humanity is due. It is a substitutionary atonement. Although many Christian thinkers have advocated a form of this atonement theory, Anselm's is probably the most influential and clear.

Anselm sets forth his account of the atonement in *Cur Deus Homo* (Why God Became Man). It takes the form of a dialogue between Anselm and Boso (a monk and former pupil from Bec where Anselm served). Boso asks the questions: Anselm provides the answers.

Towards the end of the dialogue, Boso helpfully summarizes the argument so far. He explains:

> The substance of the question was: why God became man, so that he might save mankind through his death, when it appears that he could have done this in another way. You have responded to this question with many cogent lines of reasoning, and have thereby shown that it was not right that the restoration of human nature should be left undone, and that it could not have been brought about unless man repaid what he owed to God. This debt was so large that, although no one but man owed it, only God was capable of repaying it, assuming that there should be a man identical with God. Hence it was a necessity that God should take man into the unity of his person, so that one who ought, by virtue of his nature, to make the repayment and was not capable of doing so, should be one who by virtue of his person was capable of it. Next in view of the fact that the man who was God had to be taken from a Virgin and from the person of the Son of God, you have also shown how he could have been taken sinless from out of sinful matter. You have furthermore proved that the life of this man is so sublime and so precious that it can suffice to repay the debt owed for the sins of the whole world, and infinitely more besides.[6]

There is much embedded in this summary. The problem is human sin: it has dishonored God. Now to understand "honor" here, it is important to appreciate the feudal context. It is not simply dignity or pride, but a deep challenge to the fabric of the universe and therefore the very nature of God. The dishonor needed rectification. Although God could have performed a particular action to make humanity sinless, this would not bring about the restoration of right order in the universe because humans have done the wrong. So although a human is needed to restore right order, no human has the power to do so (we are all party to the crime of sin). The only solution is the one God takes: God becomes human. Being God, this man would be sinless; being human, this man is able to restore the honor of God.

Towards the end of the dialogue, Anselm celebrates the love of God grounded in this solution. He writes:

> What, indeed, can be conceived of more merciful than that God the Father should say to a sinner condemned to eternal torments and lacking any means of redeeming himself, "Take my only-begotten Son and give him on your behalf," and that the Son himself should say, "Take me and redeem yourself." For it is something of this sort that they say when they call us and draw us towards the Christian faith. What also could be juster than that the one to whom is given a reward greater than any debt should absolve all debt, if it is presented with the feeling that is due?[7]

God has solved the problem. Redemption is restoration: we have a restored relationship with God made possible by the death of Jesus.

Christ as Victor

In the novel *The Lion, the Witch, and the Wardrobe*, **C. S. Lewis** describes the battle between good and evil in very graphic terms. The Lion and the Witch both work within the context of the Deep Magic. Edmund, the child traitor, belongs to the Witch. And the only way that Aslan, the Lion, can counteract this principle is to offer himself in the traitor's stead. This he does: he is tortured and finally killed by the Witch. However, Aslan is resurrected and explains the meaning to Susan in the following way:

> "It means," said Aslan, "that though the Witch knew the Deep Magic, there is a magic deeper still which she did not know. Her knowledge goes back only to the dawn of time. But if she could have looked a little further back, into the stillness and the darkness before Time dawned, she would have read there a different incantation. She would have known that when a willing victim who had committed no treachery was killed in a traitor's stead, the Table would crack and Death itself would start working backwards."[8]

C. S. LEWIS (1898–1963)

C. S. Lewis was born in Belfast, Ireland. He served in the army during the First World War. He was then elected fellow of Magdalen College, Oxford. He found faith in God in 1929, and became a Christian after discussions with J. R. R. Tolkien, in 1931. He married late in life to Joy Davidson. He died, still relatively young, in 1963. Along with his writing in English Literature, he is best known for his children's books and his works on theology.

Aslan is in a battle against evil. His triumph over death and evil is made possible by evil misjudging the power of goodness. The idea is that the sacrifice freely given for another trumps death and evil. C. S. Lewis is working here with the atonement image of Christ as victor.

C. S. Lewis is drawing on a very ancient tradition in Christian thinking. Starting with Irenaeus (130–202), it was developed by Origen (185–254) and Gregory of Nyssa (335–394). The idea is this: humanity is enslaved by sin and under the control of Satan. God the Father in negotiation with Satan agrees to hand over the Son as a ransom to free humanity. However, the humanity of Jesus veiled the divinity, so Satan did not entirely understand what he was getting. In addition, death could not defeat the Son of God. So Satan was "tricked" into surrendering human souls in exchange for the death of the Son. Gregory of Nyssa likens all this to a hook and bait: he writes:

> therefore, in order to secure that the ransom in our behalf might be easily accepted by him who required it, the Deity was hidden under the veil of our nature, that so, as with ravenous fish, the hook of the Deity might be gulped down along with the bait of flesh, and thus, life being introduced into the house of death, and light shining in darkness, that which is diametrically opposed to light and life might vanish; for it is not in the nature of darkness to remain when light is present, or of death to exist when life is active.[9]

Gustaf Aulén, in his highly provocative historical study of this model of the atonement, argues that the classic theory (which is his name for the victor model) dominated the first thousand years of Christianity. Then with Anselm in the eleventh century – what Aulén calls the Latin model (the one described above) – emerged. Gone was the Biblical battle with the forces of darkness, legal metaphors came to the fore. Slowly it was the Latin model in battle with the "subjective account" of Abelard (see below) that dominated the atonement debates right up to the present day. The exception

---

GUSTAF AULÉN (1879–1978)

Was a German professor and senior churchman who worked in Systematic Theology at the University of Lund and became Bishop of Lund in 1930. He was the author of several important books, including *the Catholic Christian Faith* (1923) and *The Christian Idea of the Atonement*, later translated into English as *Christus Victor* (1931). He moved to Strängmäs where he became Bishop.

---

was the Reformer Martin Luther. Aulén's point is that the classic account of the atonement has many significant qualities, which are important to recover. These include the following:

1 The New Testament sees the death of Christ as a triumph over sin, death, hell, and Satan. Paul talks of Christ destroying death (1 Corinthians 15:26) and overcoming the consequences of the Law (Romans 7:4). In Galatians Paul talks about Christ prevailing over principalities, powers, and dominions (Galatians 1:4, see also Romans 8:35ff). The ransom motif of Mark's Gospel is developed elsewhere in the New Testament (see for example 1 Timothy 2:6). And the battle with Satan is captured in the Johannine letters (1 John 3:8). Aulén concludes that: "the New Testament idea of redemption constitutes in fact a veritable revolution; for it declares that sovereign Divine Love has taken the initiative, broken through the orders of justice and merit, triumphed over the powers of evil, and created a new relation between the world and God."[10]

2 There is a continuity of divine operation. Unlike Anselm's account, where Christ becomes human to be punished for humanity, God is the agent throughout. Aulén writes approvingly of Luther that: "Time after time, Luther returns to this theme and emphasizes it with all his might: the one power which is able to overcome the tyrants is God's omnipotence. If the tyrants were victorious, then were God Himself overcome. But now almighty God Himself steps in and carries through His work to victory."[11]

3 Sin is taken very seriously. Sin is not simply the actions of bad people. It is a cosmic force with an objective identity. We literally are "slaves to sin." We struggle under bondage. Aulén writes, "The classic type regards sin as an objective power standing behind men, and the Atonement as the triumph of God over sin, death, and the devil."[12]

Atonement on this account is not easy. There is a vast array of objective evil forces that require to be fought. On the historical level, we simply have yet another unjust victim of an occupying power; however, beyond this level, is the cosmic battle with the spiritual forces of evil, death, and destruction.

Christ as Moral Example

Unlike the three accounts of the atonement described above, this theory is different. It is seen as a "subjectivist" account. With the "sacrifice," "battle," and the "legal substitution," Christ's death objectively changes the relationship with God. However, on this account, the power of the death lies in the example it affords humanity – both as an example of divine love and an example for us to follow.

Peter Abelard is the theologian most commonly associated with this view. The idea is that the death of Jesus on the cross is an example of God's love for humanity. And our redemption is made possible by humanity being inspired to follow that example and overcome sin in our own lives by giving our lives to others. Abelard's account of the atonement arises in his *Exposition of the Epistle to the Romans*. It is while he is offering a commentary on Romans 3:19–26 that he interrupts his deliberations with a question: what exactly are we saved from?

He starts by explaining that it is manifestly incoherent to believe that Christ saved us from the Devil. It just does not make sense, argues Abelard, to believe that the Devil has some inalienable rights over humanity. Abelard concludes:

> And so from these reasonings it seems proved that the devil acquired no right against man whom he seduced simply by seducing him, except perhaps (as we said before) in so far as it was a case of the Lord's permitting it – by handing man over to the wretch who was to act as his jailer or torturer for punishment.[13]

If the Devil has no rights, then God does not "deal" with the Devil. And anyway, Abelard goes on, the whole idea of blood sacrifice is problematic. Abelard explains:

> Indeed, how cruel and wicked it seems that anyone should demand the blood of an innocent person as the price for anything, or that it should in any way please him that an innocent man should be slain – still less that God should consider the death of his Son so agreeable that by it he should be reconciled to the whole world![14]

Having criticized some of the traditional atonement theories, Abelard then suggests his own solution. He explains:

> Now it seems to us that we have been justified by the blood of Christ and reconciled to God in this way: through this unique act of grace manifested to us – in that his Son has taken upon himself our nature and preserved therein in teaching us by word and example even unto death – he has more fully bound us to himself by love; with the result that our hearts should be enkindled by such a gift of divine grace, and true charity should not now shrink from enduring anything for him.[15]

In other words, Christ redeems us by providing such a powerful example of the nature of God's love that we cannot help but love Christ back. Or as Thomas Williams puts it: "On an exemplarist theory, the Passion works for our redemption only by presenting an extraordinary example of love that inspires an answering love in our hearts."[16]

Although this argument is definitely in Abelard, some scholars suspect that he is not consistent throughout his work. Thomas Williams argues persuasively that if one reads the entire "Commentary on the Epistle to the Romans," one finds that Abelard clearly includes an objective aspect. Indeed Williams writes, "Abelard says . . . that apart from the redemptive work of Christ, we are all liable to punishment for sin, and that Christ himself bore that punishment on our behalf. In other words, Abelard explicitly teaches a theory of penal substitution."[17] However, for many post-Enlightenment thinkers, this aspect of Abelard's position was ignored. For these thinkers, Abelard became a symbol (a hero perhaps) of a different way of looking at the atonement.

PETER ABELARD (1079–1142)

From an early age he displayed evidence of independent thinking and was a brilliant, if controversial, pupil. Having established himself in Paris as a lecturer, initially in dialectics, and later theology, his career was ended in 1118 because of a tragic love affair with Heloise, the niece of Fulbert, Canon of Notre Dame. He took refuge in the monastery St Denis and during this time his work on the teaching of the Trinity was condemned and his book *De Unitate et Trinitate Divina* was burnt. By 1136 he had resumed his teaching career. Always a controversial figure, by 1141 several propositions from his writings were condemned by St Bernard of Clairvaux and confirmed by Pope Innocent II. Finally reconciled to St Bernard, Abelard lived out the remainder of his life at the priory of St Marcel, Cluny. His philosophical works encompassed *Scito te ipsum* (on Ethics) and *Glossulae* on Porphyry. *Historia Calamitatum* carries his own personal history.

The power of God's loving example in Christ was considered sufficient to transform and redeem humanity.

Problems with Atonement

The atonement is difficult to explain. For those of us involved in interfaith dialogue, it is probably the hardest doctrine to defend. The objections are many and various. Jews have a problem with human sacrifice suddenly being reintroduced. From their perspective, the whole point of the Abraham and Isaac story (Genesis 22) is that human sacrifice is now forbidden. And one impact of the exile in Babylon in 597 BCE is that Jewish practice moved beyond animal sacrifices. So the news that God required Jesus as a human sacrifice is seen as a big ethical step backwards.

Muslims find it puzzling why God cannot just forgive humanity. After all, God sets the rules of the universe. Given God is omniscient, it is very unwise for God to insist that all sin must be punishable by death. Furthermore, if God decides that death is no longer the punishment for sin, then it is within the divine creator's prerogative to simply forgive humanity.

Both Jews and Muslims are appalled by the idea that Satan has "rights" over humanity. The idea of a transaction or "trick" (as some of the Fathers saw it) between God and Satan seems theologically grotesque. It undermines God's sovereignty in creation.

Perhaps an illustration of how odd atonement looks to those outside the Christian tradition might help. Imagine that there is a teacher – a Mr. Jones – in a very difficult school. In the classroom, the children are behaving very badly: they are screaming, yelling, punching each other, disobeying all instructions, and destroying chairs and tables. Imagine further that Mr. Jones has a son called Richard who is the only child behaving appropriately: indeed Richard is perfect. Now Mr. Jones decides to take some action. So he instructs his son Richard to come forward to the front of the class. Mr. Jones then takes his cane and unleashes all his anger on his son. Having finished beating his son, he then announces to the class that "his son has stood in their stead and therefore he is willing and able to forgive the rest of the class."

The objections to this teaching practice are obvious. First, it is not fair to punish an innocent person to let the guilty go free. Second, if Mr. Jones is going to simply forgive the class (which is the prerogative of the teacher), then why punish Richard at all? The teacher is entitled to simply decide to make a fresh start with his misbehaving class. Third, in our enlightened age, most of us are very uncomfortable with corporal punishment in the classroom. It works with a model of crime and punishment that ignores the complexities behind misbehaving. This is how the doctrine of the atonement looks to those outside the Church. These three reasons are why many people find the atonement problematic.

Moral Authority and Forgiveness

It is tempting to give up on atonement language. But the challenge of being a theologian is to struggle with ideas in the tradition. In terms of our central theme – doctrine as a response to evil and suffering – the atonement is vital. Given both the power and centrality of the atonement theme in Scripture and the Tradition, it is important we offer some account of it.

Let us create the parameters for our reflections. First, we have already seen in chapter seven how central to Christian theodicy is the claim that God became human and suffered and died. God knows what it is to suffer. Now Christians are claiming that God did not simply suffer but also created possibilities, which would not otherwise exist, by that suffering. Second, Christ has made it possible for us to be restored to God: as Paul writes in Romans, "Then as one man's trespass led to condemnation for all men, so one man's act of righteousness leads to acquittal and life for all men" (Romans 5:18). It is God in Christ completely identifying with humanity that makes it possible for us to be restored and forgiven. This is the truth that Christians need to continue to affirm. And we need to acknowledge that the mechanism that makes this possible is a mystery. Third, it is good that the Church never officially committed itself to a particular account of the atonement. This is partly because each theory embraces an aspect of the truth that we need to recognize and maintain, but also because theories are intelligible within a certain cultural context. Anselm's talk of God's honor makes sense in a feudal age; we would struggle to understand such talk today. Each age needs to find its own model of the atonement which expresses the mechanism by which the action of God in Christ creates new possibilities for restoration and forgiveness.

The account which follows is heavily dependent upon the work of Brian Hebblethwaite and Vernon White. Hebblethwaite in his defense of the Incarnation writes:

> Only if we can say that God has *himself*, on the cross, "borne our sorrows" can we find him universally present "in" the sufferings of others. It is not a question of "awareness" and "sympathy." It is, as Whitehead puts it, a matter of the "fellow-sufferer who understands." The whole dimension of the Christian doctrine of the incarnation, its recognition of the costly nature of God's forgiving love, and its perception that only a suffering God is morally credible, is lost if God's involvement is reduced to a matter of "awareness" and "sympathy."[18]

It is not sufficient that God in some cosmic sense feels the hurt and the pain of the creation (although I do think God does this), but that to be "morally credible" God must be the actual victim of hurt and pain. Now why is this?

It was Vernon White who developed an account of the atonement which we can call "Christ as the condition of forgiveness." The key issue for this account is what makes for sufficient forgiveness. White takes us back to *The Brothers Karamazov*, in particular the discussion between Alyosha and Ivan. Having described a landowner who set his pack of hounds on a child who had inadvertently thrown a stone and hit one of the dogs, Ivan complains that not even the mother has the right to forgive a torturer on behalf of her child.

> And, finally, I do not want a mother to embrace the torturer who had her child torn to pieces by his dogs! She has no right to forgive him! If she likes, she can forgive him for herself, she can forgive the torturer for the immeasurable suffering he has inflicted upon her as a mother; but she has no right to forgive him for the sufferings of her tortured child. She has no right to forgive the torturer for that, even if her child were to forgive him! And if that is so, if they have no right to forgive him, what becomes of harmony? Is there in the whole world a being who could or would have the right to forgive?[19]

Forgiveness is difficult complains Ivan. And no one has the right to forgive for another. A thought exercise at this point might help: there are two children. One day, John, in an unprovoked way, punches Fred. John then feels guilty about it and decides to go to Mary and ask forgiveness for his action. Now Mary cannot forgive: only Fred, who is the person wronged, can forgive. Forgiveness requires contrition on the part of the person who did the wrong to the person wronged. A third party, explains Ivan, cannot forgive sins.

However, Alyosha right at the end of the discussion introduces Christ. In a statement often overlooked because it is seen as nothing more than an introduction to the next chapter of the book, Alyosha says:

> "No, I can't admit it. Ivan," Alyosha said suddenly with flashing eyes, "you said just now, is there a being in the whole world who could or had the right to forgive? But there is such a being, and he can forgive everything, everyone and everything *for everything*, because he gave his innocent blood for all and for everything. You've forgotten him, but it is on him that the edifice is founded, and it is to him that they will cry aloud: 'Thou art just, O Lord, for thy ways are revealed!'"[20]

Alyosha insists that the innocence of Jesus gives Jesus the moral authority to forgive everything. Now White's idea is this: a morally adequate account of forgiveness requires two features: first, an agency that has been a victim of wickedness and second, an agency that is able to touch every aspect of tragedy in creation. If the agency can meet these two features, then we would have a legitimate mechanism for forgiveness. White outlines the criteria for "reconcilation which is morally demanded,"[21] when he writes:

It implies certain criteria for morally adequate reconciliation, namely that it must involve universal scope of action. If we could enter into every interlocking situation and experience, accepting the pain and effort involved in forgiving and creating good, then we can adequately forgive in any one situation . . . If Christ is able to do that, and we are "in Christ," then on that basis (but on that basis alone) forgiveness is possible.[22]

Given that Jesus is God, the suffering of Jesus is unique. The sufferer is both the creator, who is in everything and everywhere, and an individual person. In being tortured to death as a human, the creator is then able to bring about restoration and reconciliation in the creation. In much the same way as the suffering of **Nelson Mandela** (the 27 years in prison – the best years of his adult life) made his calls for the black man to forgive his white oppressor "morally authentic," so God has the same authenticity by virtue of the suffering of Jesus. White talks about the "criterion of moral authenticity," when he writes:

The heart of the model to be proposed rests on what might be called the criterion of moral authenticity, and goes something like this: *unless and until God himself has experienced suffering, death, and the temptation to sin, and overcome them, as a human individual, he has no moral authority to overcome them in and with the rest of humanity.* If this is accepted, then the Christ event becomes a constitutive action (for God) in his reconciling activity throughout history, in the sense that it helps form an essential ingredient in God's moral character.[23]

God is able to forgive because He has lived a human life – because God knows the stresses and strains of being human. God is able to forgive because God has suffered – the crucifixion is a slow death by torture.

So let us bring the threads together. First, we learn of the seriousness with which God takes the reality of evil and suffering. The Christian faith does not explain *why* evil is permitted, but the fact that God had to endure suffering and pain (the cost to God is high) strongly suggests that the reason for evil and suffering must be a very

---

NELSON MANDELA (1918–)

Mandela is famous for being the first president of South Africa who was elected by the entire country. He became leader of the African National Congress. He was imprisoned by the white regime for 27 years, spending much of his time on Robben Island, from where he was released in 1990. He was President from 1994 through to 1999.

good one. Given that God had to suffer, then God must have thought long and hard (please permit the anthropomorphic image) and determined that suffering and evil were indeed inescapable.

Second, and this is linked to the first, the fact that the creator hangs on the cross is the ultimate recognition of God taking responsibility for the hurt and pain in the creation. God is ultimately responsible for the creation: therefore God is ultimately responsible for the suffering of Ivan's children. In the tradition of "anger against God" which is found in the Psalms, sometimes in our anger and despair at the evil in this world, we need to see God suffer. Sometimes we need to see the cross as God getting God's just desserts for the hell that is the lives of millions of people. Acknowledging a legitimate anger against God is an aspect of the cross.

Third, and this is building on White, Jesus makes restoration possible because Jesus enables God to forgive. Suffering brings a certain moral authority and entitlement. The Nelson Mandela analogy is helpful. The fact he suffered gave him the authority to inspire and forgive on behalf of others who suffered. Mandela writes:

> I knew that people expected me to harbor anger towards whites. But I had none. In prison, my anger towards whites decreased, but my hatred for the system grew. I wanted South Africa to see that I loved even my enemies while I hated the system that turned us against one another.[24]

Mandela had as many reasons as anyone to hate the white oppressor. And it is because he had suffered at the hands of the white man that his calls to "love" the white man became all the more powerful. His suffering had given him the authority to reassure the white man that he can be forgiven and is still welcome in a multi-racial South Africa. With God, the authority is total: God both suffers directly in Jesus and indirectly in every instance of pain and injustice in creation. By virtue of this combination, God, through Christ, has created the conditions for us to be restored.

Conclusion

All Christian doctrine is a response to the problem of evil. And in this chapter we have seen one major aspect of that response is that God has made it possible for us to live transformed lives. We are not doomed to be a bundle of destructive egoism for all time. The promise of the atonement is that we can be forgiven. We can be forgiven for the hurt we have inflicted – often thoughtlessly, sometimes deliberately. We can be empowered to live a life reflecting the love of God to others. We have been transformed to live holy lives – to be reconcilers of people to God. Or as Paul puts it in his letter to the Church in Corinth:

So if anyone is in Christ, there is a new creation: everything old has passed away; see, everything has become new! All this is from God, who reconciled us to himself through Christ, and has given us the ministry of reconciliation; that is, in Christ God was reconciling the world to himself, not counting their trespasses against them, and entrusting the message of reconciliation to us. So we are ambassadors for Christ, since God is making his appeal through us; we entreat you on behalf of Christ, be reconciled to God. For our sake he made him to be sin who knew no sin, so that in him we might become the righteousness of God. (2 Corinthians 5:17–21)

QUESTIONS FOR REFLECTION AND DISCUSSION

1 What would you say to the Jew or Muslim who argues that Christian views of atonement are a return to human sacrifice to appease a wrathful God?
2 Of the four different atonement theories, which one do you find most acceptable?
3 Why do converts to Christianity find it so attractive that the "cross of Christ has saved them"?
4 How do we know which theory of the atonement is true? How does one decide?

Notes

1 Augustine of Hippo, *City of God* (Harmondsworth: Penguin, 1972), Book X, chapter 6, p. 380.
2 Ibid., Book X, chapter 5, p. 377.
3 Ibid., Book X, chapter 5, p. 378.
4 Ibid., Book IX, chapter 17, p. 364.
5 Ibid., Book X, chapter 21, pp. 400–1.
6 Brian Davies and G. R. Evans (eds.), *Anselm of Canterbury: The Major Works* (Oxford: Oxford University Press, 1998), p. 348.
7 Ibid., p. 354.
8 C. S. Lewis, *The Lion, the Witch and the Wardrobe* (1950) taken from *The Chronicles of Narnia* (London: HarperCollins), p. 185.
9 Gregory of Nyssa, *Catechetical Oration*, chapter 24, as found at http://www.uoregon.edu/~sshoemak/324/texts/gregory_of_nyssa.htm
10 Gustaf Aulén, *Christus Victor: An Historical Study of the Three Main Types of the Idea of the Atonement*, introduction by Jaroslav Pelikan (New York and Toronto: Macmillan Company, 1969), p. 79.

11 Ibid., p. 108.
12 Ibid., p. 147.
13 Peter Abelard, *Exposition of the Epistle to the Romans*, taken from Eugene R. Fairweather, *A Scholastic Miscellany: Anselm to Ockham*, vol. x (Philadelphia: Westminster Press, 1956), p. 281.
14 Ibid., p. 283.
15 Ibid., p. 283.
16 Thomas Williams, "Sin, grace, and redemption," in Jeffrey E. Brower and Kevin Guilfoy (eds.), *The Cambridge Companion to Abelard* (Cambridge: Cambridge University Press, 2004), p. 262.
17 Ibid., p. 266.
18 Brian Hebblethwaite, "The moral and religious value of the incarnation" in Michael Goulder (ed.), *Incarnation and Myth* (London: SCM Press, 1979), p. 94.
19 Fyodor Dostoyevsky, *The Brothers Karamazov* (Harmondsworth: Penguin Books, 1958), p. 287.
20 Vernon White, *Atonement and Incarnation: An Essay in Universalism and Particularity* (Cambridge: Cambridge University Press, 1991), p. 288. White comments on this passage from Dostoyevsky that this "represents Dostoevsky's own mature convictions. It is the solidarity of 'each and all', and all in Christ: the Orthodox concept of *sobernost*, which constitutes his own deepest response to Ivan" (p. 90).
21 Ibid., p. 89.
22 Ibid., p. 89.
23 Ibid., p. 39 (his italics).
24 Nelson Mandela, *Long Walk to Freedom* (London: Abacus, 1994), p. 680.

THE HOLY SPIRIT AND THE CHURCH

We have seen how humanity was bound to exercise its freedom and therefore fall, thereby creating the tension between aspiration (what we intuit is the good) and reality (our propensities to egoism and cruelty). We have seen how God reveals the nature of God to us and with it the appropriate way of being human by becoming human in Christ. We have seen how the death of Christ creates the possibility of restoration and redemption. It is now necessary to move to the present. This is a key role of the Spirit: Christians do not simply believe in a creator and a Redeemer, but also in a God who is present with us today, and crucially, in respect to leading a virtuous life. As Daniel Migliore observes:

> If the creed of the church ended abruptly with these first two articles of faith in God the creator and reconciler, it might seem to be speaking of events now historically remote and of truths that have little to do with our life here and now . . . The third article of the creed affirms that God is not only *over* us and *for* us but also at work *in* us. It speaks of the Holy Spirit and the new humanity in Christ.[1]

The theme of the next two chapters shows the ways in which God supports us in the present. In this one we look at the doctrine of the Holy Spirit and the community – the Church. In the next one we examine the Sacramental life of the Church.

One obvious question which arises for this chapter is this: why bring the Holy Spirit together with the Church? The answer is that these two have been connected together for centuries. When the Apostles' Creed was written in approximately 200 CE, we find Spirit and Church linked together when it claims: "I believe in the Holy Spirit, the holy catholic church, the communion of saints, the forgiveness of sins . . ." As Hughes Oliphant Old observes:

> The first thing we notice about this is that the belief in the church and its ministry is developed out of belief in the Holy Spirit. A Trinitarian understanding of God makes clear that the unity of God is not some dead, monolithic uniformity, but that in the unity of God there is communion. God is a God who reaches out. God is a communicating God, not a static, silent entity. God is a Spirit, an outpouring, inspiring, creating, and anointing Spirit, a strengthening, confirming, and comforting Spirit.[2]

The Church and the Spirit are linked: the Church is in a very real sense part of the work of the Holy Spirit.

In this chapter we shall start with the Holy Spirit. We will look at the Biblical roots of the doctrine, the development of the doctrine in the Early Church, and the work of the Holy Spirit both in the Church and beyond. Then we shall look at the Church. We will examine the Biblical images of the Church and the four defining marks of the Church (as defined in the Creeds).

Biblical Roots of the Doctrine of the Holy Spirit

The Early Church believed that the doctrine of the Holy Spirit was found throughout Scripture – both in the New Testament, but also in the Hebrew Bible. The Psalms were especially helpful. In Psalm 104, it is God's spirit that gives life:

> When you hide your face, they are dismayed;
> when you take away their breath, they die
> and return to their dust.
> When you send forth your spirit, they are created;
> and you renew the face of the ground. (Psalm 104:29–30)

It is as the spirit of God goes forth that creation occurs. In Psalm 51, it is God's spirit that is the guarantor of holy living and forgiveness.

> Create in me a clean heart, O God
> and put a new and right spirit within me.
> Do not cast me away from your presence,
> and do not take your holy spirit from me.
> Restore to me the joy of your salvation,
> and sustain in me a willing spirit. (Psalm 51:10–12)

The "holy spirit" (spelled here without capital letters because the Hebrew Bible does not hold a Trinitarian theology) is that gift that gives a sense of God. An awareness of God's presence is a gift of the Holy Spirit (which is now in capitals because that is how Christians want to interpret these texts). Elsewhere in various parts of the Hebrew Bible, it is God's spirit that is given to those called to serve God. So, for example, the servant of God in Isaiah 42 is described thus:

> Here is my servant, whom I uphold,
> my chosen, in whom my soul delights;
> I have put my spirit upon him;
> he will bring forth justice to the nations. (Isaiah 42:1–2)

It is the spirit of God which enables a person to work for truth and justice. The combination of a life-giving spirit, who assures us of forgiveness, and abides in the lives of God's people who are striving for justice, became key themes for the subsequent development of the doctrine.

In the New Testament, the Spirit is a major theme. Luke-Acts (the combined set of books written by Luke about Jesus and the start of the Early Church) is a crucial source. The Spirit, according to Luke, is prominent at every stage of Jesus' ministry. At the Birth, when the angel Gabriel comes to Mary, he says:

> The angel said to her, "The Holy Spirit will come upon you, and the power of the Most High will overshadow you; therefore the child to be born will be holy; he will be called Son of God."

And after the temptation, as Jesus starts his ministry, Luke writes:

> Then Jesus, filled with the power of the Spirit, returned to Galilee, and a report about him spread through all the surrounding country.

But it is as the story of the Church starts developing, that Luke describes the outpouring of the Holy Spirit on the Church. He writes:

> When the day of Pentecost had come, they were all together in one place. And suddenly from heaven there came a sound like the rush of a violent wind, and it filled the entire house where they were sitting. Divided tongues, as of fire, appeared among them, and a tongue rested on each of them. All of them were filled with the Holy Spirit and began to speak in other languages, as the Spirit gave them ability.

And here in this text is the link between the Holy Spirit and the Church. At the birth of the Church is this spectacular filling of the Holy Spirit. The Spirit was a vital part of the Church's experience of God, but it took several centuries for the theology of the Spirit to be sorted out.

The Development of the Holy Spirit in the Early Church

In chapter four we looked at the heresy of Arius. Arius taught that everything was created except the Father. The implication of this for the second person of the Trinity – the Son (the Redeemer) – was resolved at the Council of Nicaea in 325. However, the status of the Spirit was less clear. Indeed Nicaea did not consider the Spirit; it was Constantinople in 381 that added the sentences about the Holy Spirit to the creed. At Constantinople, the views of **Eustathius of Sebaste** were condemned. Eustathius was part of a movement known as *pneumatomachoi* (meaning "opponents of the spirit"), which was probably founded by a supporter of Arius called Macedonius (died 360).[3] Eustathius argued that the Spirit is not a divine person.

Basil of Caesarea (329–379) was a friend of Eustathius; but by the end of the controversy, they were less friendly. Basil was impressed with Eustathius' zealous

EUSTATHIUS OF SEBASTE (300–377)

He fell under the spell of the heretic Arius of Alexandra as a young man, therefore he had very ambiguous feelings about the doctrine formulated at the Council of Nicaea in 325 CE. His main interest was the monastic movement. He became the Bishop of Sebaste in Pontus in 357 CE.

monastic practice, but less impressed with his line on the Holy Spirit. In 375 CE, he wrote a treatise on the Holy Spirit, which was called *De Spiritu Sancto*. This became a key text for the Council of Constantinople. In it Basil outlines the key reasons why the Spirit is divine.

Basil addresses the text to his friend Amphiochius (a relative of Gregory of Nazianzus). He starts by complaining that his opponents are completely misusing the distinctions between God and Jesus found in 1 Corinthians 8:6, "yet for us there is one God, the Father, from whom are all things and for whom we exist, and one Lord, Jesus Christ, through whom are all things and through whom we exist (1 Corinthians 8:6)". This text is not a basis, argues Basil, for implying the inferiority of the Son from the Father. Instead the purpose is to make sure that the two persons are "not confounded." Then he moves to the arguments against the Spirit. He offers three reasons why the divinity of the Holy Spirit should be accepted. First, the baptismal formula found at the end of Matthew's Gospel. Basil writes:

> It is not permissible, they assert, for the Holy Spirit to be ranked with the Father and Son, on account of the difference of His nature and the inferiority of His dignity. Against them it is right to reply in the words of the apostles, "We ought to obey God rather than men." For if our Lord, when enjoining the baptism of salvation, charged His disciples to baptize all nations in the name "of the Father and of the Son and of the Holy Ghost," not disdaining fellowship with Him, and these men allege that we must not rank Him with the Father and the Son, is it not clear that they openly withstand the commandment of God? If they deny that coordination of this kind is declaratory of any fellowship and conjunction, let them tell us why it behoves us to hold this opinion, and what more intimate mode of conjunction they have.[4]

Basil's point is that the baptismal formula, which invokes "Father, Son and Holy Spirit," gives equal place to all three. In addition, we are exhorted to baptize in the name of all three; there are no grounds for assuming that a baptism in the Father's name alone will suffice.

The second reason is set out in chapter nineteen. Basil argues that the Biblical witness is clear in linking the Spirit to God. He writes:

> He is called Spirit, as "God is a Spirit," and "the breath of our nostrils, the anointed of the Lord." He is called holy, as the Father is holy, and the Son is holy, for to the creature holiness was brought in from without, but to the Spirit holiness is the fulfillment of nature, and it is for this reason that He is described not as being sanctified, but as sanctifying. He is called good, as the Father is good, and He who was begotten of the Good is good, and to the Spirit His goodness is essence. He is called upright, as "the Lord is upright," in that He is Himself truth, and is Himself Righteousness, having no divergence nor leaning to one side or to the other, on account of the immutability of His substance. He is called Paraclete, like the Only begotten, as He Himself says, "I will ask the Father, and He will give you another comforter." Thus names are borne by the Spirit in common with the Father and the Son, and He gets these titles from His natural and close relationship.

Basil is right. The Biblical witness repeatedly links the activities of the Spirit with God. Given that the Hebrew Bible is simply talking about the "spirit of God" (many of the references are assuming a Jewish monotheist setting), it is not surprising that the text affirms the divinity of the spirit of God.

The third reason is that the activities of the Spirit are those that God performs. Basil writes:

> if you think of the creation, the powers of the heavens were established by the Spirit, ... Working of miracles, and gifts of healing are through the Holy Spirit. Demons were driven out by the Spirit of God. The devil was brought to naught by the presence of the Spirit. Remission of Sins was by the gift of the Spirit ...

Again Basil is right. The word "spirit" is often used to describe significant and dramatic actions by God. Creation and forgiveness of sins are actions that are only possible of God. The link is clear, says Basil, the Spirit is identical with God.

These three arguments persuaded the Church. Although it is true that the Early Church was otherwise preoccupied with other major issues in the first three centuries (e.g. Christology), as it entered the fourth century the debate over the Spirit ensued. By the late fourth century, the divinity of the Spirit was secure.

The Work of the Holy Spirit Within the Church

For Christians, the primary work of the Holy Spirit is to be the presence of God for us now. Daniel Migliore explains that "a Christian theology of the Holy Spirit will give special attention to the work of the Holy Spirit in binding believers to Christ and creating new life and new community in him."[5] Migliore then identifies six features under this heading, which we will examine in detail. First, "the work of the Spirit is *re-presentative*."[6] This is the task of representing Christ to us now. As I have already stressed, the Spirit enables the gap between the present and the past to be filled. Second, "the Spirit is the *creation of new life*."[7] For the author of John's Gospel, it is the Spirit who brings about the second birth; it is the Spirit who enables us to live a transformed life, which we described in the chapter on atonement. Third, "another aspect of the work of the Holy Spirit is *liberative*."[8] Migliore stresses the "freedom" which is made possible in the Spirit. At this point there is a significant challenge to modern accounts of freedom. This is not freedom "to do anything," but a freedom to have the "mind" of Christ – to be fully human as God intended us to be. So this is freedom from egoism, self-centeredness, and frustration and, at the same time, a freedom for life, love, and harmony with God. The fourth aspect is "*communal*."[9] The Spirit can provide the glue that enables the diverse community of God to be together. As we shall see in a moment, when we discuss the Church, the community of the Church is intended to be very diverse. And the Spirit is the enabler of this diverse community. The fifth aspect is the "*promise* associated with the work of the Holy Spirit."[10] Once again this is related to the role of the Spirit as the agent of God across time. When Paul explains the significance of the Christian for the end times, he writes:

> We know that the whole creation has been groaning in labor pains until now; and not only the creation, but we ourselves, who have the first fruits of the Spirit, groan inwardly while we wait for adoption, the redemption of our bodies. (Romans 8:22–3)

We are the "first fruits of the Spirit"; we are the anticipation of the promise of God, which in this remarkable passage is extended to all creation. It is the Holy Spirit within us that creates the urge for a just order and gives us the strength to work for this just order. The final aspect of the work of the Spirit is "*the gifts or charismata of the Spirit*."[11] In Paul's famous hymn to love in 1 Corinthians 13, he describes the greatest of these gifts as "faith, hope, and love." Naturally all Christians would celebrate these gifts; however, some Christians are interested in the more spectacular gifts of the Spirit (speaking in tongues, healing, and prophecy). Indeed the fastest growing Protestant tradition is Pentecostalism, which makes these gifts central to its practice and theology. Such gifts make the experience of worship much more interesting.

The Work of the Holy Spirit Outside the Church

In Roman Catholic theology, since Vatican II, there has been a growing recognition that the work of the Holy Spirit is not simply confined to the Church. One writer who has made this central to his work is Gavin D'Costa. In *Christian Uniqueness Reconsidered*, he uses his essay to sketch out a Trinitarian theology of other religions. As an aspect of his argument, he suggests that it is part of the work of the Holy Spirit to convey insights of God through other faith traditions. The key text for D'Costa is John 16:12–15. The author of John writes:

> I still have many things to say to you, but you cannot bear them now. When the Spirit of truth comes, he will guide you into all the truth; for he will not speak on his own, but will speak whatever he hears, and he will declare to you the things that are to come. He will glorify me, because he will take what is mine and declare it to you. All that the Father has is mine. For this reason I said that he will take what is mine and declare it to you.

D'Costa draws attention to the fact that there are "truths" that Jesus cannot share with his disciples in his earthly ministry (the disciples are not in a place to receive them). However, the Spirit of truth will come, which will guide them further. The insights of the Holy Spirit will not contradict the Son (the revealer of God), but will be moving beyond what the revealer has shown in his life. D'Costa then explains:

> The significance of this Trinitarian ecclesiology is that if we have good reasons to believe that the Spirit and Word are present and active in the religions of the world (in ways that cannot, a priori, be specified), then it is intrinsic to the vocation of the church to be attentive to the world religions. Otherwise, it willfully closes itself to the Spirit of truth, which it requires to remain faithful to the truth and be guided more deeply into it.[12]

It is because we believe in the Holy Spirit that we are required to be attentive to the witness of other faith traditions. The Holy Spirit seeks to guide the Church into a deeper knowledge of the truth. Given God is active in all human cultures, we should expect to learn of God from other religious cultures.

He develops the argument in his outstanding book *The Meeting of Religions and the Trinity*. In this book, he offers a close reading of certain papal encyclicals (i.e. letters written by the Pope) and demonstrates how this approach to other religions is very much part of the Roman Catholic theology. D'Costa shows how the work of the Spirit is attempting to do the same work both inside the Church and outside. D'Costa writes:

> [I]f the Spirit within the church has the role of helping the church to follow more truthfully, and coming to indwell the trinity more completely, then this same Spirit, when outside the church must also have an analogous role within the other cultures, to help make women and men more Christ-like, individually and in community, however frustrated and thwarted.[13]

D'Costa is at this point analyzing the encyclical *Redemptoris Missio*. And the argument of both the encyclical and D'Costa is sound. It is incoherent to assume that God, through the Spirit, is related in vastly different ways to people inside the Church and those outside the Church. Therefore we should expect to encounter knowledge of God within other faith traditions. One key assumption is that complete knowledge of God will only be known at the eschaton (i.e. at the end of the age). Given this, "the very doctrine of a Trinitarian God within Christianity allows Christianity to maintain a real openness to God *in history*."[14] In other words, while we are working our way through history, there is much that the Church can and should learn. And attending to the witness of the Holy Spirit through other faith traditions is an important part of that learning.

Ecclesiology

The founding of the Church is traditionally dated from the day of Pentecost (described earlier in the chapter). This is the moment when the Holy Spirit descends on the Church. The study of the Church is called "ecclesiology," from the Greek word *ekklesia*, which means Church. We saw in chapter one how central "community" is to understanding the world. It is in a community that our worldview is shaped. Furthermore if there is no community, then, to all intents and purposes, a tradition dies. The worship of Zeus has gone out of fashion because people stopped gathering. If Christianity is to survive, then it needs people to gather. This is the work of the Church.

Roger Haight in his masterful study of ecclesiology distinguishes between "ecclesiology from above" and "ecclesiology from below." Ecclesiology from above describes a Church, which is non-historical, grounded in authoritative texts, and interpreted primarily as an agent of divine action. Ecclesiology from below faces the historical, cultural, and changing reality of the Church. The advantage of an ecclesiology from below approach is that one finds a "plurality" of models in our tradition. Haight suggests there are three criteria to distinguish appropriate views of the Church from inappropriate ones: he writes, "The three criteria are fidelity to the past, intelligibility and coherence today, and empowerment into the future."[15] So we do have, in Haight, criteria for distinguishing more or less appropriate views of the Church. However, thanks to his historical sensitivity, he also insists that there are many different models of the Church which meet this criteria. His project is one sympathetic to ecumenism.

In the remainder of this chapter, we shall look at the traditional four marks of the Church. And in each case, inspired by Haight's methodology, we shall recognize a historical dimension to the issues.

Biblical Images of the Church

Paul Minear in *Images of the Church in the New Testament* claims that there are some 96 such images.[16] Along with the well-known and central images – "Body of Christ" (1 Corinthians 12:27) and the "Bride of Christ" (Ephesians 5:23–32) – we have less well-known images, such as "a letter of Christ" (2 Corinthians 3:2–3), "the field of God" (1 Corinthians 3:9), and "salt of the earth" (Matthew 5:13). Paul Minear suggests that these images can be formed into four clusters of meaning. These are "body of Christ," "people of God," "communion of faith, hope, and love," and "creation of the Spirit." I want to modify his clusters and arrange the images slightly differently. However, before doing this, one problem needs to be stated and recognized. The problem is this: the word "church" itself is hardly ever used by Jesus. It only occurs in two passages in Matthew's Gospel (Matthew 16:18 and 18:15–17). There is a lively debate amongst New Testament scholars as to whether Jesus intended to create a church. Although this is an interesting question, which relates to the mission of Jesus, the problem can be overstated. It is clear that Jesus intended to create a community that would continue and safeguard his teaching. This is the reason why disciples were called. And theologically, the bedrock of our ecclesiology is this sense that we are called by Jesus to be disciples and empowered (as we have already seen in this chapter) by the Holy Spirit.

There are four aspects to the theme of Church in the New Testament.[17] The first is that the Church is the people of God. Building on the theme of the Jewish people being the people of God (Leviticus 26:12), the New Testament wants to claim that the Church is in continuity with the Hebrew Bible. As the author of 1 Peter puts it: "But you are a chosen race, a royal priesthood, a holy nation, God's own people, in order that you may proclaim the mighty acts of him who called you out of darkness into his marvelous light" (1 Peter 2:9). Contrary to popular opinion, a Church is not primarily a building but the people. And in this passage, we are God's own people who are called to proclaim the mighty acts of God who has transformed us.

The second aspect is the Body of Christ. This is perhaps the best known image of Church in the New Testament. It is an image developed by Paul in his letter to the Church at Corinth. Paul writes: "Now you are the body of Christ and individually members of it" (1 Corinthians 12:27). In this context Paul is stressing the value of the role of every Christian in the Church: it is, explains Paul, as silly for one Christian to turn to another and say we have no need for you as it is for the hand to suggest that it is more important than the foot. The image is striking. It suggests that the Church is the presence of Christ in the world: it brings Christ to others. It also suggests an organic connection between each Christian and Christ (a theme developed in the Gospel of John; see John 15:5). And it also captures the way each one of us matters as we build up together into an effective whole.

The third aspect is the safeguard of tradition. When Paul brings together the evidence for the resurrection for the Church at Corinth, he starts the chapter with the following declaration: "For I handed on to you as of first importance what I in turn had received" (1 Corinthians 15:3). Elsewhere, Paul talks about having a "divine jealousy," having "promised" the Church to be a "chaste virgin to Christ" (2 Corinthians 11:1–2), and his fear that an inauthentic Gospel will lure the Church away from the truth. This sort of language speaks to the Church as the community of those who have received the authentic tradition. Ideas and stories need a home. If there is not a community witnessing and celebrating certain ideas and telling the stories, then they do not survive. One key role of the Church is to be the home where the story of Jesus is told. It is to safeguard those ideas and tell the story for subsequent generations. This aspect of the New Testament is central to a Roman Catholic ecclesiology.

The fourth aspect is that the Church is the community which creates virtue. Some of the most powerful descriptions of the Church are found in Acts. Here the community is seen as one that "had all things in common" and had sold "their possessions and goods and distribute the proceeds to all, as any had need" (Acts 2:44–5). We are called to serve each other (2 Corinthians 4:5); we are called in Christ to challenge slavery, sexism, and ethnic distinctions (Galatians 3:28). This is a community that makes a difference. It should take people out of their egoism and selfish preoccupation and into a place where their human potential to live as God always intended is realized.

Building on these images, the Church entrenched into the creeds a description of itself. We shall now look at the description of the Church as it is found in the creeds.

Marks of the Church

In the Nicene Creed, we find "I believe in one holy catholic and apostolic Church." The four descriptors of the Church – one, holy, catholic, and apostolic – are known as "marks."

One and Unity

The first mark of the Church is that it is one. Traditionally this would have been understood as there is one Church, which has a variety of local expressions. So the Christians in Corinth are linked with the Christians in Rome as part of the one Church. These Christians share a theology and a narrative, which separates them from those who advocate a different theology and narrative. The fact there is one Church means that any other organizations claiming to be Churches are impostors. Therefore it is important to make sure you belong to the right Church: this was a significant tool in the emergence of orthodoxy.

With the split from the Orthodox traditions in 1054 and the emergence of the European Reformation in the sixteenth century, Christians in the same locality were not all worshipping together and significant differences of theology emerged. **John Calvin** introduced the distinction between the *visible* Church and the *invisible* Church. The visible Church is divided, perhaps corrupt and sometimes wicked; but the invisible Church (those who are truly part of God's elect) is one. This distinction means that the Church is still one, even if it does not appear to be.

In John 17, Jesus prays that his followers might be one (John 17:21). Out of obedience to the prayer of Jesus, the ecumenical movement emerged. In 1948 the World Council of Churches was constituted. For much of the twentieth century, the goal of the movement was visible institutional unity. Although certain groups have come together (mainly due to economic factors), most denominations have retained their distinctive traditions. Increasingly, therefore, the unity of the Church is seen as the shared theology and story underpinning our differences. And at the eschaton (at the end of the age), we shall finally share a complete unity.

Holy

We have already seen how the Church is intended to be a transformed community. We are called to live lives that transcend selfishness and egoism and therefore reflect the love of Christ to others. This is the challenge of holiness.

JOHN CALVIN (1509–64)

A Frenchman, who was born at Noyon in Picardy. He studied theology in Paris, before studying law at Orleans, during which time he became sympathetic to Protestant theology. He broke with the Roman Catholic Church in 1533. In 1534, he went to Noyon, where for a short time he was imprisoned. He fled to Basle, where he started writing his famous *Institutes*. The first edition was published in 1536. He was appointed Professor of Theology in 1536 at Geneva, where he had a major impact. After a spell away from Geneva, he returned in 1541, where he started to realize his theocratic vision for the city. From 1555 to 1564, he had a leadership role in the city.

One obvious question arises: what do we do when the Church behaves in ways that are "unholy"? This was raised in an acute form in the fourth century. It was the Roman emperor Diocletian (284–313) who created the circumstances that provoked the question. Diocletian had a policy of persecution towards the Church. In February 303, an edict was issued that ordered the burning of Christian books and the demolition of churches. For understandable reasons (to disobey an edict from the Emperor invited the death penalty), some of the Christian leaders handed their books over to be burned, thereby becoming *traditores* (which, from the same root, we get the English word "traitor"). Felix of Aptunga was one of many leaders who succumbed to the edict and handed books over to be burned.

So when Felix of Aptunga, in 311, laid his hands on and consecrated Caecilian as bishop of Carthage, controversy arose. Was Felix of Aptunga tainted? Was he still holy? And if not, then could the Church in Carthage be confident that his powers to consecrate were still intact? Given the Church must be holy, those who consecrate must be holy. The Donatists, so-called because they appointed Donatus to be their bishop instead of Caecilian, argued that the validity of ordination depends on the holiness of the participants. Although the synod of Aries in 314 declared the Donatists mistaken, they attracted strong support and over the next fifty years this theology persuaded many Christians in north Africa.

It was Augustine of Hippo who put forward the arguments against the Donatists. First, the holiness of the Church is the holiness of Christ. The Church is made up of people who are redeemed and are becoming sanctified by the Holy Spirit, which will only be perfected at the end of the age. Second, a crucial text for Augustine is the parable of the tares (i.e. weeds) in Matthew 13:24–31. As any gardener knows, weeds grow along with the plants (in this case wheat). If you try to separate the weeds from the wheat while they are growing, then it is likely that some of the wheat will be uprooted. So the thing to do is wait until the end of the season and then separate the weeds from the wheat. It was on the authority of this text that Augustine insisted that the Church is made up of sinners and saints, which will be separated at the end of the age. Third, as a matter of empirical fact, the Donatists are not better behaved than the Catholics. Sadly they both get drunk and use violence.

The Donatist temptation and challenge continues to arise. There are many Protestant groups that stress the redeemed community should be a righteous (i.e. completely holy) community. Some theologians believe that a redeemed person can be a holy and sinless person. However, the practice of the Church does demonstrate the wisdom of those who argued against such a theology: many Christians aspire to be good, but many do not manage it all the time.

Catholic

It was Vincent of Lerins (d. 450) who provided the classical definition of catholic. In his *Commonitorium* (meaning "a reminder"), he writes: "Now in the Catholic Church itself we take the greatest care to hold *that which has been believed everywhere, always and by all*."[18] The literal meaning of catholic is "universal." So it is stressing the shared nature of our faith across time, geography, and place.

Some Christians stumble over this word in the creed; they assume that it refers to the Roman Catholic Church. It is true that the Roman Catholic Church does claim to be, by virtue of history and size, a visible reminder of the universal Church. However, all Christians in all denominations can recognize the catholicity of the Church. Catholic means the Church is found in all places and we are obliged to recognize our kinship with all Christians everywhere.

To be catholic is difficult. We are called upon to be inclusive. Both historically and today, there are many Christians who are excluded. A constant temptation is to turn the Church into a club where membership is difficult and confined to the "right sort of people." Those writing from the vantage point of identity theologies (feminist, black, womanist, gay and lesbian, hispanic) are right to insist on inclusivity. The feminist theologian Letty M. Russell goes further. Catholicity should extend to nature. She writes:

> If God has acted in Jesus Christ to renew the whole earth, then it is important for the church's self-understanding to recognize Christ as present in the whole of creation. In this sense, to be catholic is to be connected to all of the creation in all of its groaning parts and to take responsibility for the needs of the many different churches and peoples of the world.[19]

Catholicity, then, implies an obligation to strive for justice. Humans are abusing the creation: for the Christian committed to catholicity, we are obliged to be connected to that creation and strive for a more environmentally friendly world.

Apostolic

This mark of the Church addresses the origins of the Church. The Church is a community grounded in the teachings of the apostles. The apostles are the initial witnesses to the resurrection of Jesus; they were sent out by Christ to preach the Gospel (the good news). So, for example, Peter, James, John, and Paul (although Paul sometimes had a difficult time reassuring everyone of his apostolic credentials – see 1 Corinthians 9:1–3) were apostles. A major criterion in selecting the books that became part of the

New Testament was apostolic authorship. The Early Church was determined to treat as authoritative those texts that are closest to Jesus.

It is important to note that, largely, the Church got the selection of texts right. It is true there are many gospels purporting to come from apostles (the Gospels of Thomas, Peter, Judas, and Mary), but all of these are second-century Gnostic (from the Greek word *gnosis* meaning knowledge) gospels. Although important for conveying the diversity of traditions in the Early Church, in terms of reliable history about Jesus these Gospels are unhelpful. The *Infancy Gospel of Thomas*, for example, attempts to fill in the gaps around the childhood of Jesus. It includes stories about Jesus creating clay birds and breathing life into them and moments when he is upset and makes his friends wither. As one reads these Gnostic gospels, it does look like Jesus has become more and more supernatural and less and less human.

So the word "apostolic" has two key meanings: first, it means that we are connected with the teaching of the early apostles who are the most reliable communicators of the message of Jesus. It therefore carries connotations of "authority" and "trustworthiness." Second, it means that we are required to maintain certain patterns of ministry. Traditionally, the orders of ministry are bishops, priests, and deacons. Now this is more contentious. For certain Anabaptist traditions (literally, "practice re-baptism", but normally associated with a seventeenth-century reform movement in Germany and Switzerland), it is not obvious that this structure is in the New Testament. For feminist theologians, the doctrine of "apostolic succession" is a problem because it has been used to justify male leadership in the Church. For the Roman Catholic tradition, apostolic succession means that there should be an unbroken link between a bishop and priest today, and the first apostles.

Conclusion

Part of the argument of this book is that all of Christian doctrine is a response to the problem of evil and suffering. And these two doctrines concerning the Holy Spirit and the Church are a key part of that response. The Holy Spirit is the aspect of God that makes God present to us, especially in and through the community of the Church. We do not struggle with the problems and challenges of life alone. We do so in community, which is enabled through the Holy Spirit. Christians are not called to be isolated entities. Instead we believe in living in community, which can support and help us cope.

Sometimes the institution of the Church fails to realize this vision. Both historically and today, the Church can be a cruel institution. But if one looks around, then there are vital, living, energetic communities, which continue to strive for what the Church can and should be.

QUESTIONS FOR REFLECTION AND DISCUSSION

1 Is it necessary for Christians to believe in the Holy Spirit?
2 What is the role of the Holy Spirit in Christian doctrine?
3 What is the difference between "ecclesiology from below" and "ecclesiology from above"? Which approach do you prefer and why?
4 Describe the four marks of the Church.
5 What is the difference between the Church and a regular association or club?

GLOSSARY

Anabaptists: literally re-baptisers. A nickname used to describe those Christians who emerged in the sixteenth and seventeenth centuries and taught that infant baptism is wrong and one should only be baptized as a believer

Ecclesiology: the study of the Church

Ecumenism/ecumenical movement: literally, from the Greek, the whole world. The term is used to describe the attempt to bring all the major churches together

Encyclical: a letter traditionally sent by a bishop; in Roman Catholic circles it is now confined to a letter sent by the Pope

Notes

1 Daniel L. Migliore, *Faith Seeking Understanding: An Introduction to Christian Theology*, 2nd edition (Grand Rapids MI: Eerdmans, 2004), p. 223.
2 Hughes Oliphant Old, "Why bother with the Church" in William Placher (ed.), *Essentials of Christian Theology* (Louisville, KY: Westminster John Knox, 2003), pp. 232–3.
3 It is the link with Macedonius that also leads this group to be sometimes called the "Macedonians."
4 *The Book of St Basil on the Spirit*, taken from *Nicene and Post-Nicene Father*, Series II, vol. iii (Grand Rapids, MI: Eerdmans, 1954).
5 Migliore, *Faith Seeking Understanding*, p. 227.
6 Ibid., p. 227 (his italics).
7 Ibid., p. 228 (his italics).
8 Ibid., p. 228 (his italics).
9 Ibid., p. 229 (his italics).
10 Ibid., p. 229 (his italics).

11 Ibid., p. 229 (his italics).

12 Gavin D'Costa, "Christ, the Trinity, and religious plurality" in Gavin D'Costa (ed.), *Christian Uniqueness Reconsidered: The Myth of a Pluralistic Theology of Religions* (Maryknoll, NY: Orbis Books, 1990), p. 23.

13 Gavin D'Costa, *The Meeting of Religions and the Trinity* (Edinburgh: T. & T. Clark, 2000), p. 115.

14 Ibid., p. 133 (his italics).

15 Roger Haight, SJ, *Christian Community in History: Historical Ecclesiology*, vol. 1 (New York and London: Continuum, 2004), p. 55.

16 See Paul Minear, *Images of the Church in the New Testament* (Philadelphia: Westminster, 1960).

17 In drawing up my own list of the main themes around Church in the New Testament, I have found the following discussions helpful: Daniel Migliore's *Faith Seeking Understanding*, Paul Minear's *Images of the Church in the New Testament*, and Hughes Oliphant Old, "Why bother with the Church?"

18 Vincent of Lerins, "Commonitorium," ed. R. St Moxon, *Cambridge Patristic Texts*, taken from http://www.fordham.edu/halsall/ancient/434lerins-canon.html (accessed 25 April, 2006).

19 Letty M. Russell, "Why bother with the Church?" in William Placher (ed.), *Essentials of Christian Theology*, p. 245.

Chapter 10
SACRAMENTS AND THE LIFE OF VIRTUE

LEARNING OUTCOMES

By the end of this chapter you should be able to:

- Understand the classical Roman Catholic account of the sacraments
- Appreciate some of the differences amongst Protestants over the sacraments
- See how it is possible to defend a sacramental theology.

Definition of Sacraments

We have Tertullian (b. 260 CE) to thank for the application of the term "sacraments" to baptism and communion. Sacraments is a Latin word – *sacramentum*. Originally, the term was a legal one involving the pledge of money – sometimes property – in a contractual arrangement, which took place in a temple. However, by the time of Tertullian, the Romans were using the term to mean "a sacred oath." Roman soldiers were required to take an oath of strict obedience and allegiance to the Roman gods and to their commander; so, by analogy, Tertullian saw the sacraments of baptism and Eucharist as equally binding loyalty symbols on Christians.

Although Tertullian might not have been the first, he used the word "sacrament" when translating the Bible. He translated the Greek word *mysterion* (a mystery), as sacrament. In these two ways, two characteristics of sacraments became defined: The first is that they are practices in the Church that bind the Church together; the second is that they are grounded in the mysterious work of God.

The contemporary Roman Catholic theologian, Joseph Martos, offers a broad definition, one which sees sacrament as "a sign or symbol of something which is sacred and mysterious."[1] He goes on to observe that all religions have sacraments; they operate as "doors to the sacred, that is, as invitations to religious experiences."[2] They are ways to connect with the divine.

In Christianity the understanding of sacrament varies from tradition to tradition. In this chapter we shall start by looking at the Roman Catholic view of sacraments. Then we shall compare their views with Protestant and Reformed accounts, before culminating in my own analysis of what the sacraments are and how they should be understood.

The Classical Roman Catholic Understanding

In the *Catechism of the Catholic Church* we find a very clear description of the sacraments. Unlike the broad definition offered above, a more precise and more Christian definition is offered:

> The sacraments are efficacious signs of grace, instituted by Christ and entrusted to the Church, by which divine life is dispensed to us. The visible rites by which the sacraments are celebrated signify and make present the graces proper to each sacrament. They bear fruit in those who receive them with the required dispositions.[3]

This definition makes clear the key aspects of the Catholic account of the sacraments: they are instituted by Christ; they enable divine life to be dispensed to us; and they work in the lives of those with the appropriate attitude.

For Roman Catholics, the sacramental life is the basis of the Church's liturgy. This is what it is all about. All three members of the Trinity are involved in the liturgy. God the Father is "blessed and adored as the source of all the blessings of creation."[4] So it is the Father who is the proper object of worship. God the Son is found explicitly in the sacramental nature of the liturgy because "his mystery of salvation is made present there."[5] And "the mission of the Holy Spirit in the liturgy of the Church is to prepare the assembly to encounter Christ."[6] The liturgy is a powerhouse of divine activity. The heart of the experience is an encounter with the divine.

For Roman Catholics, there are seven sacraments, instituted by Christ. There are three sacraments of Christian initiation, namely Baptism, Confirmation, and Eucharist. These "lay the foundations of every Christian life."[7] However, once inside the Christian life, we find life difficult, both spiritually and physically. Therefore there are two sacraments of healing. These are the sacraments of Penance and of Anointing of the Sick. The last two sacraments are "at the service of communion and the mission of the faithful."[8] These are Holy Orders and Matrimony. Holy Orders is the practice of ordination to one of the three orders of ministry: bishop, priest, and deacon. Matrimony is the sacrament of bringing together a man and a woman to create a family.

For our purposes, we shall concentrate on the two sacraments of baptism and Eucharist. These raise fundamental issues that divide Christians. For Roman Catholics, baptism is the "basis of the whole Christian life, the gateway to life in the Spirit, and the door which gives access to the other sacraments."[9] This is grounded in Scripture. In the Hebrew Bible, the Jewish people escape from slavery in Egypt by crossing the Red Sea, and receive the promised land by crossing the River Jordan. The point is, one passes through water both to escape captivity and to receive the freedom of new life. So by analogy, baptism plays the same role in the life of the Christian.

In being baptized, we are following the example of Jesus, who was baptized by John. And in being baptized, the stain of original sin is removed. The Catechism claims that "By Baptism *all sins* are forgiven, original sin and all personal sins, as well as all punishment for sin."[10] Both adults and infants can be baptized. On infants, the Catechism writes:

> Born with a fallen nature and tainted by original sin, children also have need of the new birth in Baptism to be freed from the power of darkness and brought into the realm of the freedom of the children of God, to which all men are called. The sheer gratuitousness of the grace of salvation is particularly manifest in infant Baptism. The Church and the parents would deny a child the priceless grace of becoming a child of God were they not to confer Baptism shortly after birth.[11]

Now, on this point, Christians disagree. Members of the Baptist tradition, for example, insist that baptism needs to be grounded in the testimony of the person who has already decided to accept the offer of God's grace. Given babies cannot yet decide for themselves, infant baptism is improper. Roman Catholics do recognize that "faith must grow *after* baptism."[12] They also argue that infant baptism is found in the New Testament because the book of Acts talks about entire "households" receiving baptism, which presumably would have included infants.

Because of its foundational character, any person can perform a baptism. Ideally, it should be a bishop or priest or deacon. However, "in case of necessity, any person, even someone not baptized, can baptize, if he has the required intention. The intention required is to will to do what the Church does when she baptizes, and to apply the Trinitarian baptismal formula."[13] Even today, there are many parts of the world where a devout midwife will take a sick baby and perform a discreet baptism. Although the Catechism does concede that God's mercy and Christ's injunction towards children "allow us to hope that there is a way of salvation for children who have died without Baptism,"[14] it is clearly preferable that the stain of original sin has been removed and that the sick baby can be guaranteed its place in heaven.

The Eucharist is based on the Last Supper. Jesus brings his disciples together hours before he is going to be arrested (see Luke 22:7–20; Matthew 26:17–29; Mark 14:12–25; 1 Corinthians 11:23–26). In this meal, Jesus explains to the disciples that the bread is his body and the wine, his blood. Paul, in 1 Corinthians, explains that Jesus took bread

> and when he had given thanks, he broke it, and said, "This is my body which is for you. Do this in remembrance of me." In the same way also the cup, after supper, saying, "This cup is the new covenant in my blood. Do this, as often as you drink it, in remembrance of me." (1 Corinthians 11:24–5)

At this extremely poignant moment, Jesus asks his disciples to eat bread and drink wine in remembrance of him. From the time of Jesus onwards, the Eucharist (which means thanksgiving) or the Lord's Supper became a central Christian ritual.

Once again, we find that all three members of the Trinity are involved in the Eucharist. The Catechism explains:

> "We must therefore consider the Eucharist as:
> – thanksgiving and praise to the *Father*;
> – the sacrificial memorial of *Christ* and his Body;
> – the presence of Christ by the power of his Word and of his *Spirit*."[15]

It is a thanksgiving because we are celebrating the works of creation and salvation. God has given us the opportunity to become children of God by the gracious acts of creation and redemption. The memorial is not "merely the recollection of past

COUNCIL OF TRENT

Held by Roman Catholics in response to Protestantism. Considered by Roman Catholics to be a major reforming council.

events"[16] but the making present of Christ's sacrifice on the cross. And it is this work of "making present" that the Holy Spirit brings about. It is at this point we find the Catechism talking about transubstantiation. The Catechism quotes from the ruling at the **Council of Trent**, which was held between 1545 and 1563:

> The Council of Trent summarizes the Catholic faith by declaring: "Because Christ our Redeemer said that it was truly his body that he was offering under the species of bread, it has always been the conviction of the Church of God, and this holy Council now declares again, that by the consecration of the bread and wine there takes place a change of the whole substance of the bread into the substance of the body of Christ our Lord and of the whole substance of the wine into the substance of his blood. This change the holy Catholic Church has fittingly and properly called transubstantiation."[17]

Transubstantiation is grounded in Aristotelian terminology and philosophy. Aristotle (384–322 BCE) distinguished between "substance" and "accidents." The essential nature is "substance," while the shape, color, and general outward appearance are "accidents." Using this distinction, although the appearance of bread and wine remains the same, it does, nevertheless, become the body and blood of Jesus. The Eucharist, then, is a miracle of divine grace. In the act of taking the Eucharist, one takes into one's body the divine and redeeming power of God in Christ.

Reformation and Protestant Views

One of Martin Luther's targets at the Reformation was penance. It was the practice of indulgences that provoked his ire. However, as his views developed, he became increasingly suspicious of the use of Aristotelian philosophy in Christian doctrine. In *Babylonian Captivity of the Church* (1520), he insists that there are not seven sacraments. At the start of the tract, he implies there are three (baptism, Eucharist and penance), but towards the end concludes:

Nevertheless, it has seemed proper to restrict the name of sacrament to those promises which have signs attached to them. The remainder, not being bound to signs, are bare promises. Hence there are, strictly speaking, but two sacraments in the church of God – baptism and the bread. For only in these two do we find both the divinely instituted sign and the promise of forgiveness of sins. The sacrament of penance, which I added to these two, lacks the divinely instituted visible sign, and is, as I have said, nothing but a way and a return to baptism.[18]

So for Luther, a sacrament needs to be a "divinely instituted visible sign." The sign is the "water" (in the case of baptism) and the "bread" and "wine" (in the case of the Eucharist). On baptism, Luther is as equally committed as Roman Catholics to infant baptism. On the Eucharist, he wants Christ present in both the accidents and the substance. He draws an analogy with the doctrine of the Incarnation: in the same ways Godhead permeated all of humanity so Christ permeates all the bread. He writes:

And why could not Christ include his body in the substance of the bread just as well as in the accidents? In red-hot iron, for instance, the two substances, fire and iron, are so mingled that every part is both iron and fire. Why is it not even more possible that the body of Christ be contained in every part of the substance of the bread?[19]

Luther then believes in the "real presence", sometimes known as "consubstantiation." For Luther, because Jesus states that "this is my body" in the Bible, it must be so. The power of the sacraments is made possible by God and received by the faith of the believer.

John Calvin took the line that the sacraments were signs of a reality that God had already performed. When defining a sacrament, he writes:

It seems to me that a simple and proper definition would be to say that it is an outward sign by which the Lord seals on our consciences the promises of his good will towards us in order to sustain the weakness of our faith; and we in turn attest our piety towards him in the presence of the Lord and of his angels and before men.[20]

The emphasis here is that sacraments are signs of work that God has already done. So, says Calvin,

baptism should be a token and proof of our cleansing; or (the better to explain what I mean) it is like a sealed document to confirm to us that all our sins are so abolished, remitted, and effaced that they can never come to his sight, be recalled or charged against us . . . Accordingly, they who regarded baptism as nothing but a token and mark by which we confess our religion before men, as soldiers bear the insignia of their commander as a mark of their profession, have not weighed what was the chief point of baptism. It is to receive baptism with this promise: "He who believes and is baptized will be saved." (Mark 16:16)[21]

ULRICH ZWINGLI (1484–1531)

Zwingli was born in Switzerland; he was educated at Berne, Vienna, and Basle and became a priest in 1506. He was an admirer of the work and teaching of Erasmus and was a major player in the Swiss Reformation, which was partly provoked by his lectures on the New Testament, which were delivered in 1519. He came to prominence in Zurich, where he won arguments against the Roman Catholic's Vicar General Joann Faber. Thanks to the support of the city, he continued to promote his Protestant views. He married Anna Meyer in 1524. Some of his most distinctive theological views were developed later in his life, including the claim that the Eucharist should be understood as entirely symbolic. In defending these views, he found himself periodically under attack. It was while he was marching under a military banner as the army's chaplain that he was killed on October 11, 1531.

This, then, is a nuanced account. Baptism is not simply a public witness, but remains a mechanism that witnesses to a work that God has performed. On the Eucharist, the bread and wine witness to a spiritual reality of redemption. In both cases, for Calvin, the agent at work is the Holy Spirit.

Ulrich Zwingli is the most radical of the big three reformers. For him, the sacraments are just "signs or ceremonials."[22] When baptizing a baby, one is simply saying this: "with this external sign you are to dedicate and pledge them to the name of the Father, the Son and the Holy Ghost, and to teach them to observe all the things that I have committed to you."[23] And on the Eucharist, he finds it absurd to say that "Christ is literally there." It would mean that Christ is literally "broken, and pressed with the teeth."[24] Instead we should interpret the phrase "this is my body" more metaphorically. It is analogous, explains Zwingli, to a wife who shows someone her husband's ring and says "This is my late husband."[25] In short, the Eucharist is a memorial.

While Luther, Calvin, and Zwingli were comfortable with infant baptism, it was the Anabaptists who insisted that it was wrong. Anabaptists emerged both in Saxony and Switzerland during this period of upheaval and reformation. **Menno Simons**, writing in 1539, claims that:

Young children are without understanding and unteachable; therefore baptism cannot be administered to them without perverting the ordinance of the Lord, misusing His exalted name, and doing violence to His holy Word. In the New Testament no ceremonies for infants are enjoined, for it treats both in doctrines and sacraments with those who

MENNO SIMONS (1496–1561)

Menno Simons was the founder of the Mennonite Church. He was a Catholic priest in Dutch Friesland, but left the Catholic Church in 1536 to become Anabaptist (i.e. insisting on believers' baptism rather than infant baptism). His movement has a strong commitment to non-violence.

have ears to hear and hearts to understand . . . Faith does not follow from baptism, but baptism follows from faith.[26]

Anabaptists (whose modern heir is the Baptist denomination) believed that a valid baptism involves an adult who wants to confess Christ in a public witness. It is simply a sign of a work of grace already performed in a life. It is not a vehicle of that grace.

Standing Back

It is the Roman Catholic theologian Edward Schillebeeckx who has led the way in the modern debate. For Schillebeeckx, sacraments should be understood as a deep encounter with Christ. The disciples around the historical Jesus had a sacramental encounter with God all the time. Schillebeeckx writes: "The man Jesus, as the personal visible realization of the divine grace of redemption, is *the* sacrament, the primordial sacrament, because this man, the Son of God himself, is intended by the Father to be in his humanity, the only way to the actuality of redemption."[27] Given Christ has ascended, today we now receive that encounter through the seven sacraments. Schillebeeckx writes: "In an earthly embodiment which we can see and touch, the heavenly Christ sacramentalizes both his continual intercession for us and his active gift of grace. Therefore the sacraments are the visible realization on earth of Christ's mystery of saving worship."[28]

The modern debate around the nature of the Eucharist has been dominated by the introduction of two new terms to the debate. The first is *transfinalization*, coined by F. J. Leenhardt in 1955. Joseph Martos helpfully explains:

The basic idea behind it was that the "final reality" of any created thing is determined by its maker and not by what it is made of. A carpenter who made a cabinet, for example, made something whose final reality was a cabinet even though he made it out of wood.

He had actually produced something new, since before only the wood existed but now there was a new reality, brought into being through the intention of the creator.[29]

So if you apply this idea to the Eucharist, then at the end of the process of consecration, the purpose of the bread and wine has changed. At the start of the service it is just "bread" and "wine," but by the end the creator, who is Jesus Christ, has made body and blood.

The second term is *transignification*, which stresses significance and meaning. On this view certain actions are symbolic. A slap across the face is on one level just a hand touching a face; but on another level it can represent anger, even fury. The latter explanation is as real as the former: indeed one would completely misunderstand the slap across the face if one interpreted it as just a hand touching a face. So by analogy sacraments transignify a human and divine reality. On the human level, the practice of baptism involves a baby being marked by the sign of the cross with water; on a divine level, it is the life being transformed by grace. The latter is as real as the former.

These two terms are taking the debate to a new level. It should be completely clear we are not talking about cannibalism – this is not the consumption of a human person. In fact Christians do not consume the bread and wine for food, but to enable the divine life to become part of their lives.

Keith Ward is very helpful on this point. He has clearly been influenced by the debate on transignification. Ward argues that one completely misunderstands the Eucharist if it is seen as simply bread and wine. It is symbolic; but in an echo of Paul Tillich, he then explains "a symbol, in this sense, participates in and conveys the reality which it symbolizes."[30] When Jesus initiates the practice, he

> gives the disciples a foreshadowing symbol of that revealing and redeeming act. The broken bread presents both the sacrifice of the faithful servant and the divine passion. The wine originates a new covenant, sealed by the sacrifice of Jesus, already completed in intention, by which the life of the eternal Word begins to transform the lives of men and women. Every subsequent celebration of that supper makes present the same reality, whose significance is greatly enriched by knowledge of the resurrection and outpouring of the Spirit.[31]

The reality of the redeeming work of God, according to Ward, is made present every time we celebrate the supper. Ward believes that there is a real change in the bread and wine. However, unlike many mechanical accounts of the sacraments, he wants to advocate a relational model. He starts by suggesting that we need to revisit the meaning of the bread.

> A piece of bread, when perceived by a human consciousness, is not just a chemical compound. It takes on a complex set of symbolic associations. It is something to be eaten,

with a certain taste and texture, perhaps to be shared, a product of sowing, growing, reaping, and baking, and so of a joining of natural forces with human cultivation. The chemical compound takes on the properties of its causal origin, its intended use, its relation to human senses, and its social context.[32]

He objects strongly to the view that these additional properties are not really part of the bread. Indeed Ward argues the property of "having been prepared in order to be eaten"[33] is part of its Platonic Form. If this point is conceded, then Ward comes to the heart of his argument:

> One might then say that, if bread is used in a ritual context, its essence (its substance in the sense of that which defines what it essentially is) is significantly changed. The mode of preparation remains the same, and yet part of that preparation becomes its setting apart by an act of blessing. By that act, it is consecrated to God set apart from common use. It is no longer ordinary bread, and its intended purpose becomes quite different.[34]

The intended purpose is to enable the divine life to become part of the worshipper. The social context, purpose, and perception of the bread has all changed. For Ward, this can be called "transubstantiation." He writes, "If one means that the essential nature of the bread has been changed, even though all its essential properties remain the same."[35] And it has objectively changed: God has made it possible for the divine life to be "truly expressed and conveyed by the rite."[36]

How is it possible for Christ to be present in the sacrament? Ward suggests that the basic operation is the same as the Incarnation. In the Incarnation, the Eternal Word (the second person of the Trinity) becomes present in the human life of Jesus. In the Eucharist, the Eternal Word becomes present in the bread and wine. Ward writes:

> Even though the particular acts of the Word in Jesus are not exactly repeatable (there will never again be a young man teaching in a remote province of the Roman Empire) there is a sense in which the liberating action of the Word in Jesus can be repeated in different contexts. What is present on the altar is the eternal Christ in the particular form he took in Jesus, acting to convey divine love and power as he did in Jesus.[37]

So from the divine perspective, God, through the Spirit, is making the Eternal Word present in a distinctive way in the bread and wine. From the human perspective, the liturgical context and the prayer of consecration imbues the bread with a new and distinctive purpose. In so doing, we can properly speak of the bread changing into the body and blood of Jesus.

This chapter started by looking at sacraments in general and has culminated in focusing on the Eucharist. This is right and proper in a textbook which is stressing how Christian theology provides an answer to the problem of evil and suffering. God's redemption was made possible by a cruel act of an occupying power against an innocent man. All Christians are required to remember the act and celebrate it afresh in the Eucharist. The Eucharist reminds us of that central paradox of Christianity: our salvation has been made possible by suffering. We remember the involvement of God in our suffering. We recognize how that suffering has transformed us. We remain confused about the reasons for suffering, yet recognize its power to change our lives.

QUESTIONS FOR REFLECTION AND DISCUSSION

1 How many sacraments do you think there are?
2 What do you think Jesus meant when, at the last supper, he said "this is my body" and "this is my blood"?
3 Can a modern person believe in transubstantiation?
4 What happens at baptism?

GLOSSARY

Catechism: (from a Greek word which means "to make hear, or to instruct.") An outline of Christian doctrine
Liturgy: (literally, the work of the people.) A term to describe structured worship
Sacraments: term used to describe certain basic Christian practices (Eucharist and baptism or, for Roman Catholics, an additional five). Traditionally defined as "an outward and visible sign of an inward and spiritual grace" (Book of Common Prayer)
Transubstantiation: the doctrine that the bread and the wine become the body and blood of Jesus

Notes

1 Joseph Martos, *Doors to the Sacred: A Historical Introduction to Sacraments in the Catholic Church*, revised edition (Liguori, MO: Liguori/Triumph, 2001), p. 4.
2 Ibid., p. 7.
3 *Catechism of the Catholic Church* (Mahwah, NJ: Paulist Press, 1994), p. 293.
4 Ibid., p. 288.
5 Ibid., p. 288.
6 Ibid., p. 288.
7 Ibid., p. 311.

8 Ibid., p. 311.

9 Ibid., p. 312.

10 Ibid., p. 321 (italics in the text).

11 Ibid., p. 319.

12 Ibid., p. 320 (italics in the text).

13 Ibid., p. 320.

14 Ibid., p. 321.

15 Ibid., p. 342.

16 Ibid., p. 343.

17 Ibid., p. 347.

18 Martin Luther, *Babylonian Captivity of the Church* (1520) found in James F. White, *Documents of Christian Worship: Descriptive and Interpretive Sources* (Louisville, KY: WJK, 1992), p. 131.

19 Ibid., p. 198.

20 John Calvin, *Institutes of the Christian Religion*, IV, 13, 1–26 (1559) found in White, *Documents of Christian Worship*, p. 132.

21 John Calvin, *Institutes of the Christian Religion*, IV, found in White, *Documents of Christian Worship*, p. 172.

22 Ulrich Zwingli, *Commentary on True and False Religion* (1525) found in White, *Documents of Christian Worship*, p. 132.

23 Ulrich Zwingli, *Of Baptism*, found in White, *Documents of Christian Worship*, pp. 170–1.

24 Ulrich Zwingli, *On the Lord's Supper*, found in White, *Documents of Christian Worship*, p. 201.

25 Ibid., p. 201.

26 Menno Simons, *Foundations of Christian Doctrine* (1539) found in White, *Documents of Christian Worship*, p. 169.

27 Edward Schillebeeckx, *Christ the Sacrament of the Encounter with God* (New York: Sheed & Ward, 1963), p. 15.

28 Ibid., p. 44.

29 Joseph Martos, *Doors to the Sacred: A Historical Introduction to Sacraments in the Catholic Church*, revised edition (Liguori, MO: Liguori/Triumph, 2001), p. 263.

30 Keith Ward, *Religion and Community* (Oxford: Oxford University Press, 2000), p. 194.

31 Ibid., pp. 195–6.

32 Ibid., p. 197.

33 Ibid., p. 197.

34 Ibid., p. 197.

35 Ibid., p. 198.

36 Ibid., p. 198.

37 Ibid., p. 199.

Chapter 11

RELIGIOUS
DIVERSITY:
WHAT IS
GOD UP TO?

LEARNING OUTCOMES

By the end of this chapter you should be able to:

- understand the challenge of religious diversity
- appreciate the three main positions in the debate

One aspect of this world, which is proving a real challenge, is living with religious diversity. Although one can overstate the problem of religious conflicts (there are often cultural, economic, and nationalist factors at work), it is true that there are plenty of examples of religious traditions that have problems in living together. Again, learning to live with religious diversity is an important part of the Christian doctrinal response to evil and suffering. And the challenge of living with religious diversity requires a thoughtful theological response.

Religious diversity has always been a problem. Ancient Israel had long been pre-occupied, so the sources say, with the assertion of exclusive rightness for its devotion to Yahweh and his Law, and the documents are full of attacks on those of other, i.e. false, religious allegiance. In the New Testament, there is both a confirmation of the rejection of pagan cults as idolatrous and a many-sided controversy about the question of the newness of the Christian faith. How far was it in conformity with Judaism? Had there been a radical break, or was there substantial continuity – and if the latter, then in what respects? In other words, was the faith that centered on Jesus a new dispensation or in some ways (what ways?) in continuity with the faith to be found in the Jewish scriptures?

As the Western Church developed, relations between the developing Christian tradition and other religions became more complex. Generally a commitment to the truth revealed in Christianity meant that those who disagreed needed to be confronted with their error. So the tradition is rich in vehement denunciations of Judaism.[1] However, this attitude also ran parallel with a willingness (whether deliberate or almost unconscious) to learn from and often build upon the insights of other traditions. Christianity was born into a Jewish culture which was strongly influenced by Hellenism (i.e. Greek culture). Platonism and Stoicism are two leading schools of Greek thought that significantly influenced the Christian faith. The fifth-century Bishop of Hippo, Augustine, explicitly acknowledges, in *The Confessions*, his debt to the Neo-platonists. Much later in the thirteenth century, the Dominican Friar, Thomas Aquinas, helped to reintroduce Aristotelian philosophy into the Church as a result of his wide reading of Islamic thinkers. For many Christian thinkers, the Church constantly has much to learn from non-Christian thinkers, as these two examples illustrate. The indebtedness has of course sometimes been conscious, sometimes virtually unconscious.

The combination of hostility combined with occasional accommodation and mutual influence probably characterized the Christian attitude to other religions right up until the start of this century. It was at this point that certain distinctively modern questions came to the fore.

Other Religions as a Problem

The twentieth century has seen a significant change in Christian attitudes to other religions. This was the century when "Religious Studies" as opposed to "Theology" became popular. (Convention uses the word "Theology" to denote the study of Christian theology, while Religious Studies refers to the study of a range of religions.) Instead of simply judging other traditions by the central doctrines of Christianity, the first task is understanding. Other faith traditions must be understood on their own terms. This tendency opened up a further set of problems. The ancient religions of India (rather inappropriately subsumed under the label "Hinduism") suddenly became more attractive: where the West had insisted for centuries that the world was a relatively recent creation, Hinduism found itself vindicated by contemporary science in believing that the world is millions of years old; and for all sorts of reasons the insistence in the West that a baby dying at two has enjoyed the same unique life as the person dying at seventy makes much less sense than reincarnation. When a religion comes to be treated on its own terms, it is no longer manifestly false or foolish.

So the first factor in shaping the problem of "other religions" was understanding the other on its own terms. The second factor was more philosophical; many Westerners, including Christians, had come to feel that they did not know for sure whether Christianity was the truth; in short there was a problem about epistemology (theory of knowledge). For the West it was chiefly the Scottish philosopher David Hume who created the problem. The argument was simple: a condition of knowledge is that we know with some certainty that something is true. Given that we know virtually nothing with that sort of certainty, we should stop using the category of "knowledge." Immanuel Kant talked about David Hume as "shattering his slumbers." For Hume, especially, knowledge of God was particularly problematic. How can you know whether it is a triune God or an Allah or a Hindu Brahman underpinning everything?

With the reliability of Scripture being tested by the critical study of the texts and with the reliability of the Church being undermined by a critical study of history, the Church seemed to many to be no longer sure how best to justify faith with authority. This in itself created a further problem: if Christianity is true, then why did God not make it more obvious? Were the old authorities (scripture, Church decisions, papacy) capable of exercising their traditional weight? The problem of epistemology became more acute when set alongside religious diversity. There are so many options: it is not obvious which one is the truth at all.

The third factor which shaped the problem for Christianity was internal to Christian doctrine. Traditionally, Christians do not simply believe that they hold a true description of the way ultimate reality is, but also such knowledge is essential for salvation. In short, one will be condemned to hell unless one is a Christian. However, although the Christian religion is the largest religion in the world, it still leaves at least 68 percent of the population who are not Christians. Is a loving God really going to condemn the majority of people to hell? Christianity here had an internal problem – in terms of reconciling some of its long-held but contradictory tenets and traditions.

The traditional response has been to insist that the Church should preach the Gospel to these other cultures and that people should be encouraged to convert. Studies have shown that only a small minority of people convert from one tradition to another. Religion is closely linked with cultural identity; converting from one tradition to another is often interpreted as an act of betrayal. To put it crudely, a devout Roman Catholic grandmother of traditional outlook may understand the lapsed grandson who is "rebelling" against the Church, but will be deeply upset if he converts to Anglicanism, or even worse, Islam. It is because we feel committed to our families and cultural communities that conversion is so difficult – unless there has been some kind of cultural liberation.

So there are three factors which have come to pose the problem of religious diversity in a particularly acute form, namely (a) a growth in our understanding of other traditions, (b) a belief that it is difficult to know for sure which tradition has the truth, and (c) the problem of a loving God who is presented traditionally as condemning large numbers of people to hell simply because of their commitment to their culture and faith.

The Christian theology of other religions has become, in recent decades especially, a well-established branch of Christian systematic theology. Any theological account must provide some explanation within the Christian schema of the role and status of the majority of the human race. The recent debate has been shaped by the British philosopher John Hick, whose student Alan Race,[2] created the taxonomy that has come to be dominant. This taxonomy suggested three different Christian responses: pluralism which insists that all religions are equally salvific (i.e. able to save), inclusivism which believes that Christianity is the true religion, yet other religions are discovering the truths of Christianity without realizing it, and exclusivism which insists that conscious knowledge of and commitment to Christianity is essential for salvation.

These three options will now be considered in detail.

The Pluralist Hypothesis

John Hick started formulating his pluralist hypothesis as a direct result of his encounter with other faith traditions. It was as the H. G. Woods Professor at the University of Birmingham that he started developing links with the local faith communities. In *God Has Many Names* he compares various prayers taken from the Sikh, Hindu, Islamic, and Christian traditions. He notes the striking similarities and then argues that it is unlikely that only one tradition has effective prayers or that there is a different recipient for the prayers of each tradition. Given this, the best explanation is that each tradition is praying to the one true God using the resources and language of that tradition.[3]

This is the heart of the pluralist hypothesis – a single reality that is accessed and partially revealed in all the major religions of the world. Over the next twenty years, Hick clarified the details.

To start with, Hick was advocating a "theistic pluralism." A single God, who was loving and good, was underpinning all the major faith traditions. He makes much in his earlier work of a contradiction embedded in Christianity: 1 Timothy 2:6 describes a God who "desires the salvation of all people," while John 14:6 insists that Jesus is the only way to salvation. If only one religion is salvific, then it cannot be true that God *effectively* desires the salvation of all people. The only way to overcome this contradiction is to believe that all religions are salvific.

"Theistic pluralism" works reasonably well for the Abrahamic faiths (i.e. Judaism, Islam, and Christianity). It might even, in certain ways, extend towards Hinduism, but it completely fails to cope with Buddhism. Buddhism takes innumerable different forms, but there are significant strands that hardly talk about "God" at all. God hardly figures in the four Noble Truths, which are the central teaching of the **Buddha**. So in Hick's Gifford Lectures, published as *An Interpretation of Religion*, he argues for a "Real" which no tradition can describe or claim to know exactly. In this way, the significance of Nirvana in Buddhism can be accommodated in the experience of the Real.

To explain this shift, Hick turns to the Kantian distinction between the noumenal and the phenomenal. The noumenal is knowledge of the divine as "it is in itself." The phenomenal is knowledge of the divine as "it appears to mind." The noumenal is inaccessible. All we know is that each culture is interpreting an "objective" experience of the Real in its own language and concepts. We cannot claim any particular culture is more or less right, because none of us can transcend our own culture and find out exactly what the Real is really like.

Now there are a whole host of obvious questions facing Hick, which, to his credit, he confronts with complete clarity. The first is: how does Hick know that the major

BUDDHA

The founder of Buddhism. His life is shrouded in mystery and tradition. Born in Northern India in the sixth century BCE, he was a "prince" who renounced the life of luxury for a quest for enlightenment. Having explored a variety of "Hindu" schools, he arrived at a distinctive account of Enlightenment, which stressed the cultivation of certain dispositions that cope with suffering.

world faiths are all viable means of accessing the Real? He starts by acknowledging that the best explanation for the global phenomenon of religious experience is to assume that there is an objective reality which is being accessed.[4] In addition, he suggests that if only one tradition was effective in accessing the Real, then presumably that tradition would be more effective in producing saints (i.e. for Hick, persons who are ego-transcending Reality centered).[5] Empirically this does not seem to be the case. Insofar as one can judge, most traditions have been both deeply damaging and at the same time effective in saint production. Christianity is the tradition responsible for both the Crusades and the spirituality of St Francis of Assisi. So, argues Hick, it looks as if all world religions are equally able to produce saints and therefore are vehicles for the transforming power of the Real.

This flows into the second issue. On what criteria does Hick exclude traditions? Can witchcraft or the Branch Davidians become vehicles for the Real? Hick is careful here. Traditions that can be shown to be ethically destructive are not vehicles of the Real; so Nazism, insofar as it has certain similarities with a religion, is excluded on the grounds that it arrived at conclusions that are fundamentally opposed to the growing awareness of ethical insight in the major world faiths.

He provides a further argument that appeals to the longevity of, at least, the big five (Hinduism, Buddhism, Judaism, Christianity, and Islam). He makes use of Karl Jaspers' concept of the "axial period"; a golden age (starting *c.* 800 BCE) when in different parts of the world, at about the same time, a common discovery about objective moral obligations that are grounded in the transcendent confronts humanity. The combination of Socrates in Ancient Greece, the Upanishads in India, Confucius in China and the eighth-century prophets of Israel, gave birth to the main traditions that shaped the major world faiths. For Hick, it is likely that traditions emerging out of this period are likely to be valid vehicles of the Real.

The third issue is the status of distinctive doctrines within each religion: so Judaism believes that Yahweh gave a chosen people a land; Islam believes that the **Qur'an** is the final and definitive revelation from God; and Christians insist that Jesus is the Incarnation of God. What is the status of these doctrines in Hick's scheme? His position is simple: any distinctive doctrine that conflicts with the pluralist hypothesis must now be interpreted differently from its traditional ways. As a Christian minister, he has attempted to offer alternative interpretations of certain key Christian doctrines. He was the editor of *The Myth of God Incarnate*. This volume formulates a range of arguments; some emerging from Biblical criticism (many New Testament scholars think it unlikely that Jesus claimed to be God or that the earliest texts about Jesus thought of him in such a way), but others stressing rather more the implications of certain other doctrines and insights. It is the latter point that Hick makes central. He writes, "[W]e have to present Jesus and the Christian life in a way compatible with our new recognition of the validity of the other great world faiths as being also, at

QUR'AN

The Qur'an is the holy book of Islam. Revealed to the Prophet Muhammad in Mecca and Medina (both in Saudi Arabia) in the seventh century CE. The text is written in Arabic and believed by Muslims to be the very Word of God.

their best, ways of salvation. We must therefore not insist upon Jesus being always portrayed within the interpretative framework built around him by centuries of Western thought."[6] For Hick, the pluralist hypothesis requires that we think of Jesus as a person who *shows us* God rather than *is* God: what Keith Ward, in *A Vision to Pursue*, calls a "functional" Christology rather than an "Ontological" one. Paul Knitter, who develops Hick's arguments, suggests that the "exclusive" claims made for Jesus reflect the enthusiasm of Christians – it is analogous to the language used between lovers.[7] "My partner is the most beautiful person in the world" is rarely meant literally, nor is it always (ever?) verifiable; for most of us, it simply means my love for this person is so significant that I feel that my partner is very beautiful and the overwhelming object of my attention and devotion.

John Hick sets forth his hypothesis with commendable clarity. It offers an account of religious experience and religious diversity that makes sense of many puzzling features. However, it is interesting to note that the academy (not to mention the churches!) has tended to be suspicious of his position. And this is for good reason: central to Christian epistemology (how we know what God is like) and also theodicy (why God allows evil) is the claim that Jesus was really God. In addition, Hick's accommodation of all this diversity has left us knowing nothing about the nature of the "Real." Is the Real personal or non-personal? We do not know. We do not even know whether God is good or bad. The ideology of modernity is operating here. As Gavin D'Costa puts it:

> Hick's "pluralism" masks the advocation of liberal modernity's "god" in this case a form of ethical agnosticism. If ethical agnostics were to suggest that the conflict between religions would be best dealt with by everyone becoming an ethical agnostic, not only would this fail to deal with plurality, in so much as it fails to take plurality seriously, it would also fail to take religious cultures seriously by dissolving them into instrumental mythical configurations best understood within modernity's mastercode.[8]

D'Costa is right: Hick solves the challenge of religious diversity by asking us all to become ethical agnostics. It is not going to work. It will not provide a significant contribution to peace making. So we turn now to consider the "exclusivist" alternative.

Exclusivism

Exclusivism is characteristic of most conservative forms of religion. Amongst Christians, the strongest defenders are found amongst conservative evangelicals. They almost always start with a commitment to (a) truth and (b) revelation. Truth is important because they reject the tendency of pluralists to insist that contradictory religions can all be vehicles of the Real. Muslims believe that Jesus was (no more than) a prophet of Allah; Christians insist he is the Incarnation of God. If you accept the correspondence theory of truth (namely, a correspondence with "reality" determines the truth or falsity of a statement), then these two assertions cannot both be true. One must be true and the other false.

If one decides that there are good reasons to believe in the Incarnation, then pluralism is not an option. The claim that in "reality" God became human in Jesus means that at least in one respect Christianity has knowledge of the Real which is both distinctive and superior. This links to the second commitment made by exclusivists. Knowledge of God, as opposed to guesswork or speculation, explains Karl Barth, depends on "revelation." Humans can guess about the Real as much as they like, but it does not become knowledge unless the Real breaks in and reveals its nature to us. All religions base their claims for knowledge on revelation; in most cases, this takes the form of an authoritative text. The point is that unless there is some form of authoritative revelation, one cannot make a claim to knowledge.

One problem facing Hick is that he doesn't seem to know very much about the "Real." To accommodate Buddhism, he cannot know whether the Real is personal or non-personal. All Hick has is an "objective" something, that is applying global pressure which generates religious experience; for many this seems tantamount to agnosticism.

But how does one know which revelation is the truth? Different exclusivists provide different answers. Some attempt to offer criteria to distinguish between different positions. For example, Harold Netland sets out ten principles that provide criteria to distinguish between different religions. He lists those principles as follows, where P stands for Principle and R stands for a particular religion:

P1: If a defining belief p of a religion R is self-contradictory then p is false.

P2: If two or more defining beliefs of R are mutually contradictory at least one of them must be false.

P3: If a defining belief p of R is self-defeating it cannot reasonably be accepted as true.

P4: If the defining beliefs of R are not coherent in the sense of providing a unified perspective on the world, then R cannot plausibly be regarded as true.

P5: Any religious worldview which is unable to account for fundamental phenomena associated with a religious orientation or which cannot provide adequate answers to central questions in religion should not be accepted as true.

P6: If a defining belief p of R contradicts well-established conclusions in other domains, and if R cannot justify doing so, then p should be rejected as probably false.

P7: If a defining belief p of R depends upon a belief in another domain (e.g. history) which there is good reason to reject as false, then there is good reason to reject p as probably false.

P8: If one or more defining beliefs of R are incompatible with widely accepted and well-established moral values and principles; or if R includes among its essential practices or rites activities which are incompatible with basic moral values and practices, then there is good reason for rejecting R as false.

P9: If the defining beliefs of R entail the denial of the objectivity of basic moral values and principles; or if they entail the denial of the objective distinction between right and wrong, good and evil, then there is good reason for rejecting R as false.

P10: If R is unable to provide adequate answers to basic questions about the phenomena of moral awareness this provides good reasons for rejecting R as false.[9]

Having provided this extensive set of criteria, which includes coherence, historical, and ethical principles, Netland then concludes triumphantly: ". . . I should state that the reason I believe one is justified in accepting the Christian faith as true is because it is the only worldview that satisfies the requirements of all the above criteria."[10]

Most contemporary theologians are not persuaded by this approach. The problem with criteria is that the tradition you are in will tend to determine which ones are chosen. There is a danger of creating a mutually affirming circle.

Therefore most academic exclusivists prefer the route suggested by Lindbeck. In his highly influential book, *The Nature of Doctrine*, Lindbeck argues for the "cultural-linguistic" approach to religion, where "emphasis is placed on those respects in which religions resemble languages and together with their correlative forms of life are thus similar to cultures."[11] He sets this approach against experiential-expressivism, which is very similar to Hick's pluralism, and cognitive propositionalism, which is very similar to Netland's exclusivism. For him, the cultural-linguistic approach comes into its own when it comes to making sense of other religions. On the unsurpassability of a tradition, the experiential-expressivist is able to claim "that there is only one religion which has the concepts and categories that enable it to refer to the religious object, i.e., to whatever in fact is more important than anything else in the universe,"[12] although he does note that traditions on this view will almost certainly embody both true and false claims about the nature of the religious object. On interfaith dialogue, he argues that there are reasons internal to the Christian tradition which justify its position. For example, writes Lindbeck, "it can be argued in a variety of ways that Christian churches are called upon to imitate their Lord by selfless service to neighbors quite apart from the question of whether this promotes conversions."[13] And on the salvation of other religious traditions, Lindbeck suggests the following: "The proposal is that dying itself be pictured as the point at which every human being is ultimately and expressly confronted by the gospel, by the crucified and risen Lord. It is only then that the final decision is made for or against Christ; and this is true, not only of unbelievers but also of believers. All previous decisions, whether for faith or against faith, are preliminary."[14]

Lindbeck is a highly sophisticated "exclusivist." Religious schemes are analogous to "cultures." One learns the language and the form of life. The cosmic claims within a tradition need to be taken seriously. One accommodates other religious traditions by recognising that, for example, sharing the commandment to love your neighbour should be sufficient to compel dialogue; and the decision for or against Christ is ultimately made at the moment of death.

Many conservative evangelicals consider Lindbeck's maneuvering unnecessary. They start with "truth" and "revelation," and then work out the implications. The Biblical witness, they insist, teaches the following about religious diversity. First, many alternative traditions are guilty of idolatry, and are perhaps even inspired by a force of evil. Second, the Christian obligation is to preach the Gospel and attempt to convert those of other traditions. Third, apart from our confidence that the judge of the Earth shall do right, we should not try to speculate on matters that are not revealed; so we do not know exactly what will happen to those who have not heard, though Scripture certainly points us in certain directions.

The problems with exclusivism are overwhelming. It seems to forget that the central claim is that there is one God who is the creator of the whole world. Before Christ, this God was interested in the lives of humans who emerged on earth some 300,000 years ago. It is a denial of the doctrine of creation to imply that God's only interest was Abraham, the Jewish people, and then the Church. To confine God's activity and grace to Israel, and then slowly to Europe as Christendom developed is to advocate an attenuated God who is hardly deserving of the appellation "creator." In addition, anyone who gets to know people of other faith traditions finds countless examples of lives exhibiting, what the book of Galatians calls, "the fruit of the spirit" which is "love, joy, peace, patience, kindness, generosity, faithfulness, gentleness, and self-control" (Galatians 5:22–3). To account for this goodness, we need to recognize the work of the Spirit in these lives. Exclusivism is not only manifestly unjust, but also not true to the key themes of Christian doctrine.

Inclusivism

It is partly out of a sensitivity to the problem of the ignorant that many Christians are attracted to the third option. Inclusivism is the view that even though salvation is exclusively in Christ, faithful adherents of another faith tradition may be saved through Christ, even though they do not realize it in this world.

The best known exponent of Inclusivism is the Roman Catholic theologian Karl Rahner. He was enormously influential on Vatican II, which took his line. Rahner proposed four theses, of which the first three are the most significant. Rahner writes:

> 1st Thesis: We must begin with the thesis which follows, because it certainly represents the basis in the Christian faith of the theological understanding of other religions. This thesis states that Christianity understands itself as the absolute religion, intended for all men, which cannot recognise any other religion beside itself as of equal right . . .
>
> 2nd Thesis: Until the moment when the gospel really enters into the historical situation of an individual, a non-Christian religion (even outside the Mosaic religion) does not merely contain elements of a natural knowledge of God, elements, moreover, mixed up with human depravity which is the result of original sin and later aberrations. It contains also supernatural elements arising out of the grace which is given to men as a gratuitous gift on account of Christ. For this reason a non-Christian religion can be recognised as a lawful religion (although only in different degrees) without thereby denying the error and depravity contained in it . . .
>
> 3rd Thesis: If the second thesis is correct, then Christianity does not simply confront the member of an extra-Christian religion as a mere non-Christian but as someone who can and must already be regarded in this or that respect as an anonymous Christian.[15]

Rahner is attempting to "make sense" of the phenomenon of religious diversity. The first thesis stresses that it is part of Christian self-identification that we believe that Christianity is true. But then, given that Christians believe that God is active in the whole world, we must believe that God is active in all religious traditions. Granted this runs parallel with much error, sin, and self-deception, supernatural elements of those traditions are still not excluded. As it is therefore possible for a tradition to be "lawful," then it must be possible for such a tradition to be a means of salvation.

The use of the term "lawful" is deliberately drawing attention to the status of the Hebrew religion in the Old Testament. Christians who insist that salvation is only possible through conscious acknowledgment of Christ have a problem with all those in the Hebrew Bible. Abraham, Jacob, David, the prophets are all clearly "saved," despite not consciously acknowledging Christ during their lives. One traditional response to this problem is to follow the traditional interpretation of 1 Peter 3:19 in suggesting that between his death and resurrection, Jesus descended into hell and preached the gospel to the Old Testament patriarchs. One problem with this is that the passage in 1 Peter probably did not carry this sense. It is better to suggest that God's salvific power in the Cross extends beyond time to reach many lives without their realizing it. The traditional doctrine of Christ as God's Eternal Word suggests a mission extending throughout time and space.

The strongest argument for inclusivism, then, is that it is already embedded within the Christian tradition. When we try to make sense of the millions who have never heard of Christianity and all those who pre-date Christianity, we are led to postulate that God is able to save men and women without their realizing it.

Inclusivism represents the position of most more liberal Christians today. In the reply to John Hick and Paul Knitter's influential book *The Myth of Christian Uniqueness*,[16] called *Christian Uniqueness Reconsidered: The Myth of a Pluralist Theology of Religion*, almost all the contributors are inclusivists. Gavin D'Costa, in this volume, suggests in his own five theses that inclusivism is the natural expression of a Trinitarian world-view. D'Costa's five theses are:

> THESIS ONE: A trinitarian Christology guards against exclusivism and pluralism by dialectically relating the universal and the particular.
>
> THESIS TWO: Pneumatology allows the particularity of Christ to be related to the universal activity of God in the history of humankind.
>
> THESIS THREE: A Christocentric trinitarianism discloses loving relationship as the proper mode of being. Hence love of neighbor (which includes Hindus, Buddhists, and others) is an imperative for all Christians.
>
> THESIS FOUR: The normativity of Christ involves the normativity of crucified self-giving love. Praxis and dialogue.
>
> THESIS FIVE: The church stands under the judgement of the Holy Spirit, and if the Holy Spirit is active in the world religions, then the world religions are vital to Christian faithfulness.[17]

D'Costa's position is simple: exclusivists make much of Jesus (the second person of the Trinity), though not so much of Jesus as Logos, but lose sight of the Father and the Son: the Father who creates and sustains the whole world and the Spirit who "blows where it wills." Pluralists have a God (a Father) at the heart of the universe and sustaining everything that is, but have no revelation or knowledge of that God (in effect God the Son and God the Holy Spirit are missing). What we need is a Trinitarian understanding of God, which provides both an account of the nature of the love that we should demonstrate to others and a way of seeing how God interacts with other religions.

Critical of the Categories

Many theologians have found the categories that have dominated the debate problematic. Some have pointed out that they conflate a variety of different issues. On the one hand, the central question is soteriological: are those outside the Christian religion saved? On the other hand, that question cannot be answered without considering a whole range of related matters: which religion is true and how do you know which one is true or where and whether truth resides in the various great faiths? What about the status and significance of natural theology? What sort of knowledge of God is possible outside revelation?[18]

Consider, for example, the issue of truth. Anyone committed to the correspondence theory of truth will find themselves forced to a version of inclusivism. The correspondence theory states that "x is true if and only if x corresponds to the way things are in reality." So if Christians really believe that God, the creator of the universe, is a trinity, Father, Son, and Holy Spirit, then the trinitarian description of God must be better and more accurate than any other description of God. And if that is the case, then worshippers of other faith traditions might imagine that they are encountering Brahman or Allah or whatever, but in point of fact their encounter is with the triune God. This is a form of inclusivism.

Even a pluralist, at this point, operates as an inclusivist. Pluralists insist that religious believers may imagine that they are encountering a particular God, described in their tradition as, say a trinity, but in point of fact they are encountering a Real which transcends all particular descriptions. If the pluralist hypothesis is true, then it means that the vast majority of adherents of most religions are mistaken and the "symbol system" (i.e. the vocabulary embedded within a particular worldview) of pluralism is what the orthodox are really discovering. A commitment to the truth of pluralism, ironically, makes the pluralist a kind of inclusivist.

Granted, the inclusivism of pluralism only applies to "truth" and not to "soteriology," nevertheless Hick does provide a description of the way things are (albeit a highly attenuated one) which he believes is more accurate (corresponds more closely) than alternative accounts (i.e. those held by orthodox believers within each tradition).

Once one sees that the debate obscures a range of technical questions, then there are other options. Keith Ward has suggested a "soft pluralism" at the heart of his "open orthodoxy." Ward is unhappy with Hick's pluralism because it seems to rest on a "pragmatic theory of truth."[19] Instead Ward wants to talk about more or less adequate accounts of ultimate reality and to say that all traditions contain some false beliefs. He rejects the label inclusivist because an inclusivist assumes that his or her tradition includes the best of other traditions, while a soft pluralist believes that other traditions have insights not known (or perhaps not known sufficiently well) within one's own.

There are others who have suggested that the traditional paradigm is much more problematic than has been recognized. Mark Heim in a thoughtful book called *Salvations* argues that the triune God will bring about the differently conceived "salvations" for each tradition. For Heim, there are real differences between traditions. And it therefore matters which tradition one is in. Kenneth Surin in a brilliantly provocative article, suggests that pluralism is analogous to the infamous McDonald's hamburger. In much the same way that McDonald's sweeps the world, eradicating difference, and offering the same bland global food, so Hick's pluralism does the same thing. So Surin writes,

> The McDonald's hamburger is the first universal food, but the people – be they from La Paz, Bombay, Cairo or Brisbane – who eat the McDonald's hamburger also consume the American way of life with it. Equally, the adherents of the world ecumenism canvassed by the religious pluralists align themselves with a movement that is universal, but they too consume a certain way of life. Not quite the American way of life itself . . . , but a single, overarching way of life which has become so pervasive that the American way of life is today simply its most prominent and developed manifestation: namely, the life of a world administered by global media and information networks, international agencies and multinational corporations.[20]

For Surin the whole question requires location. It represents the triumph of the Western values of tolerance and imperialism. Instead of imposing a pluralist description of other faiths on the rest of the world, we should listen and politically empower other faith traditions and free them from the tyranny of American power. The theological problem, argues Surin, needs to be eased out of our line of vision: the political problem is much more significant. We need to become "post-pluralistic."[21]

Moving the Debate Forward

The taxonomy of "pluralism, inclusivism, and exclusivism" remains a useful introduction to the issues. Pluralism is a problem for most religious traditions. The particular truth claims made within each tradition are central to its identity. The Qur'an is central to Islamic identity; and the Qur'an certainly does not teach Hick-type pluralism! The Incarnation and Trinity are key to the Christian understanding of God; and no Church is planning to surrender such key doctrines.

Inclusivism is not popular in Interfaith circles. Bilal Sambur – a Muslim – is typical when he writes about Rahner's concept of the "anonymous Christian": "This concept does not have any contribution to interfaith relations, because people have freely chosen religion as their independent religious identity. Furthermore, that concept includes the disrespectful approach to human freedom and humiliates the religion of the other."[22] What Sambur ignores is that the equivalent of Rahner's concept is found in the Islamic doctrine of "people of the book." When the Qur'an affirms Christianity and Judaism as traditions of the book, it means that although Islam has the complete truth, Christianity and Judaism have a partial insight into that truth.

Given that any commitment to the truth of a tradition will entail some form of inclusivism to explain the phenomenon of disagreement, it is not surprising that such devices are found in all the major world faiths. The *Bhagavad Gita* for example is explicit: the followers of other gods are really discovering Krishna. Judaism talks about the Noachide Laws that provide a mechanism for gentiles to have a covenantal relationship with their creator. Islam as we have noted has the "people of the book," while Christians have come to talk about "anonymous Christians" and formerly saw Christ the eternal Logos as having inspired both prophets and Greek philosophers.

However, inclusivism is inclined to suggest that we are all simply trapped in our traditions. It does assume that a tradition "includes" or "embraces" the other. Ward's "soft pluralism" is helpful here. Our growing historical and philosophical sensitivity has made us much more aware of the diversity within traditions. For example, there are strands within the Christian tradition which affirm panentheism, which has striking similarities with certain Hindu strands. Broadly "liberal" strands, those that take seriously the achievement of the Enlightenment, have more in common with liberals in other traditions than the conservatives in their own tradition. Liberal Christians and Jews often find much common ground.

Our historical sensitivity makes us realize that all traditions have been influenced by other traditions. Christianity was born out of a combination of Hellenistic influences and Judaism. St Thomas Aquinas in the thirteenth century learnt about Aristotle from Islamic thinkers and writers. Buddhism is clearly linked to Hinduism. And Sikhism emerged out of the clash between Hindu and Islamic cultures.

Learning of God from the other has always characterized our traditions, however little people like to recognize it. Continuing to do so is a social and political necessity.

Conclusion

Pluralism and Exclusivism are both temptations which will continue to exacerbate conflict between traditions. Pluralists are insisting we become "ethical agnostics." In their conceit, they imply that world peace depends upon such a position. However, this excludes every conservative believer in every tradition, which is by far the vast majority. Exclusivists ignore the dynamics in their own tradition that obliges us to reach out and recognize the work of God in other faith traditions.

So as with all traditions, it is a version of inclusivism which is most helpful. Ward is right: our version of inclusivism must recognize the fact of truths beyond and outside the Christian tradition. We can learn of God from a Muslim and a Buddhist. Indeed, we are obliged to do so.

Understood in this way, we remain located in and belonging to our tradition. We have an obligation to work hard to understand and learn from the other. And we should do so because we need to learn of God from these traditions. As we shall see, one's destiny in the life hereafter is not determined by the tradition with which one happens to identify. It is all much more complicated.

This sort of Christian theology of other religions offers the possibility of constructive, mature relations between the traditions. In offering that possibility, then once again we have a constructive response to religious diversity, which creates the possibility of peaceful relations between the traditions.

QUESTIONS FOR REFLECTION AND DISCUSSION

1 Are you a pluralist, inclusivist, or exclusivist? Explain why.
2 Can you be a pluralist and a Christian?
3 If you were a Muslim or a Jew, which position would you prefer a Christian to take?
4 Why did God allow so many religions to emerge?

GLOSSARY

Noumenal: a technical term used in philosophy and central to the work of Immanual Kant, which describes the world as it is "in itself"
Phenomenal: a technical term in philosophy which describes the world as "it appears to mind"

Notes

1 See Dan Cohn-Sherbok's comprehensive survey of Christian anti-Semitism in *The Crucified Jew* (London: Fount, 1992).
2 See Alan Race, *Christian and Religious Pluralism* (London: SCM Press, 1983).
3 See John Hick, *God Has Many Names* (Basingstoke: Macmillan, 1980), chapter 4.
4 See John Hick, *An Interpretation of Religion* (Basingstoke: Macmillan, 1989), chapter 13.
5 Ibid., p. 303.
6 John Hick, "Jesus and the world religions," in John Hick (ed.) *The Myth of God Incarnate* (London: SCM Press, 1977), p. 182.

7 Paul Knitter, *No Other Name? A Critical Study of Christian Attitudes to Other Religions* (London: SCM Press, 1985).

8 Gavin D'Costa, *The Meeting of Religions and the Trinity* (Edinburgh: T. & T. Clark, 2000), p. 26.

9 Harold Netland, *Dissonant Voices. Religious Pluralism* (Grand Rapids, MI, and Leicester: Eerdmans and Apollos, 1991), pp. 192–3. Keith Yandell is another philosopher who has suggested a slightly different list of rational criteria which can be used to evaluate religions. See Keith Yandell, *Christianity and Philosophy* (Grand Rapids, MI: Eerdmans, 1984). For a good discussion of this approach see Brad Stetson, *Pluralism and Particularity in Religious Belief* (Westport: Praeger, 1994).

10 Ibid., p. 193.

11 George Lindbeck, *The Nature of Doctrine. Religion and Theology in a Postliberal Age* (London: SPCK, 1984), pp. 17–18.

12 Ibid., p. 50.

13 Ibid., p. 54.

14 Ibid., p. 59.

15 Karl Rahner, *Theological Investigations*, vol. v (Oxford: Oxford University Press, 1994), pp. 118, 121–5, 127, 131–2.

16 John Hick and Paul Knitter (eds.), *The Myth of Christian Uniqueness* (London: SCM, 1987).

17 Gavin D'Costa, "Christ, the Trinity, and religious plurality," in Gavin D'Costa (ed.), *Christian Uniqueness Reconsidered. The Myth of a Pluralistic Theology of Religions* (Maryknoll, NY: Orbis, 1990), pp. 16–26. In a later book, Gavin D'Costa argues that inclusivism collapses into a version of exclusivism that concedes that non-Christians can be redeemed. See D'Costa, *The Meeting of Religions and the Trinity* (Edinburgh: T. & T. Clark, 2000), p. 22. Just as an aside, I do not see why D'Costa does not recognize that many of the more liberal forms of exclusivism collapse into inclusivism. Inclusivity does capture the theme of the Trinitarian account that he develops later in the book.

18 This is the theme of my article called "Creating options: shattering the 'exclusivist, inclusivist, and pluralist' paradigm," *New Blackfriars*, 74 (867) (1993): 33–40. See also Gavin D'Costa's reply to my article which follows that article.

19 Keith Ward, *Religion and Revelation: A Theology of Revelation in the World's Religions* (Oxford: Oxford University Press, 1994), p. 310.

20 Ken Surin, "A 'politics of speech'. Religious pluralism in the age of the McDonald's hamburger," in Gavin D'Costa (ed.), *Christian Uniqueness Reconsidered. The Myth of a Pluralistic Theology of Religions* (Maryknoll, NY: Orbis, 1990), p. 201.

21 Ibid., p. 209.

22 Bilal Sambur, "Is interfaith prayer possible?" in *World Faiths Encounter* 23 (1999): 30.

Chapter 12
HOPE
BEYOND
THE GRAVE

LEARNING OUTCOMES

By the end of this chapter you should be able to:

- understand the centrality of the resurrection of Jesus in a Christian account of life after death
- understand the author's argument for animal immortality

STRUCTURE

- Accounts of life after death in the different religions
- The Christian tradition – the Resurrection of Jesus, Jesus as a model of the life to come
- A redeemed creation – hell

A vitally important part of the doctrinal response to the problem of evil is the idea that this life is not everything. We are not complex bundles of atoms that face extinction when we die. We are created for a purpose – that purpose is to discover the centrality of love and overcome our propensities to egoism. As we discover love so we discover that which will endure for eternity – a loving relationship with our creator.

In the modern period life after death has been increasingly questioned. And as life after death has become a problem so the problem of theodicy has become more significant. As Keith Ward observes in *Holding Fast to God* "without life after death, making sense of evil and suffering is very difficult."

In this chapter, we shall start by briefly looking at the different accounts of life after death found around the world. Then we shall look at distinctively Christian sources. For Christians, the resurrection of Jesus is central. Using the resurrection of Jesus, I shall then sketch out an account of life beyond the grave. Then we shall examine the three traditional destinations: heaven, hell, and purgatory.

Accounts of Life After Death in the Different Religions

Ted Peters helpfully describes the six main options outside of Christianity. The first is "scientific naturalism."[1] This is the view that when the brain dies the person is dead; on this view there is no continued existence beyond the grave. The second is the immortal soul. It was Plato who introduced this idea to the West. Upon death the body dies, but the immortal and immaterial soul continues to exist. The third is reincarnation. This is a Hindu belief, although also found in many indigenous traditions. The idea here is that the essence of a person continues to live on in a different bodily form. The fourth is astral projection. This is popular in New Age worldviews. The astral body is our star body, which upon death is released from the physical body and ascends up the seven planes. The fifth is "ancestral presence as the living dead."[2] This involves deceased ancestors who continue to influence the present through their continued spirit. The sixth is out of body experiences. These are well documented experiences of individuals who are pronounced dead yet see the process from above and tell us about them when they are resuscitated. Having surveyed all these options, Ted Peters then observes:

> What Christian eschatology teaches conforms to none of these options. What each of the last five options share in common is an individual eschatology with a *soulechtomy* ("soul-removing operation") – that is, they tend towards extracting a nonmaterial essence or soul from a person and slating this soul to live on without the body and without the physical world. In contrast, it appears quite clear that followers of Jesus affirm a future resurrection of the body; and our bodies in the resurrection require an accompanying renewed world, the new creation or kingdom of God.[3]

Although there are Christians who defend the immortality of the soul, it is true that the resurrection of Jesus is central. Partly because no one knows what life beyond the grave is going to be like, we are at this point forced to resort to revelation. This means any account will be tradition-specific. So if one asks a Hindu, he or she would give a different answer from a Christian. Furthermore the answers given from within different strands of a tradition will vary considerably. Anyone with a sense of history will appreciate that there is no uniform, universal, Christian position. It is, however, worth noting at this point that the answers given by different religious traditions are not completely at odds. Although Peters is right to draw attention to the contrasts, there is still a shared emphasis across these traditions. Most traditions stress some element of judgment (we must take responsibility for the decisions made in this life); most aspire to some state of harmony, where love and freedom finally coincide (the radical flaws in earthly life are absent). However, it is true that there are differences. And it is the distinctively Christian account of life beyond the grave, which is grounded in the Bible, that we turn to next.

The Christian Tradition

As Christians we turn to the resources of our tradition. Life after death is relatively unimportant in the Hebrew Bible. God's judgment of the nations tends to occur in this world. The word Sheol is used in Ecclesiastes (see 9:10), which seems to refer to an abode of the dead, but it is not attractive. However, as we approach the end of the time covered by the writings of the Hebrew Bible, a new movement emerges. Israel was being perpetually battered by more powerful opponents; in response, the *apocalyptic* genre was born. Apocalyptic means "reveal." Instead of expecting the present age to get better, it will get worse, until God decisively steps in and ends history. As a strategy of coping with the endless pain of disappointment and powerlessness, it is a good one. The struggles of this moment are a sign of the end of time. We cope with the devastation because it is a sign of God's impending judgment and action in history. In addition, the author of Daniel argues that those who are dying in this devastation will be resurrected. Daniel writes: "Many of those who sleep in the dust of the earth shall awake, some to everlasting life, and some to shame and everlasting contempt" (Daniel 12:2).

By the time of Jesus, expectations of the end of the age, coupled with a general resurrection, were widespread. Jesus himself taught about the imminent rule of God (the Kingdom of God). Indeed there is a lively debate in New Testament scholarship about whether Jesus holds a realized eschatology (the end is somehow being realized in the ministry of Jesus) or a futuristic eschatology (Jesus is simply preaching about an end which will occur in the future). The disciples continued to stress the teaching around the end. Indeed it is a theme that permeates the New Testament writings. And of course this theme was given a new direction because the Early Church believed that Jesus had risen from the dead.

The Resurrection of Jesus

The New Testament is in agreement: Jesus who was once dead is now alive. However, the precise nature of the historical event is subject to much controversy. Scholars divide between those who think that at the heart of the resurrection experience is a vision (and presumably the body of Jesus has long since decomposed), and those who think the tomb was empty and the physical body became a resurrected "spiritual" body. For the vision group, the argument is that there is a gradual developing sophistication in the resurrection accounts. And the earliest narratives imply strongly that the resurrection was a vision. They point to the resurrection narrative found in 1 Corinthians 15. This is an important passage. Paul is bringing together all the evidence for the resurrection in a systematic way. Crucially, Paul links his experience with the rest of the apostles. And we know from Acts that this was an intense vision of the resurrected Jesus while he was on the road to Damascus (Acts 9:1–9), after the ascension of Jesus. So the argument is then developed: Paul seems to be implying that it is a "vision" experience in this early passage outlining the evidence for the resurrection. Working then in chronological order, the next text written discussing the resurrection is Mark's Gospel. And in this Gospel, we have the empty tomb, but no appearances. It is not until Matthew and Luke that we have everything – an empty tomb, appearances, and the capacity to "teleport."

It is N. T. Wright who has provided the most substantial rebuttal of these arguments. The empty tomb is in 1 Corinthians 15: Paul distinguishes the state of being buried from the state of being raised from the dead (verse 4), which implies strongly that being raised contrasts markedly with being buried.[4] In addition, in the rest of the chapter, Paul uses the resurrection of Jesus as his justification for resurrection of all humanity. "[T]he rest of chapter 15," explains Wright, "does not . . . speak of that interesting oxymoron, a non-bodily 'resurrection'."[5] The whole chapter is assuming a bodily resurrection. And although it is true that the traditions do develop in Matthew, Luke, and John, the bodily resurrection is central. Wright summarizes his own argument when he writes:

We have seen that early Christian resurrection-belief has a remarkable consistency despite varieties of expression, and that this consistency includes both the location of Christianity at one point on the spectrum of Jewish belief (bodily resurrection) and four key modifications from within that point: (1) resurrection has moved from the circumference of belief to the center; (2) "the resurrection" is no longer a single event, but has split chronologically into two, the first part of which has already happened; (3) resurrection involves transformation, not mere resuscitation; and (4) when "resurrection" language is used metaphorically, it no longer refers to the national restoration of Israel, but to baptism and holiness.[6]

Wright makes a strong case that throughout the New Testament (both in the earlier writings and the later ones) there is a bodily resurrection of Jesus and therefore an empty tomb. The body of Jesus was not resuscitated (because if that was all that happened, then due to the injuries inflicted on Jesus on the cross, he would probably have just died again) but transformed.

What is striking about Wright's argument is that unlike Karl Barth and Wolfhart Pannenberg, he wants to insist on the availability of sufficient historical evidence for this amazing event. Karl Barth would share Wright's emphasis that the resurrection is an event that took place in space and time, but, because of its striking nature, it is unavailable to critical evaluation by historians. Barth writes, "We cannot read the Gospels without getting the strong impression that as we pass from the story of the passion to the story of Easter we are led into a historical sphere of a different kind . . . There is no proof, and there obviously cannot and ought not be any proof, for the fact that this history did take place (proof, that is, according to the terminology of modern historical scholarship)."[7] For Barth, it is history, but it is not susceptible to the tools of modern historical scholarship. For Wolfhart Pannenberg, history is where it is at. God must and has acted in history. He argues that all history should be seen from the vantage point of the eschaton (the end of the age). And the meaning of the resurrection in its complete fullness will only be known then. However, against Barth, he does want to affirm that historians who are not prejudging the plausibility of the resurrection should be able to see the possibility of the resurrection. Wright is sympathetic to Pannenberg, but wants to go further and insist that the bodily resurrection is the best reading of the New Testament data.[8]

For the purposes of this chapter, a transformed bodily resurrection is what is needed. The Christian claim is not simply that the experience of "Jesus is alive" was "real" and life transforming, but also that it is to be a model of the general resurrection to come (see especially I Corinthians 15:50ff, Philippians 3:21, and Romans 8:18ff). This will provide the basis of the Christian account of life after death.

Jesus as a model of the life to come

On the whole, the Christian tradition is committed to a view of humanity as a psycho-somatic unity, that is an integrated unity of body and soul[9]. The immortality of the soul has never been the dominant view of the Church. In fact in the western Church it was not required until the fifth Lateran Council which was held in 1513. According to David Brown, most philosophers believe that the mutual interdependence, yet irreducibility, of soul and body makes sense. Brown writes,

> Admittedly, earlier this century, discussion still tended to solidify into two opposed camps, with one side being reductionist materialists and the other insistent upon two distinct substances or entities in human beings, a body and a soul. Now, however ... there is in fact emerging a general consensus among believer and non-believer alike, which advocates a mediating position. According to this, while the mind or the soul is incapable of existence independent of the body, it is nonetheless not reducible to, or explicable purely in terms of, the material. One technical way of drawing this distinction commonly employed is to say that dual aspect (mental/physical) has replaced dualism (soul and body as two distinct entities).[10]

Fortunately, modern philosophy and the majority within the Christian tradition seem to converge. When we imagine life beyond the grave, we will have a mental life located within a body, what St Paul sees as a transformed self. The precise nature of the body is difficult to describe. Just as there is a different flesh for animals and humans, so there will be different bodies for earth and heaven (see I Corinthians 15:39). It seems then that we will have an individual body that will operate significantly differently from our present one.[11] Presumably we will need some sort of space–time framework (it is difficult to see how bodies could operate without such), but courtesy of perhaps teleporting or telepathy, we will not be subject to the restrictions that we currently endure. We will be recognizable (as Jesus was to his disciples) and will meet up with those we love.

This brief sketch is grounded in the New Testament talk about resurrection. We are not required to try and imagine millions of disembodied entities existing and communicating. The resurrected life is sufficiently similar to this world to be conceivable. Also the problem of personal identity is not as great for resurrected bodies as it would be for disembodied souls.

How do you know that the Fred you are meeting this week is identical with the Fred you saw last week? John Locke suggested that you would search for the continuity of memory. If Fred can recall the previous meeting, then he is the same person. The memory criterion has the enormous advantage that even if Fred had changed dramatically (say in appearance), you would still be able to establish Fred's identity. However, there are problems, such as memory loss. Quinton has suggested a modified Locke position.[12] He wants to link identity with the soul: and he defines the soul as "a series of mental states connected by continuity of character and memory."[13] However, this rather neat move is still left with the logical possibility of a clone or replica emerging. In other words, let us imagine that in the intervening gap between the death of

John Smith and his resurrection, the cosmic machine goes slightly wrong and two appear.[14] Both share identical memories and character. Which one is identical with the dead John Smith? And since it is axiomatic that there is only one person, then you cannot say that both John Smiths are identical. This nice little problem has led some philosophers to insist that personal identity depends on bodily continuity. And once death breaks bodily continuity, then meaningful identity becomes impossible.

It is rather unreasonable to insist that the logical possibility of a replica appearing should exclude the logical possibility that our unique self survives death. When the time comes and we find ourselves in the next life, it will not do to insist that despite the vast similarities in appearance, memory, interests, character, and relationships I am not the same person because there was a break in my bodily continuity. It is true that bodily continuity through space and time is the great constant of human life. And this is our problem: we find it difficult to imagine personal identity transcending gaps in bodily continuity.

So imagine the following thought exercise. All children at the age of eight suddenly disappear for two minutes and reappear as humanoid-birds. The process is much like a caterpillar changing into a butterfly, but with a short gap to enable the transformation to take place. Now I grant you that this sounds odd to us, but if it were universal it would appear completely normal. The humanoid-bird would share many of the characteristics of the child: it would remember being a child; it would have the same basic character and personality. Once a humanoid-bird, the character would inevitably change, in much the same way that the character of a person who recovers the ability to walk after being confined to a wheelchair for ten year changes. The point is simple: if this were merely a part of the natural process, we would rapidly become accustomed to talking about a humanoid-bird as identical with the child. Now if the process went wrong, which from time to time it probably would, and two humanoid-birds emerged, then we would probably talk about the child splitting into two birds and require that each should now be treated as an autonomous individual.

Life beyond the grave will be a similar change. We are the children who will become transformed into humanoid-birds. Our characters will transfer from our existing bodies into the heavenly body. This heavenly body will enable different possibilities that will bring about change and development in our character. It is important to build on our character similarities and yet embrace them within certain differences. This life matters because it provides the resources that God, through his grace, will prepare for eternity.

The argument thus far has been loosely built on the resurrection of Jesus. I have attempted to defend the coherence of postulating a resurrection, with a redeemed space–time framework, in which individuals will be recognizable. The focus, however, has been exclusively on people; the question I want to conclude with is, what about the rest of the creation?

A Redeemed Creation

Traditionally, creation seems a much more dramatic project than redemption. Creation is made up of mountains, plants, and animals. It is rich in diversity and beauty. Traditionally, redemption is confined to humans, and often not many of them. One cannot help but wonder why God bothered with animals and plants, if the end result involved their exclusion. A priori we have every reason to expect the scale of redemption to be at least equivalent to that of creation.

In Romans, Paul insists that the "creation itself will be set free from its bondage to decay and will obtain the freedom of the glory of the children of God" (Romans 8:21). The book of Revelation talks about a "new heaven and a new earth" (Revelation 21:1). There is a strand that strongly implies that all of creation will ultimately be redeemed. I think this strand needs to be taken seriously.

Granted this will be speculative, but it seems reasonable to believe that in some way, analogous to the transforming of the human life, all matter and life will be transformed. Jurgen Moltmann brings the significance of the resurrection together with a cosmic Christology to justify the redemption of the entire creation. He writes,

> If the day of Christ's resurrection is the first day of the new creation, then it also brings the creation of new light, a light which lights up not merely the sense but the mind and spirit too, and shines over the whole new creation . . . In the Epistle to the Colossians a vision of cosmic peace is *christology*. Through Christ everything will be reconciled "whether on earth or in heaven, making peace by the blood of his cross, through himself (1:20) . . . He (Christ) died . . . so as to reconcile everything in heaven and on earth, which means the angels and the beasts too, and to bring peace to the whole creation . . ." If Christ has died not merely for the reconciliation of human beings, but for the reconciliation of all other creatures too, then every created being enjoys infinite value in God's sight, and has its own right to live; this is not true of human beings alone.[15]

Although I would hesitate to say that "every created being enjoys infinite value," he succeeds in showing how the immortality of animal life is embedded in the logic of a cosmic christology and atonement.

Keith Ward reaches a similar conclusion, but by a different route. His problem is animal suffering. One of the cruel features of the evolutionary process is the enormous waste of sentient life. Species come, go, and change. To do this, death and suffering are an essential part of the process. Ward is rightly disturbed by any attempt to justify the suffering on the grounds that it made humanity possible. God would then become a cosmic utilitarian who inflicts pain as a means to a greater end. However, if the suffering of sentient life cannot be justified as a route to a greater end, then an alternative is needed. Ward writes:

Despite the many pointers to the existence of God, theism would be falsified if physical death was the end, for then there could be no justification for the existence of this world. However, if one supposes that every sentient being has an endless existence, which offers the prospect of supreme happiness, it is surely true that the sorrows and troubles of this life will seem very small by comparison. Immortality, for animals as well as humans, is a necessary condition of any acceptable theodicy; that necessity, together with all other arguments for God, is one of the main reasons for believing in immorality. This theodicy consideration, taken with the internal logic of a Christ redeeming the entire world, provides strong reasons for believing that non-human life will be part of the life to come.[16]

It is because of the dramatic impact of God dying at the hands of God's creation that everything in creation is affected. The result is that God does not simply have the authority to forgive and reconcile humanity to God, but also the reconciliation extends to everything in creation.

This poses an obvious question: what about hell? Does hell exist?

Hell

Traditionally, hell is the state of unrelenting punishment by God for the wickedness that we have done on earth. For some Christians, hell is believed to be the destination for all those who are not Christians.[17] Hell was especially popular in the Middle Ages. **Dante Alighieri** produced the poetic masterpiece *The Divine Comedy*, in which he described the nature of hell, purgatory, and paradise. Many of Dante's targets are his contemporary political and civic leaders in Florence in 1300. However, for our purposes, it is interesting to see how hell is constructed. It has nine circles: Limbo, the Lustful, the Gluttonous, the Avaricious, the Wrathful, Heretics, the Violent, the Fraudulent, and the Treacherous. For Dante, a pain-free limbo is the destination for Aristotle and Virgil, while Muhammad is found in the eighth circle with his guts spilled out.

Although it is true that we will all have to face up to the consequences of our behavior on earth, I am not persuaded about such a reality as hell. The problems with such a straightforward doctrine of hell seem overwhelming. To divide humanity into those deserving of heaven and those deserving of hell seems impossible. There are plenty of Christians who thwart love while there are equally plenty of non-Christians who exhibit all the "fruits of the Spirit" (love and kindness, etc) that Paul writes about in Galatians. An eternity of punishment seems disproportionate for a lifetime of wickedness, even if one has been exceptionally wicked. Beside this, the Christian good news (the gospel) is about Christ dying for the whole world so that the whole world is redeemed.

DANTE ALIGHIERI (1265–1321)

Dante was born and lived in Italy. Tragically, he lost his parents as a child. He grew up under the influence of the Dominicans. As a young man, he fell in love with Beatrice (we suspect a daughter of Portinari – a prominent citizen in Florence), who died in 1290. This loss continued to affect Dante throughout his life; indeed Beatrice has a starring role in the most famous of Dante's work *The Divine Comedy*. His life was made complicated by his anti-Papal sympathies, which became an issue in Florence in 1301. As a result, he found himself moving from town to town for much of his life.

Hell, as traditionally described, is very unlikely. Instead hell is a state of "selfishness" and "loneliness" that we create for ourselves. Hell is very much a state of mind that we can and do create here on earth. As we discover love, so we discover the life of God, and as we create barriers of hatred, so we create hell. It is possible that when we die some of us, perhaps most of us, will still have barriers that need to be destroyed. This is the problematic area that the doctrine of purgatory set out to resolve.

Purgatory emerged in the sixth century with Gregory the Great. Traditionally, in Roman Catholic thought, it provides a state for those who die redeemed yet need to repent of venial sins (venial as opposed mortal sins – i.e. love coexists with a venial sin and can be repaired by love). The assumption here is that sin requires some form of temporal punishment, even though God has forgiven it. So it is a place of purification. It was confirmed at the Council of Florence (1431–45) and the Council of Trent (1545–63). The text from the Apocrapha (2 Maccabees 12:39–45), along with 1 Corinthians 3:11–15, were often cited to justify the doctrine.

The doctrine was misused in the Middle Ages. It assumed disproportionate significance in the life of the medieval Christian. The "suffering Church" beyond the grave can receive our prayers, and the grace from a mass said on their behalf can ease their time in Purgatory and enable release to come more quickly.

Naturally, it is unhelpful for us to become too literal in our understanding of purgatory. C. S. Lewis has the right idea when in the *Great Divorce* he suggested that purgatory ought to be understood as the continuing availability of God's love to all. God does not give up on us. Purgatory understood in this way is helpful. My argument in this chapter is that human barriers created by individuals need to be destroyed by love, and that this process should start in this life and might require some time in the life to come to bring it to completion.

Conclusion

There are many temptations to avoid when thinking about this topic. We must resist the temptation to capitulate to modernity and accept a scientific naturalism. We need the bigger picture: the suffering of this life is utterly obscene unless there is the larger canvas. This is a central part of our response to the problem of evil and suffering. We must resist the temptation to dismiss Biblical talk of resurrection. To some, resurrection just seems implausible. However, plausibility is a cultural judgment: we should not imagine that the universe is confined to the limits of our "plausible" imaginations. And finally, we must resist the temptation to limit redemption to humans. The promise is that the entire creation will be redeemed. There is no reason why the redemption project should be smaller than the creation one.

The Christian hope is important. We need to retain, constantly, the sense that our life is a small part of a greater whole. It is only from that perspective that much that appears difficult and odd now will ultimately be seen to form a pattern that can be used by God for eternity.

QUESTIONS FOR REFLECTION AND DISCUSSION

1 Why do some people find life after death implausible?
2 Do you think bad people should go to hell?
3 Does the text in Romans 8 justify a belief that all creation will participate in redemption? If so, what does this mean for the mosquito?
4 Is it possible to be a Christian and not believe in life after death?

GLOSSARY

Ancestral presence: the belief that deceased ancestors continue to influence the present

Astral projection: the New Age belief in a star body, which on death is released and then ascends

Hell: a place of punishment after death

Purgatory: traditionally understood in Roman Catholic theology as the place where those who die in the "grace of God" can receive due punishment for their venial sins (as opposed to mortal sins)

Reincarnation: the belief that the self is reborn. A widely held belief found in many traditions (for example, Hinduism)

Resurrection: the claim that both the body and the spirit of a person survives death

Sheol: a Hebrew term which describes the place of the departed. The term occurs in the Hebrew Bible

Soul: understood in several different ways to describe the "spirit" or "essence" of a person that survives death

Notes

1 Ted Peters, "Where are we going?" in William Placher (ed.), *Essentials of Christian Theology* (Louisville, KY: Westminster John Knox, 2003), p. 349. The entire list of positions is taken from Ted Peters survey in this chapter (see especially pp. 349–50).

2 Ibid., p. 350.

3 Ibid., p. 350.

4 See N. T. Wright, *The Resurrection of the Son of God* (Minneapolis, MN: Fortress Press, 2003), p. 321.

5 Ibid., p. 383.

6 Ibid., p. 681.

7 Karl Barth, *Church Dogmatics*, vol. iv, Part 1 (Edinburgh: T. & T. Clark, 1956), pp. 334–5.

8 See Wright, *The Resurrection of the Son of God*, p. 17.

9 It is important to note that historically there are many theologians who combined the resurrection of the body with the immortality of the soul (even in some of St Paul's epistles).

10 David Brown, "The Christian heaven," in Dan Cohn-Sherbok and Christopher Lewis (eds.), *Beyond Death: Theological and Philosophical Reflections on Life after Death* (Basingstoke: Macmillan, 1995), p. 44.

11 I am aware that Karl Rahner uses the seed analogy also found in I Corinthians 15 to suggest that we will not have individual bodies but unite with the "all" (i.e. the whole world). See Karl Rahner, *On the Theology of Death* (New York: Herder & Herder, 1971), p. 31.

12 See Anthony Quinton, "The Soul," reprinted in W. L. Wainwright and W. J. Rowe (eds.), *Readings in the Philosophy of Religion* (New York: Harcourt Brace Jovanovich, 1989), pp. 462–75.

13 Ibid., p. 466.

14 For a good discussion of the problem of multiple replication see John Hick, *Death and Eternal Life* (Basingstoke: Macmillan, 1985), pp. 290–5.

15 Jürgen Moltmann, *The Way of Jesus Christ: Christology in Messianic Dimensions* (London: SCM Press, 1990), pp. 254–6.

16 Keith Ward, *Rational Theology and the Creativity of God* (Oxford: Blackwell, 1982), pp. 201–2.

17 Some of the material which follows was written with my co-author Giles Legood for the *Funeral Handbook* (London: SPCK, 2003), pp. 36–7.

Chapter 13
THE END
OF THE AGE

LEARNING OUTCOMES

By the end of this chapter, you should be able to:

- understand the differences between the scientific narrative of the end of the universe and the fundamentalist narrative
- recognize the fact that the belief the world will end was a key feature of the ministry of Jesus
- know how the author attempts to reconcile science and theology

STRUCTURE

- The scientific account
- The fundamentalist account
- Standing back

Both science and theology agree that this universe will not go on forever. However, their visions surrounding this end contrast markedly. In this chapter, we will examine these two contrasting visions and then attempt to formulate an account that makes both scientific and theological sense.

The Scientific Account

The cosmic battle between gravity and expansion will determine the likely outcome at the end of the universe. The question is: was the expansion of the universe rapid enough to escape the ultimate gravitational pull? If so, then scenario one will be realized: We will find ourselves in a universe full of "dark energy" (the energy that encourages expansion). And in this expanding universe, the night sky will become dark – stars will cease to twinkle – and everything will become cold. This universe could not sustain life. If the expansion of the universe was not sufficient to escape the gravitational pull, then we will face the gravitational scenario: This is called the "big crunch." All matter will be crushed and will cease to be. The physicist John Polkinghorne sums up the situation thus: "Neither of these catastrophes will happen tomorrow; they lie tens of billions of years into the future. Nevertheless, one way or the other, the universe is condemned to ultimate futility, and humanity will prove to have been a transient episode in its history."[1]

So although none of this is particularly imminent, it is not encouraging. In addition, of more immediate concern (i.e. only four billion years away), there is the death of our star. The sun generates light and heat by converting hydrogen into helium. As the hydrogen from the core gets depleted, the sun will become a red giant star. At this point, the sun starts to lose its outer layers, which drift into space. The next stage is the white dwarf – a small star, which is stable but has no nuclear fuel. And in time, as the leftover heat is dispersed, we will be left with a dark, cold, black dwarf.

Given the vast distances in space, it is difficult to see how significant numbers of humans could be moved to another hospitable planet, which would have to be outside our solar system. Our star's death is inevitable and, in cosmic terms, soon; therefore it looks inevitable that humanity is doomed to extinction (assuming we don't destroy ourselves in the meantime). For science, modern cosmology assumes that certain fundamental forces will determine the future of the universe. And these forces do not bode well for life.

The Fundamentalist Account

In contrast, the fundamentalist account of the end of the universe offers a very different picture. Instead of inanimate forces determining the outcome, we have God, acting in Christ, to bring about the end of the age. One very popular example of this fundamentalist account (it is important to stress that many, perhaps most, evangelical Christians would disagree with this account) is the premillennial dispensationalist account. It is premillennial because the return of Christ occurs before the 1000 years promised in Revelation 20:4, "They came to life, and reigned with Christ a thousand years." It is dispensationalist because it is shaped by the dispensationalist theology of **John Nelson Darby**.

This particular version of the end times has been popularized by the best-selling *Left Behind* **series** written by Tim LaHaye, who founded the PreTrib Research Center, and Jerry B. Jenkins, who is the ghostwriter and former editor of the *Moody Magazine*. The series captures events from the rapture through the tribulation to the millennium.

JOHN NELSON DARBY (1800–82)

Originally Darby was an Anglican priest who resigned from the Church of England to become a member of the "Brethren." A talented hymn-writer, translator, and theologian, he rapidly established himself as a major figure in the movement. In 1845, a disagreement led to Darby taking a more strict line. He became the leader of the Exclusive Brethren, which is a small sect which teaches absolute separation from the world. He traveled widely throughout America and Europe. His dispensationalist schema had a major impact on American Fundamentalism.

LEFT BEHIND SERIES

A popular series of American books, written by Tim LaHaye and Jerry B. Jenkins, which offer a fictional portrayal of the end of the age based on a dispensationalist reading of the Bible. The first in the series was called *Left Behind*, rapidly followed by *Tribulation Force, Nicolae, Soul Harvest, Apollyon, Assassins, The Indwelling, the Mark, Desecration, The Remnant, Armageddon,* and *Glorious Appearing.*

The *Left Behind* series is not the first attempt to reach a mass market with the theology of the end times (Hal Lindsey's *The Late Great Planet Earth* became one of the biggest selling nonfiction works of the 1970s), but with 62 million copies sold, and rising, it is the most successful yet.

The first novel sets the scene. Starting in the present, it starts with a night flight from Chicago to London, midway across the Atlantic, on a 747 jetliner, when an elderly woman discovers that her husband is missing. Upon investigation a hundred passengers have disappeared, nothing left save for their clothes which are neatly set out on their seats. The mysterious disappearance of people on the aircraft is part of a worldwide spontaneous disappearance of millions of people. This is the "rapture" – the call of the Church out of the world to be saved from the judgment of God that will follow in the tribulation.

The theology of the novels comes out in the plot. Generally Roman Catholics are viewed with suspicion: although the current Pope is raptured (because he has strong Reformed sympathies), Cardinal Mathews replaces him (an evil pluralist out to create a syncretistic religion). The Antichrist is Nicolae Carpathia from Romania who becomes Secretary General of the United Nations. The UN becomes the Global Community, which moves its headquarters to Babylon and takes control of all weapons (decommissioning 90 percent of them). Those who disappear are "born again" Christians and the unborn – the novel describes the bewilderment of a pregnant mother whose new born baby disappears at the moment of delivery.[2] It is the evangelicals and the innocent who are saved at the Rapture. As the series progresses, we also find that there is a small group of Gentiles (who turn to Christ during the tribulation) and a Jewish remnant (those that survive the slaughter during the tribulation) who are redeemed.

It is important that we understand why this theology is so attractive to so many people. First, the Bible is taken seriously. For LaHaye, this theology is what the Bible teaches. They are simply setting out what the word of God says. The only book in the Bible which contains a promise of blessing to those who read it is Revelation – "Blessed is he who reads aloud the words of the prophecy, and blessed are those who hear, and who keep what is written therein" (Revelation 1:3). Yet this is the book of the Bible that most Christians avoid.

Second, the fact this theology builds on dispensationalism makes it attractive to some people. To give dispensationalism its due, it is an attempt to explain why God deals with humanity in different ways at various different periods of human history. This structure was suggested by John Nelson Darby. According to Darby, there are seven dispensations: first, the dispensation of Innocence (Genesis 1:28) – this runs from the creation to the Fall; second, the dispensation of conscience or moral responsibility (Genesis 3:7) – from the Fall to Noah; the third is the dispensation of human government (Genesis 8:15) – from the flood to the call of Abraham; the fourth is promise (Genesis 12:1) – from Abraham to Moses; the fifth is the important and major dispensation of law (Exodus 19.1) – from Moses to the death of Christ; the sixth is the dispensation we are currently in called the Church (Acts 2:1) – from the resurrection and continuing; and the seventh is the dispensation of the Kingdom or Millennium (Revelation 20:4). Building on this overarching structure, Darby then divided the return of Jesus into three stages. Stage one is the Secret Rapture (see Matthew 24:40–1 and 1 Thessalonians 5:2 – and earlier). Stage two is the seven year tribulation, when the Antichrist will come to prominence. (Daniel 9:24–26a, do note that a week equals seven years, cf Genesis 29:27). Stage three is after the Battle of Armageddon (Revelation 19:11–21) when Jesus will usher in the millennium (Revelation 20:4–6).

Third, as a recruitment tool, it is very powerful. The claim that "any day now the rapture will occur" is one that can never be falsified. It is an event, which will occur only once. The fact it doesn't occur today means it might occur tomorrow: and one carries on believing that until it happens. Preachers stress the dangers of the tribulation and the promise of God to save the redeemed from the tribulation. The fear of "being left behind" (from friends and relatives) and the horrors of the tribulation are sufficient to persuade many people of fundamentalist Christianity.

Although I have attempted to identify the attractions of this theology, there are significant problems with it. Carl E. Olson identifies some of the key difficulties. After documenting the publishing achievement of the *Left Behind* series, he writes, "That's a serious number of people learning the secrets of the Book of Revelation. Unfortunately for them, the secrets are stale, recycled, and false."[3] In a perceptive critique, he looks at the capacity of the "Bible prophecy experts" to organize the Scripture to fit whatever the "signs of the time" are at the moment. So Olson writes:

> Reading quotes by *Left Behind* enthusiasts who are convinced The End is nigh, I recall how many "Ends" have come and gone in my short lifetime. The "signs of the times" were many and varied: the fledgling modern state of Israel, any and every Middle Eastern conflict, the European Market, Jimmy Carter, the energy crisis, Ronald Reagan, communism, the Persian Gulf War – the list goes on.[4]

The apocalyptic images of Scriptures are very malleable. Different ages have no problem "reading into" the images the political problems of their time. Kenneth Newport's magisterial study *Apocalypse and Millennium*, appropriately subtitled "Studies in Biblical Eisegesis" demonstrates this very well. Eisegesis, explains Newport, is "the fundamental concern . . . to see the vital link that exists between the beliefs and concerns of the reader (which are of course dependent upon his or her cultural and historical context) and the kind of interpretation which that reader then gives to the text."[5] Newport then goes on to show very effectively through eight different case studies, how communities "read into" the book of Revelation their concerns and preoccupations. It is especially interesting to see how "in the hands of some, indeed most, eighteenth-century Protestant interpreters, the book became a means of divinely sanctioning their contemporary society's anti-Catholicism. Catholics were servants of the Antichrist and Satan, and hence their influence upon Christendom must be negated."[6] It is, however, even more interesting to see how Roman Catholics then interpreted the book of Revelation to counter this anti-Catholic interpretation.

Along with the capacity of Christians of all ages to read into the book of Revelation the various villains of their age, there are fundamental problems with the entire schema of dispensationalist theology. It is an odd theology in several ways: some of the consequences are often not appreciated by Christians. Technically, for example, the Lord's Prayer is not a Christian prayer because it was taught by Jesus for the dispensation of the kingdom. Olson is spot on with his summary of the key problems with this theology:

> John Nelson Darby, the ex-Anglican priest who constructed the premillennial dispensational system in the 1830s, based it on three premises: Jesus Christ failed in his initial mission, the Church has become apostate and is in ruins, and the Old Testament promises to the Israelites have yet to be fulfilled. Inevitably and logically this meant that the Church is not connected to Old Testament Israel, nor is she even as important, at least in earthly terms. The Church is, Darby taught, a "heavenly people" meant for a Christ who was relegated to a heavenly status once he was rejected by the Jews, God's "earthly" people. Fast forward to the future millennial reign, complete with a new Temple and reinstituted animal sacrifices. During this "Davidic reign" the Church will exercise authority from heaven – possibly in a huge, cubed New Jerusalem hovering over the earth. Meanwhile, the earth will be occupied by those non-Raptured and non-glorified believers, mostly Jewish, who accepted Jesus as Savior during the Tribulation. After all, that horrific time will be for punishing an evil humanity and will be a means of bringing the Jews back to God in an ultimate display of tough love. How odd to think that Christians who believe that the Church is composed of "Jew and Greek" alike (Romans 10:12) are sometimes suspected of anti-Semitism by those who believe that in the future, earthly millennium the Jews will be rewarded with earth while pre-Rapture Christians will achieve heaven, the grand prize.[7]

So this is a problematic theology, which has given birth to an unhealthy preoccupation. Instead of thinking of the end of the age in these terms, we need to search for an alternative. And as with creation, this alternative needs to recognize the timeframe of the cosmologists. It is to the quest for this alternative that we turn next.

Standing Back

Although perhaps the two options set out above – the rather pessimistic scientific picture and the rather implausible evangelical picture – are the best known accounts of the end, there are plenty of other possibilities which are being discussed by theologians. In this concluding section, I shall group some of these other theological discussions around three key points, which I shall argue are essential aspects of a Christian theology of the end of the age.

The first is that the Christian promise of a divine action to bring about the kingdom of God is not an excuse for ignoring political and social challenges now. Indeed the promise of the end is a challenge to unjust structures now. It was Karl Marx (1818–83) who argued that the Christian hope of a just world in the hereafter is an oppressive tool, or to use his famous phrase it is the "opium of the people." This quote comes from "Towards a Critique of Hegel's *Philosophy of Right*": the context is as follows:

> Religious suffering is at the same time an expression of real suffering and a protest against real suffering. Religion is the sigh of the oppressed creature, the feeling of a heartless world, and the soul of the soulless circumstances. It is the opium of the people.[8]

Marx believed that built into the structures of capitalism is an unjust economic relationship between the proletariat and the capitalist classes. And to cope with the pain of this injustice, the proletariat is offered the dream of a just world after death. Marx argued that such a theology serves the interests of the rich and powerful; it is part of the superstructure supported by the unjust economic base. For this reason, it should be rejected and instead we should work for justice now.

Marx does have a point. The nineteenth-century children's hymn writer Mrs Cecil Frances Humphreys Alexander (1823–95) included in her famous hymn, "All things bright and beautiful," the following verse:

> The rich man in his castle
> The poor man at the gate
> God made them high and lowly
> and ordered their estate.

This is hardly a call for social justice. And we find both today, and in the past, examples of theologies that are happy with an unjust status quo – in South Africa under the apartheid regime or in the United States at the time of the civil rights movement. Marx is right to sound a prophetic warning against the ways in which theology can serve the interests of the rich and powerful.

It was Jürgen Moltmann who challenged the Marxist view of the Christian hope. In his classic *A Theology of Hope*, he argued that the purpose and value of the Christian eschatology is to provide a standard for human relations, which we are called to strive for and realize. Moltmann writes:

ALBERT SCHWEITZER (1875–1965)

Schweitzer was born in Kaisersberg in Alsace. He was educated at the University of Strasburg, and later at Berlin and Paris. He became a pastor in 1899. He was a prolific writer: he argued that the eschatology (beliefs about the end of the world) of Jesus was not being taken seriously. He provoked considerable controversy. Later in his life, he decided to go to Africa to serve as a doctor.

The Christian Church has not to serve mankind in order that this world may remain what it is, or may be preserved in the state in which it is, but in order that it may transform itself and become what it promised to be. For this reason "Church for the world" can mean nothing else but "Church for the kingdom of God" and the renewing of the world. This means in practice that Christianity takes up mankind – or to put it concretely, the Church takes up the society with which it lives – into its own horizon of expectation of the eschatological fulfillment of justice, life, humanity and sociability, and communicates in its own decisions in history its openness and readiness for this future and its elasticity towards it.[9]

For Moltmann, the Christian hope starts with the resurrection of Jesus. This is the start of the promise of God being realized amongst us. The challenge then is to continue to work to realize the "kingdom on earth as it is in heaven." It is because Christians know that, ultimately, injustice will be overcome that we can work in the now, confident that the victory has already been won.

The second aspect is that *Jesus believed that in his life and ministry he was inaugurating the kingdom of God, which is still to be completed*. A major reason why a Christian is required to take the discourse of the end seriously is that it is clearly grounded in the message of Jesus. It was **Albert Schweitzer** in his famous *The Quest of the Historical Jesus* (1906) who argued that the only way to properly understand Jesus is as an apocalyptic prophet, firmly located in the first century. (The term "apocalyptic" comes from the Greek word *apocalypsis* meaning "revealing" or "unveiling": so the idea is that apocalypticism is a belief that God has revealed the secrets of the end times.) Although the details of Schweitzer's picture are contested, the sense that Jesus was heavily shaped by apocalyptic theology is widely affirmed. In the earliest sources for the historical Jesus (e.g. Mark's gospel), we find this robustly apocalyptic worldview:

"Those who are ashamed of me and of my words in this adulterous and sinful generation, of them the Son of Man will also be ashamed when he comes in the glory of his Father with the holy angels." And he said to them, "Truly I tell you, there are some standing here who will not taste death until they see that the kingdom of God has come with power." (Mark 8:38–9:1)

or

But in those days, after that suffering, the sun will be darkened, and the moon will not give its light, and the stars will be falling from heaven, and the powers in the heavens will be shaken. Then they will see "the Son of Man coming in clouds" with great power and glory. Then he will send out the angels, and gather his elect from the four winds, from the ends of the earth to the ends of heaven. "From the fig tree learn its lesson: as soon as its branch becomes tender and puts forth its leaves, you know that summer is near. So also, when you see these things taking place, you know that he is near, at the very gates. Truly I tell you, this generation will not pass away until all these things have taken place." (Mark 13:24–30)

The New Testament scholar Bart Ehrman summarizes the worldview of Jesus thus: "Jesus thought that the history of the world would come to a screeching halt, that God would intervene in the affairs of this planet, overthrow the forces of evil in a cosmic act of judgment, and establish his utopian Kingdom here on earth. And this was to happen within Jesus' own generation."[10] Ehrman sets out the evidence for this account of Jesus with some care. First, within first-century Judaism apocalypticism is widespread. The apocalyptic worldview flourishes in a climate where people are suffering: and the Jewish people, who had been forced to cope with endless occupations, knew what suffering involved. Provoked by the Romans, in 66 CE there was a revolt, which resulted in thousands of Jews in Jerusalem being slaughtered. Given this context, it is not surprising that some Jews "publicly proclaimed the imminent end of their suffering through the supernatural intervention of God."[11] A major group, the Essenes, a community seeking to live an appropriately rigorous observant life in the desert (about whom we know a great deal through the Dead Sea Scrolls) believed in the imminent end of the world. So apocalypticism is an important part of the context of Jesus' ministry.

Second, the passages from Mark's Gospel makes perfect sense in this context. Ehrman is right to argue that there is a consistent apocalyptic worldview that can be assembled from those texts that most likely go back to the historical Jesus. We have a vision of what the rules for the coming reign of God will look like: a "reversal of fortunes"[12] – the values and priorities of the current evil age will be reversed; and "salvation for sinners"[13] – the lost and needy. In addition, Jesus believes in a judgment that is both universal and imminent.[14] As Ehrman admits, much of this message is in continuity with the prophetic tradition of the Hebrew Bible, but it is also different – the Kingdom will be established by a dramatic act of God. Ehrman summarizes thus:

[T]his message was like that proclaimed throughout the writings of the prophets in the Hebrew Bible. Judgment was coming, people needed to repent in preparation or they would be condemned. Those who turned to God, though, would be saved. At the same time, Jesus' message was different, for his was framed within an apocalyptic context. As a first-century Jew, Jesus lived when many Jews expected God to intervene once and for all for his people, to overthrow the forces of evil that had gained ascendancy in the world and to bring in his good Kingdom on earth. There would then be no more war, poverty, disease, calamity, sin, hatred, or death. The kingdom would arrive in power, and all that was opposed to it would be destroyed and removed.[15]

It is clear then that the message of Jesus was about the reign of God which will be ushered in through a decisive divine action. It is also clear that Jesus believed he was the agent of God that makes it possible for the kingdom to arrive. As Ehrman puts it: "Jesus maintained that people who heard his message and followed it would enter into the future Kingdom of God. Thus Jesus portrayed himself as the herald of this Kingdom, who knew when it was coming and how it would arrive. More than that, he evidently saw himself as having a special standing before God. After all, whoever accepted his message would enter God's Kingdom."[16] As we saw in the chapter on the Incarnation, I would go further than Ehrman: to make sense of the subsequent worship of Jesus, there must be a sense in which the disclosure of God to his disciples was so remarkable that people recognized in this life the reality of God. Jesus is so intimate with God that Jesus was believed to be identical with God. So Jesus is not simply an agent of God but an authoritative teacher about and facilitator of the end of the age.

Many contemporary Christians are embarrassed by this sci-fi type vision of the future. However, there is no reason to be. Naturally, we should not take the picture-language too literally. Jesus shared a belief in a first-century cosmology (he had to otherwise he would not have been understood); and it is only in that cosmology that stars can fall from the heavens (see Mark 13:25). We need to work with these images in a different way. In addition, we should locate this apocalyptic strand within the rest of the New Testament. We can trace very clearly the way the Church came to terms with the delay in the parousia (second coming – literally it means presence). But more importantly, we need to recognize how the resurrection of Jesus was interpreted as the start of the end of the age. As we saw in the last chapter, the resurrection of Jesus is the model and promise to all of us (all creation). The end has started with the resurrection.

This leads to the third aspect. The scale of time for cosmologists needs to be taken more seriously. It is more likely to be millions or billions of years rather than next year. Most Christians have adjusted their understanding of the past. No longer do we assume that the universe was created in 4004 BCE, but we understand it all started 13 to 14 billion years ago. However, we have not modified our understanding of the future. This is where the scientific narrative is helpful. It helps modify our perspective. In cosmological time, the time lapse between the Jesus event and now is nothing – virtually insignificant. If the end of the world occurred tomorrow, then, in cosmological time, that would be remarkably soon. The scientific narrative does set some parameters: it seems likely that it will occur before the death of our star.

This leads to the fourth aspect. It might be objected that the scientific narrative is deeply depressing. So how can that narrative be reconciled with our expectation of a kingdom where God and God's values will reign? The answer must be that the *end of the age will be divine action analogous to creation*. Indeed as we have just seen, this is precisely what Jesus claims. In the same way that God worked with the forces of gravity and expansion to enable life to emerge, so God will work with those forces at the eschaton (the end of the universe).

Polkinghorne struggles to make sense of how God is going to work with the forces in the universe to realize the redeemed creation. He stresses that unlike the first creation (which was *ex nihilo* – out of nothing), this creation will be *ex vetere* (out of the old creation). Polkinghorne acknowledges his debt to Moltmann and Gabriel Daly when he compares the first creation with the new creation. Polkinghorne writes:

> [T]he old creation has the character which is appropriate to an evolutionary universe, endowed with the ability through the shuffling exploration of its happenstance to "make itself." It is a universe, certainly not lying outside the sustaining and providential care of God, but nevertheless it is given its due independence to follow its own history. The historical process cannot avoid the cost of suffering which is the price of independence. The new creation represents the transformation of that universe when it enters freely into a new and closer relationship with its Creator, so that it becomes a totally sacramental world, suffused with the divine presence. Its process can be free from suffering, for it is conceivable that the divine ordained laws of nature appropriate to a world making itself through its own evolving history should give way to a differently constituted form of "matter," appropriate to a universe "freely returned" from independence to an existence of integration with its Creator.[17]

For Polkinghorne, the end of the world is a transformation from a matter that is more autonomous of God to a "matter" that is totally "suffused with the divine presence." God will bring about a "spiritualizing" of the universe. In this way all of creation will be redeemed.

Jesus was right to believe that he was ushering in the end of the age. In living his life, witnessing to the nature of God, and dying, Jesus enables us to see what God is like. In rising again, Jesus anticipates the possibility, which will be realized for all humanity and the entire cosmos. I have already noted that, working with the time scale of the cosmologists, the time lapse between the resurrection and now is virtually insignificant. We should expect that this world will continue for many years to come. With that expectation, we should continue to be good stewards of the creation – respecting the intrinsic value of everything in creation and ensuring that the environment is protected so subsequent generations can enjoy this world.

Our propensities towards egoism and selfishness make it possible that we could significantly damage this world. Although humans have considerable power, it is unlikely that we could actually so damage the world that it would disappear – at the very least mountains, rocks, and sea life would probably survive a cataclysmic disaster. We could, however, make parts of the world completely uninhabitable for humans and mammals. We should not assume that a divine intervention would prevent this from happening. God in Christ has already ensured that everything in creation will be redeemed; but in the meantime we are still responsible with God for the next segment of creation. Humanity needs to listen more carefully to the Spirit of God who is seeking to lure us to live lives of love and respect.

Instead of endlessly offering a redemption timetable, we need to "be ready" for the work that God is calling us to do now. One should live in the now, aware of the demands and standards of the end. The fact that a just universe will emerge (God has promised that this is so) provides a goal for which we must strive. Keith Ward alludes to the Lord's Prayer, when he explains:

> Christian prayer for the contemporary world should perhaps be that the world should not end soon, but should realize the will of God "on earth as in heaven." But it should also be that, whenever the world ends, the perfected Messianic kingdom should make present the pleroma of the cosmic Wisdom, in the Spirit-filled community of a transfigured earth, which can fully manifest the glory of the creator God. If the end of history is soon, the Christian belief is that even that tragedy is not unredeemable. The world of humanity will not simply cease to be. Christ will "come again," in the form of his cosmic glory, and in a transfigured world, to usher in the Messianic kingdom in a new earth. Whether late or soon, the ultimate hope is for the resurrection of the natural order, and the participation of all the souls which have ever been created in a divine and incorruptible life.[18]

For Ward, we are called to live in the present, but aware of the Christian hope. As we look around our dangerous world, it is possible that disaster could strike. It is possible that global warming will lead to significant suffering and loss of human life. Indeed it is possible that we could make ourselves extinct as a species. Yet the divine intention to realize the work started at the resurrection will continue. God will continue to work with everything in creation to realize a different form of matter which is permeated with divine grace. This universe will be recreated and molded to be a place where love and justice are truly reconciled.

Expect to be surprised at the end of the age. It is likely that there are other sentient creatures on other planets to whom God has disclosed Godself. We should expect all the diversity of God's creation to participate in the redeemed creation. It will reflect the complexity of the God we worship. A God who is full of constant surprises. At every moment God has surprised humanity. The end of the age will be no different.

QUESTIONS FOR REFLECTION AND DISCUSSION

1 Is it necessary for a Christian to believe that the world will end?
2 How do you think Christians should accommodate Jesus' mistaken belief in the imminent end of the world?
3 If the world does not end before the death of our star, then would that be a decisive disproof of Christianity?
4 Why are so many Christians attracted to the *Left Behind* series?

GLOSSARY

Dark energy: the term used by cosmologists to describe the energy in the universe that encourages expansion
Dispensationalism: the doctrine that the history of God's treatment of humanity can be divided into different periods
Rapture: the belief that the second coming of Jesus will be marked by a first stage when the true Church will disappear and meet Christ in the skies

Notes

1 John Polkinghorne, *Science and Christian Belief: Theological Reflections of a Bottom-Up Thinker* (London: SPCK, 1994), p. 162.
2 Tim LaHaye and Jerry B. Jenkins, *Left Behind: A Novel of the Earth's Last Days* (Wheaton, IL: Tyndale House Publishers, 1995), pp. 46–7.
3 Carl E. Olson, "No end in sight," *First Things* 127 (2002), p. 12.
4 Ibid.
5 Kenneth Newport, *Apocalypse and Millennium* (Cambridge: Cambridge University Press, 2000), p. 21.
6 Ibid., p. 62.
7 Olson, "No end in sight," p. 14.
8 Karl Marx, "Towards a critique of Hegel's *Philosophy of Right*" in David McLellan (ed.), *Karl Marx: Selected Writings* (Oxford: Oxford University Press, 1977), p. 64.

9 Jürgen Moltmann, *Theology of Hope* (London: SCM Press, 1967), pp. 327–8.
10 Bart D. Ehrman, *Jesus: Apocalyptic Prophet of the New Millennium* (Oxford: Oxford University Press, 1999), p. 3.
11 Ibid., p. 119.
12 Ibid., p. 148.
13 Ibid., p. 150.
14 Ibid., p. 158.
15 Ibid., p. 161.
16 Ibid., p. 217.
17 Polkinghorne, *Science and Christian Belief*, p. 167.
18 Keith Ward, *Religion and Human Nature* (Oxford: Oxford University Press, 1998), p. 294.

Chapter 14
PARTICIPATING IN THE CONVERSATION

From the outside, doctrine can look very strange. For the Church to split, for example, over whether the Holy Spirit proceeds from both the Father and the Son, seems both arcane and irresolvable. This is the reason why this book tries to ease you in. If you start with the arguments over the atonement, then you are going to be in trouble. Instead we start with the sense of the divine that surrounds us. To presume that we are simply complex bundles of atoms that emerged by accident and will face extinction when we die is one way to look at the world. But it is a very implausible way. We do not normally explain complex events as "a giant fluke." The "accident hypothesis" for everything that is seems very unlikely: it does not explain our experience of love, music, and morality.

It also does not explain our "experience" of God. Thanks to a faith-filled environment as a child, I have been blessed with the sense of God throughout my life. This is not an invisible person constantly talking to me. Rather it is an abiding awareness of love upholding and supporting me, even through the hardest times. In much the same way as you can sit at a table in a restaurant, perhaps with a friend or two, and be aware, at the periphery of your vision, of other diners in the restaurant, so I find God simply there – at the edge – calling and reminding me of what I can and should be.

Certain disciplines can help to cultivate this sense of God. The Muslim who finds the hour a day (which is approximately the amount of time needed to do the five obligatory prayers) will live life much more conscious of the divine than the non-observant one. As a Christian, I attempt to find time to say the Daily Office in the morning. It refocuses me on what really matters: it shifts my priorities: and it helps me to reengage with the love which I sense is constantly around me.

Getting into religion is much like getting into opera (or into any demanding practice). Attendance at an opera is obligation; one must learn to listen so one can appreciate; and one should meet up with others who can show you the complexity of the opera. It is the same with faith. And in the same way that it might take some time before the operatic aria gets inside you and really affects you, so it is with faith.

So underpinning this book are two related arguments. The first is that "faith in the divine" makes sense. The "God hypothesis" is much more likely to be true than the "accident hypothesis." The second argument is that faith is a training, where one starts to see and feel the transcendent around you. It is this second consideration which explains why the arguments (in themselves) rarely persuade. The sense that God is likely needs to run parallel with the cultivation of a sensitivity to the God that is.

Sensitivity to faith requires a grounding in a particular tradition. Each tradition is different. One cannot be introduced to all traditions simultaneously: it takes time to learn to appreciate a particular tradition. One cannot be introduced to the essense of all traditions: some have tried to make this available, but they end up just offering yet another tradition. The Unitarian Universalists, for example, try to offer a tradition which includes and affirms all, but in so doing they create a distinctive tradition, with a strong emphasis on ethics and a deep suspicion about metaphysics. One must grow up in a particular tradition: this is inescapable.

All traditions are a constant movement between "core convictions" and "contemporary complexities." We are in the business of discerning what God requires of us. Our "core convictions" are the basis on which we determine what God requires of us; our "contemporary complexities" are the problems that require analysis and thought. The "core convictions" in all religions are some form of "revelation" (some disclosure of God that tells us what God is like). For Jews, it is the Torah; for Muslims, the Qur'an; for Hindus, the Upanishads; and for Christians, it is the life, death, and resurrection of Jesus.

Now how do you know which claim to revelation is true? One can grade claims to revelation: so David Koresh of Waco is much further down the list than, say, the Prophet Muhammad. And certain interpretations of the revelation by certain groups are much less likely to be true; so for example, both the Christian fundamentalist and the Muslim Salafi are problematic. The criteria to form this list include the following: coherence, plausibility, explanatory power, compatibility with knowledge learned elsewhere, and so on. One's task is to engage constructively with one's tradition and arrive at an account of God and God's relations with the world that makes sense of the complexity of one's experience of the world. One does this work with humility; and one does this work aware that there are many accounts of God and God's relations with the world that make sense (perhaps even as much sense as your own account). And one task, therefore, that one's theology must take into account is the variety of plausible accounts (i.e. well thought out) of God that are out there.

So, then, the task of doctrine is to explicate the core convictions and relate them to the contemporary complexities (one might recognize Paul Tillich's method of correlation here). For Christians, our definitive disclosure of God is a life. It is the life, death, and resurrection of Jesus. The author of the Gospel of John describes Jesus as the Word of God (in Greek, *logos*). This life is the Christian equivalent of the Qur'an. Our task is to look at this life and attempt to interpret it as a disclosure of God.

This is difficult. One reason why there are so many different forms of Christianity is because it is not immediately obvious what we learn about God from Christ. There are some basics: Jesus identifies with the marginalized and outcast, thereby we know that God does the same. Jesus calls on us to make the "reign of God" a priority, thereby we know that God so calls us. Jesus demonstrates love to humanity to a point of a total giving of his life, so we know God is doing the same. Jesus lived through despair and discovered the triumph of the resurrection, thereby God promises to do the same to our despair. But what exactly God thinks of "homosexuality" or "stem cell research" is less clear.

There are, of course, passages in the Bible which talk about homosexuality. And given it is through the Bible that we learn about the Logos of God, the Bible is enormously important. Karl Barth helpfully explains the relationship of the Word of God (Christ) with the book that becomes the word when it witnesses to the Word. 2 Timothy 3:16 explains that Scripture is "inspired." Granted the word here is "God-breathed," but even that is not the same as, for example, the Qur'anic claim to be dictated. Our definitive disclosure of God is Christ. The Bible is the inspired text which points us constantly to the Word of God. However, what we learn of God in Christ is also the criterion by which we judge the rest of the Bible. So passages in the Bible that institute and condone slavery are judged to be an inauthentic disclosure of what God wants because such passages are incompatible with what we know of God in Christ.

With our core convictions about what we know of God in Christ, we are in a position to examine what God might be doing in allowing the diversity of religious traditions to emerge. This diversity is partly due to the complexity of our subject matter. It is complicated working out what God is like. Given this complexity, it is not surprising that different views have emerged. And we also see in the life, death, and resurrection a constant willingness to accept people where they are. Where Zacchaeus was ostracized, Jesus includes; where woman were ignored and not allowed to learn, Jesus speaks and teaches. The God revealed in Christ is the God who is speaking to the Muslim and the Jew. Jesus constantly tells us to expect to learn of God from the surprising places (for example, the child); so we should expect to learn of God from the Muslim and the Jew. Truth about God, which is compatible with what we know of God in Christ, can be discovered in modernity, in science, and in other faith traditions.

This is Christian doctrine. This is the challenge of living within our tradition and struggling to discern what the Spirit of God is saying. Our constant reference point is the life, death, and resurrection of Jesus as witnessed to in the pages of the Scripture. Our external reference point is the gathered community, which meets together to allow the life of God to transform us through the Eucharist. Our challenge is those countless contemporary complexities, which drive us back to think and pray anew about what God is communicating.

Theology is never going to stand still. We constantly find ourselves revisiting the debates of the past to see more clearly what is really going on. We constantly find ourselves with fresh challenges that involve more imaginative engagement. We constantly find ourselves needing to listen to fresh and different voices. And this is where everyone has a contribution to make.

Participating in the Tradition

The Word of God (i.e. the life, death, and resurrection) stands in judgment on the Christian tradition. Where God in Christ reached out to the marginalized, the Christian tradition is dominated by the established. Where God in Christ includes the poor, the Christian tradition is dominated by the privileged. Where God in Christ engages with women, the Christian tradition is dominated by men. In so many ways, the Christian tradition has – in my view – discovered much that is true about God, yet done so while excluding many of the voices that God, through Christ, is commanding us to include.

The emergence of the "identity theologies" (i.e. theologies that concentrate on the distinctive experience of those who are traditionally excluded – women, blacks, gays, etc.) is an exciting development. In a limited way, this book has been shaped by their insights – the emphasis on Process theology, the complex account of an inevitable fall that facilitates growth, and the obligation to see the Church as an inclusive community. However, there is more that is happening and more work that I need to do.

The experience of other faith traditions is another important avenue. The work of seeing links and parallels across traditions can make an important difference to our sense of self-understanding. Again in a limited way, the experience of other faith traditions is in the background. But more needs to be, and can be, done.

So the ending of this book is not intended to bring closure. It is not the last word in the conversation. Instead the end is a start. It is an invitation for the reader to continue the work that God in Christ calls us all to do. A textbook introduction to doctrine is very different from the definitive systematic theology. A textbook is intended to provide a training to enable the student to leap beyond the words on the page of this particular book. The theology of this book invites the reader to see all theology as a textbook. It is no coincidence that Thomas Aquinas (the great theologian of the thirteenth century) saw his massive *Summa Theologica* as an introduction for beginners in the faith. The textbook model of theology invites growth and moving beyond.

Participation in the conversation is conditional. It is conditional on listening. An incoherent musing that does not struggle with the tradition is not conversation. The tradition is entitled to be heard. We are not inventing a new religion: we are building on the struggles of all those who have gone before. Even though the tradition has problems, we should still listen to it. And we should listen to each other. We should be bringing our own voices and struggles to the conversation.

Please argue with this book. Disagree with the conclusions. Dig deep into your own experience of the God revealed in Christ and reflect on its significance. Then start to contribute to the conversation. Theology is complicated because our subject matter is complicated. Therefore theology needs your contribution. Hopefully, this end is just a beginning.

INTERNET RESOURCES

Both students and teachers will find a vast array of materials on the internet, which explore many of the issues that are discussed in this book. Some of the finest are:

The Wabash for Teaching and Learning in Theology and Religion
http://www.wabashcenter.wabash.edu/home/default.aspx
This is not simply an excellent resource on content, but also extremely helpful on teaching.

Christian Classics Ethereal Library
http://www.ccel.org
It is important for any student to read the "classics." This website makes them available in a form that is very user friendly.

The New Advent Catholic Website
http://www.newadvent.org/
Understanding the Roman Catholic tradition is absolutely essential for anyone who wants to understand Christianity. This is the finest Roman Catholic website.

Religion on-line
http://www.religion-online.org/
Major articles by major scholars in theology.

Intute: Arts and Humanities
http://www.intute.ac.uk/artsandhumanities/religion/
An excellent way in to many outstanding resources in religion and theology.

Religion Compass
http://www.blackwell-compass.com/home_religion_compass
Although this needs a library subscription, it is an excellent resource, which is aimed at students.

INDEX